Crime Without Punishment

Crime Without Punishment

David A. Jones
The University of Pittsburgh

Lexington Books
D.C. Heath and Company
Lexington, Massachusetts
Toronto

Library of Congress Cataloging in Publication Data

Jones, David Arthur, 1946-
  Crime without punishment.

  Bibliography: p.
  Includes index.
  1. Pleas (Criminal procedure)—United States. 2. Plea bargaining—United
States. 3. Criminal justice, Administration of—United States. I. Title.
KF9654.J66   345'.73'072   78-19538
ISBN 0-669-02512-7

Published simultaneously in Canada

Printed in the United States of America

International Standard Book Number: 0-669-02512-7

Library of Congress Catalog Card Number: 78-19538

To Christopher

Contents

List of Figures
and Tables

Acknowledgments

I wish to express my gratitude to everyone who participated in any way in the studies upon which I have drawn to assemble this book. These people include the researchers and the respondents who became involved in the many studies which I have cited as well as in the few studies in which I played an active role. Special appreciation is directed to practitioners within the criminal justice system across the United States, such as judges, prosecutors, defense attorneys, their clerks and other staff members, police and correctional officers, as well as defendants themselves, who generously spared some of their valuable time talking with the author. There are at least one hundred such persons.

Catherine M. Jones worked closely with me on the compilation, summary, and analysis of the data contained within this book. She worked with me continuously over a period of more than two years as different data bases were made compatible, and quantitative information was reconciled with qualitative information. I am indebted to the faculty of the Graduate Program in Administration of Justice at the University of Pittsburgh for bearing with me as I devoted a substantial portion of my nonteaching time preparing this manuscript.

Crime Without Punishment

1 Introduction

Alexander Solzhenitsyn capsulized the current weakness of the American criminal justice system in his speech to the 1978 graduates of Harvard University in which he observed that our preoccupation with the defense of individual rights has made society defenseless against some criminals. He urged the United States to defend human obligations as well as human rights. A relatively small number of persistent criminal offenders avoid punishment for the majority of their serious crimes by infrequently negotiating a few guilty pleas to offenses that are, by comparison, trivial. Partially as a result of this country's extreme deference to individual human rights, vicious and often violent criminals secure one bargain after another with the law. Consequently, both these criminals and the persons who attempt unsuccessfully to administer criminal justice in most parts of the United States fail to fulfill their human obligations to the rest of society.

Criminals in the United States, with a few exceptions, do not enjoy formal political or governmental authority as they tend to in some totalitarian nations. Nevertheless, many criminals dominate the streets of most American cities, and they continue to terrorize innocent citizens and to paralyze a judicial system that should be capable of neutralizing a much greater proportion of their wrongful conduct. Although many citizens contend that police services are inadequate to prevent or to deter the commission of serious crimes, greater popular dissatisfaction seems to be directed toward the judicial process and those whose duty it is to adjudicate the guilt or the innocence of suspected criminal offenders and to impose sanctions upon those who are convicted. Even popular disenchantment with the correctional component of the American criminal justice system is attributed by many to the shortcomings of the judicial process.

Virtually everyone who has experienced any significant contact with the American judicial process in recent years will admit that it functions poorly in civil as well as in criminal cases. One reason it functions so poorly is because the job is done so slowly. Courts in general, but particularly the criminal courts, have become besieged with a formidable backlog of pending cases that involve defendants accused of committing crimes months or even years ago but who cannot be scheduled for trial until months or even years ahead. Justice delayed is justice denied, not only to defendants but to the victims of crime and to the public at large.

Why is Justice Delayed?

Why cannot the judicial process be accelerated to a faster pace? The answer is not clear. Those who are charged with administering justice in the courts argue that too many crimes are being committed by too many separate offenders, and that the supply of judges and prosecutors is too small in relation to the demand for their services. This book will look at the current demand for justice in the courts compared with this demand historically, in an effort to assess the relationship, if there is one, that may exist between increases in the population, a rising crime rate, and burgeoning constraints on the ability of American courts to deliver justice expeditiously.

In addition to being criticized for delaying justice, courts are criticized for denying justice altogether. Convicted criminal offenders allege that they were coerced or misled into admitting guilt for their offenses without being given an opportunity to defend themselves. Victims of crime complain that they are not afforded an opportunity to recount in court the details surrounding attacks by criminals, that offenders are not punished on the basis of each crime perpetrated, and that a victim has little or no opportunity to participate in the selection of the sanction that is imposed against an offender that has caused him harm. Police say they have lost respect for the courts and hesitate to charge suspects with many crimes because the conduct is hard to prove and, even if proven, an offender will receive a "slap on the wrist" and be set free again right away.

Why is Justice Denied?

Why cannot the judicial process precisely determine the guilt or the innocence of each person who has been charged with committing a serious crime as to each charge of which he stands accused? The answer is not clear once again. Those who are charged with administering justice reiterate that too many crimes are committed by too many offenders, and that most judicial units do not have enough prosecutors, judges, or financial resources to pinpoint criminal responsibility for the average known crime. This book will look at operations in the courtrooms and behind the scenes to gain some insight into how criminal cases are handled from initial charging through disposition by trial, guilty plea, or dismissal, in an effort to assess the effectiveness and the propriety of criminal prosecutions within judicial units of different size and demographic characteristics across the country. Is it true, for example, that the larger the population served by a judicial unit the fewer trials it can have and the more guilty pleas it must have?

There is no doubt that in the past twenty years appellate courts in the United States, and particularly the United States Supreme Court, have established rigid standards of criminal procedure that must be followed not only at trial but prior to trial in order for incriminating evidence to be used to convict defendants. Lower court judges and prosecutors have complained that the "criminal law revolution" and its aftermath have shackled their ability to bring the guilty to justice, forcing them to stay out of the courtroom and to rely upon the willingness of many defendants to admit their guilt in consideration of promises for leniency in punishment. This book will examine a variety of rates that are associated with the disposition of criminal cases by various means including dismissal, trial, and guilty plea. Is it true that trial rates are lower or that guilty plea rates are higher since the "criminal law revolution?"

Many offenders who have been convicted of serious crimes complain, usually after being convicted, that the judicial process was a sham for them. Offenders may allege that they were coerced or beguiled into pleading guilty to crimes they did not commit or to crimes they feel could never have been proven against them at a trial. Offenders may charge that they were induced into pleading serious charges, guilty or not, in order to minimize the risk of a harsh sentence when in fact the sentence that was imposed subsequent to their admission of guilt was as severe or even more severe than they imagined they could receive had they maintained their innocence, gone to trial, and been found guilty by a judge or a jury. Is the judicial process a charade, or are these offenders exaggerating the truth or lying? The purpose of the adjudicative process is to determine accurately, fairly, and swiftly who is guilty of what, and to separate the guilty from the innocent. Justice is not served when defendants who have been wrongfully charged are persuaded they will "get off easy" if they go along with efforts to convict them, whereas if they exercise their constitutional right to have the charges against them proven at a trial, they will be punished even if they are innocent or penalized more severely than they deserve to be.

The Chief Justice of the United States has accused at least half of the legal profession of being incompetent, particularly so in the courtroom. Is this true? Are lawyers who have been assigned to prosecute or defend persons accused of crimes capable of doing a credible job? Are lawyers ready, willing, and able to serve as advocates in adversarial proceedings? The assumption that only the guilty will be convicted and the innocent acquitted is faulty unless both prosecution and defense counsel are functioning up to par.

Are judges of American courts competent by reason of experience, temperament and training to fulfill their critical responsibility of supervising the judicial processes? The awesomeness of the judicial office may be used to intimidate lawyers and clients alike. A wrong ruling by a judge even if it is an honest mistake in a minor proceeding may inspire a defendant, with or without advice of counsel, to terminate by agreement the charges pending against him then and there rather than to proceed further in the courts where "the cards are stacked against him anyway." Not just the bar, but the bench also, requires ongoing scrutiny to ensure that justice is administered equitably in practice as well as in theory.

Society has reached the point where truly it has become almost defenseless against many of the vicious and violent criminal offenders who roam the streets as predators. Clearly, many criminals who remain at large have walked out of court free to resume their predations. Is this the fault of the criminal exclusively? It seems that some of the blame should be shared by the courts and by lawyers who practice criminal law on either side of the aisle. It is easy to pass the blame on to legislators who have decriminalized or diminished the criminality of some forms of conduct, or to criticize the police for failing to prevent crime, or to scold penologists for being unsuccessful at altering the warped personalities of known offenders. It is harder for members of the legal profession to admit that procedures that have been the foundation of Anglo-American jurisprudence for nearly one thousand years at least have ceased to operate in practice the way they were designed to do in theory. Diagnosis precedes both prognosis and treatment, however, and it is evident that the judicial process has become sick and in need of treatment. How sick? What treatment? What prospects, if any, for recovery? A comprehensive examination is needed to begin with. This book may be viewed as an examination—as an examination before trial, before the trial of the courts.

2 Research Design and Methodology

The principal aim of this book is to study the disposition of criminal cases across the United States during the mid-1970s, from the detection and arrest of criminal suspects through the formal charging process, pretrial discovery and screening procedures, and on to guilty plea or trial, conviction, acquittal or dismissal. The purpose for doing so is to assess the strengths and weaknesses of the prosecution, defense, adjudication and sentencing functions within representative American jurisdictions of different geographic size and population density located within each major region of the nation.

There is little, if any, need to conduct an in-depth study merely to determine the extent to which our system of administering criminal justice is chaotic. That much is well known to almost everyone who has ever interacted within any component sector of the criminal justice system but particularly within the courts. It is the conclusion reached by lawyers, judges and other professionals who purport to administer justice, as well as by lay citizens such as the victims of crime, witnesses to crimes, and even criminal offenders themselves. A more penetrating question is *why* the system of administering criminal justice throughout the United States has reached such a state of disarray? The most urgent issue is *how*, if at all, this undesirable situation may be changed?

A number of practitioners and theoreticians alike have pointed to the practice of "plea bargaining" as the root of the trauma that surrounds the disposition of criminal cases throughout the country. One writer has said: "The sum and substance of the whole matter is that when the . . . police get a case disposed of in the courts . . . their troubles are over; they are more interested in conviction than punishment. . . ."[1] Another has noted: "In political terms, it is far more important for a prosecutor to secure convictions than it is for him to secure adequate sentences."[2]

One of the most pervasive commentaries on plea bargaining was delivered by Chief Justice Warren Burger as part of the opinion of the United States Supreme Court in the case of Santobello v. New York (1972):

> Disposition of charges after plea discussions is not only an essential part of the process but a highly desirable part for many reasons. It leads to prompt and largely final disposition of most criminal cases; it avoids much of the corrosive impact of enforced idleness during pretrial confinement for those who are denied release pending trial; it protects the public from those accused persons who are prone to continue criminal conduct even while on pre-trial release; and, by shortening the

time between charge and disposition, it enhances whatever may be the rehabilitative prospects of the guilty when they are ultimately imprisoned.[3]

The Chief Justice has prophesized frankly that if plea bargaining were to decline, the backlog of criminal cases pending in most criminal courts would increase.[4]

Not everyone agrees that plea bargaining is either so beneficial or so necessary. One observer has pointed out that negotiated guilty pleas are not new to the administration of criminal justice in America, but have evolved over time and have endured at least in part on account of the relatively little effort required to dispose of criminal cases by negotiation rather than by trial.[5] Another has postulated that the guilty plea has grown largely as a "product of circumstance, not choice."[6] A strong critic of plea bargaining alleges that this practice "permits a prosecutor to avoid making decisions in the system of justice he is morally and legally obligated to make;" that it "tends to indicate to a judge that the prosecutor does not feel strongly about a case;" that it "causes a loss of public confidence in our system of government;" and that it "makes it easier to have corruption within a prosecutor's office."[7] An earlier critic concluded that the "chief loss to the orderly administration of the criminal law which comes from bargaining for pleas of guilty, pleas to lesser offenses and the 'immunity bath' is that it is all extra-legal, secret and undercover."[8]

Nor does everyone believe that plea bargaining is inevitable. A British observer has remarked that plea bargaining is "less an independent ill than a symptom. More properly it is part of a collection of symptoms of a general sickness. It is but one manifestation, albeit a significant one, of a system which is not operating properly."[9] Several prosecutors around the nation have experimented to reduce or eliminate guilty plea negotiations, but the practice continues in most jurisdictions, nearly to the point of becoming an institution. Those who administer criminal justice (judges, prosecutors, defense counsel) in urban centers point to a rapidly rising rate of serious crime as constituting a drain on their manpower and limiting their ability to take many cases to trial. Those who administer criminal justice in rural areas point to the low budgetary resources available to them, low staff salaries that result, and their inability to prosecute criminal cases as efficiently as they could do if they were located in urban centers where they could draft more manpower, enjoy shorter travel distances, and attract the best professional staff including investigators.

To criticize the functioning of any organization, but particularly a unit of government, is much easier than to implement reform by means of planned change. This is true especially in relation to a dynamic system of interfacing organizational units such as the criminal justice system, and most certainly true of the judicial process. It is extremely difficult, if not utterly impossible, for measurable and lasting change to occur within any system or unit of a system unless a great deal of information is known about the characteristics of every component and operational gear. Unfortunately, too little data has been obtained that reflects the operational capabilities of the judicial processes within most jurisdictions in the United States, be they federal, state, county, or municipal.

One objective of this book, therefore, is to attempt to isolate and identify practices and problems that are common to many judicial units across America insofar as the disposition of criminal cases is concerned. Do the practices and the problems relating to the disposition of criminal cases vary significantly from north to south, east to west, and from urban to rural areas? The existing literature does not answer this question.

A second objective is to attempt to delineate the roles that are played by key defense, judicial, and prosecutorial personnel (actors) within most American judicial units, as well as the roles played by ancillary court personnel such as clerks, investigators, probation officers, and statisticians, together with the recognized goals envisioned by each. One scholar has asserted that the process of pleading defendants guilty to criminal charges without trial consists of normative procedures coupled with clearly defined roles and goals.[10] Do these roles and goals vary significantly across different judicial units throughout the country? Are they a function, in whole or in part, of outside variables such as the political orientation of key personnel (e.g., liberal or conservative), the manner in which key officials are selected to hold office (e.g., appointed or elected), the length of time that key officials will remain in office, the existence of a challenge to their authority at the polls or in the press, and the sentiments of the citizenry toward crime in general, toward a "crime wave," or toward highly visible or serious crimes? Previous studies have not shed much light on the answers to these and related questions, except with respect to a very limited number of jurisdictions that may not be representative of the nation.

A third objective is to measure the self-perceptions of key officials (actors) as to their roles and goals; to measure self-assessments made by these officials as to their success or failure at fulfilling their self-perceived roles and goals; and to compare these self-perceptions and self-assessments with more objective perceptions and assessments reached by the author during the course of his research.

A fourth objective is to delineate, as precisely as possible, a typology of criminal case dispositions that reflects the characteristics of case-flow in jurisdictions that are representative of judicial units throughout the United States during the mid-1970s.

A fifth objective of this book is to unravel implications for responsible action that must be taken, and to recommend planned change that needs to occur, in order that the chaos presently associated with the adjudication and sentencing of criminal offenders throughout the United States may be reduced immensely.

To fulfill these objectives, a vast amount of both qualitative and quantitative data has had to be gathered, summarized, and analyzed, sometimes at rather great lengths. Not all of the information that is cited in this book was gathered or originally evaluated by the author. Much of the quantitative data presented herein has been obtained from a number of earlier studies and represents the triangulation of various research products. Some of this quantitative data was generated by one or more systematic-empirical studies of national scope that were conducted during or immediately prior to the mid 1970s. These studies include the National Crime Survey,[11] the National Parole Outcome Study,[12] and the National Study of Plea Bargaining.[13] The author served as the deputy director of the National Study of Plea Bargaining during its execution in 1975 and 1976, during the course of which he traveled to many American judicial units.

In addition, some of the empirical data has been generated by ongoing surveys of federal, state, county, and municipal law enforcement and judicial activities, including annual reports of most state and some county courts for recent years,[14] the Federal Bureau of Investigation's Uniform Crime Reports for recent years,[15] and the annual reports of the director of the Administrative Office of the United States Courts for each year since 1967.[16] Some of this information is historical and was drawn from the Office of Administration of the United States Courts for years between 1945 and 1967;[17] from the annual reports of the Attorney General of the United States for years between 1908 and 1937;[18] and from annual studies conducted by the United States Bureau of the Census during the years 1936 through 1941.[19] Finally, some of this data was generated by various published or unpublished studies of regional or local scope in areas such as the detection of crime by the police, judicial administration, and corrections.

Most of the statistical information that is summarized or paraphrased within this book has been validated and found to be reliable, more or less,[20] by the research teams that compiled the data. For this reason, and due to a lack of space, the research designs and the methods that were used to gather and to authenticate such preexisting data will not be reported again here. Instead, the interested reader should refer back to the original publication of each respective study or else communicate with its author or authors for insight into its statistical significance or other value.

On the other hand, most of the qualitative information that is presented within this book has not been published previously, chiefly because it is the product of research conducted by the author. For this reason, some elaboration on the design and the methods that were used is warranted. The data is the product of the author's visit to more than thirty criminal court jurisdictions[21] located throughout the United States, each selected as part of a stratified random sampling effort. During these visits, the author supervised and in many instances conducted interviews with judges, prosecutors, public, and private defense counsel, some police and correctional officers, some criminal defendants, some crime victims, and many ancillary court personnel. During these visits, also, the author observed numerous criminal proceedings take place, including internal charging and screening activities within prosecutors' offices, pretrial hearings and motions, plea negotiations, pleadings, presentence hearings and sentencings. Obviously, some of these proceedings occurred inside courtrooms while others took place elsewhere such as in judicial chambers, lawyers' offices, corridors of public and private buildings, police stations and jails.

Sampling the Nation

The research on which this book is based has been concerned with studying process characteristics pertaining to judicial units throughout the United States. These judicial units have served as the principal subjects for this research. The study has been interested less in measuring observables (differences or similarities) between or among individuals who function within any given judicial unit, than in measuring observables among different judicial units as organizational entities. For this reason, an initial task in the investigation was to sample American judicial units rather than to sample defendants, defense counsel, judges or prosecutors as individuals.

There are 3,100 separate state judicial units in the United States including the District of Columbia Court of Appeals and Superior Court following their creation in this decade.[22] Of these units, twenty-nine in Alaska are known as divisions, sixty-four in Louisiana are called parishes, forty-one are independent cities including thirty-eight in Virginia plus one each in Maryland (Baltimore), Missouri (St. Louis), and Nevada (Carson City). The balance of the state judicial units in the United States are referred to as counties. These 3,100 separate state judicial units include 2,460 units that serve respective populations of less than 50,000 as of April 1, 1970.[23] As of the same date, 338 state judicial units served respective judicial units of 100,000 or over, and by the end of 1975 at least ten more judicial units served populations in excess of 100,000. Federal judicial units were omitted from this study, as were local units such as police courts, since by far the majority of criminal cases pass through state courts located within county-level units of government.[24]

Twenty sample judicial units were selected for field visitation, and these were obtained at random using a table of random numbers from a sampling frame of the 338 state jurisdictions serving respective populations of one hundred thousand and over. The sample judicial units are located in eighteen different states. California and New York were represented twice. Three of the sample judicial units serve populations in excess of one million, and four others serve populations in excess of five hundred thousand. In addition, six sample judicial units serve a geographic land area in excess of one thousand square miles. There is little doubt but that this sample is representative of the major American state judicial units, and as table 2-1 reflects the sample jurisdictions are well-balanced according to regions of the country.

In addition, another twenty judicial units were selected for field visitation,

Table 2-1
Twenty Sample Judicial Units Randomly Selected for Field Visitation

Judicial Unit (County)	State	County Seat	Land Area (Square Miles)	Population (April 1, 1970)
Alameda	California	Oakland	733	1,073,184
Allen	Indiana	Fort Wayne	671	280,455
Bergen	New Jersey	Hackensack	234	897,148
Bernalillo	New Mexico	Albuquerque	1,169	315,774
Clark	Nevada	Las Vegas	7,874	273,288
Cook	Illinois	Chicago	954	5,493,766
Dallas	Texas	Dallas	859	1,327,695
El Paso	Colorado	Colorado Springs	2,157	235,972
Guilford	North Carolina	Greensboro	655	288,645
Hamilton	Tennessee	Chattanooga	550	255,077
Hartford	Connecticut	Hartford	739	816,737
Henrico	Virginia	Richmond	229	154,365
Jefferson	Alabama	Birmingham	1,115	644,991
Kalamazoo	Michigan	Kalamazoo	562	201,550
Pima	Arizona	Tucson	9,240	351,667
Plymouth	Massachusetts	Brockton	654	333,314
Richmond	New York	Saint George	58	295,443
Rockland	New York	New City	176	229,903
San Bernadino	California	San Bernadino	20,117	682,233
Trumbull	Ohio	Warren	608	232,579

Source: United States Bureau of the Census, 1970 Census of Population in the United States.

but these were not obtained at random. Instead, these jurisdictions were selected purposefully for a variety of reasons to complement the jurisdictions that were selected at random. Some, but not all, of these purposefully selected jurisdictions were chosen because unusual plea bargaining practices or other characteristics of criminal case disposition are reputed to take place (or to have taken place) there. Others were chosen as part of the study's pretest. Still others were selected on account of the author's familiarity with their judicial operations, having either practiced law or conducted previous research there. Table 2-2 indicates that these jurisdictions reflect a cross-section of the larger, urban judicial units in the United States. Included among these jurisdictions are seven that serve populations in excess of one million and another seven that serve populations in excess of five hundred thousand. As is the case with the judicial units that were chosen at random, those that were selected purposefully are located within all major geographic areas of the United States.

Altogether, the judicial units that were sampled at random serve a population of 14,383,786 and cover a land area of 49,354 square miles. These jurisdictions serve an aggregate of 7 percent of the United States population, although they encompass only 1.4 percent of the nation's total land area. Collectively, the judicial units that were studied purposefully serve a population

Table 2-2
Twenty Sample Judicial Units Deliberately Selected for Field Visitation

Judicial Unit (County, District, Division, Independent City, or Parish)	State	Seat of Judicial Unit	Land Area (Square Miles)	Population (April 1, 1970)
Allegheny	Pennsylvania	Pittsburgh	728	1,605,133
Anchorage[a]	Alaska	Anchorage	927	126,133
Arlington	Virginia	Arlington	25	174,284
Black Hawk	Iowa	Waterloo	568	132,916
Dade	Florida	Miami	2,042	1,267,792
Davidson	Tennessee	Nashville	508	447,877
Delaware	Pennsylvania	Media	184	601,715
District Of Columbia		Washington	61	756,510
El Paso	Texas	El Paso	1,057	359,291
Erie	New York	Buffalo	1,058	1,113,491
Hillsborough	New Hampshire	Nashua	887	223,941
Kings	New York	Brooklyn	70	2,602,012
Los Angeles	California	Los Angeles	4,059	7,040,697
Montgomery	Maryland	Rockville	495	522,809
Multnomah	Oregon	Portland	423	554,668
New York	New York	New York	23	1,539,233
Orleans[b]	Louisiana	New Orleans	197	593,471
Saint Louis[c]	Missouri	Saint Louis	61	622,236
San Diego	California	San Diego	4,261	1,357,854
Worcester	Massachusetts	Worcester	1,509	637,037

Source: United States Bureau of the Census, 1970 Census of Population in the United States.
[a] Anchorage Division.
[b] Orleans Parish.
[c] Independent City of Saint Louis.

of 22,279,378 and cover a land area of 19,142 square miles. These jurisdictions serve an aggregate of 11 percent of the United States population, but encompass only 0.5 percent of the country's total land area. When the twenty judicial units that were selected at random are combined with the twenty that were chosen purposefully, these forty jurisdictions serve an aggregate of 18 percent of the United States population (36,663,164 people) and cover almost 2 percent (68,496 square miles) of this country's total land area. On April 1, 1970, the total population of the United States was 203,235,298 and its total land area was 3,540,989 square miles.

Among the twenty judicial units that were sampled at random for this study plus the twenty that were studied purposefully, a little more than half (twenty-seven) of the fifty states in the United States are represented. More than one-third (eighteen) of the states are represented in the random sample alone. By looking at Tables 2-1 and 2-2, it becomes apparent that the forty judicial units that are the foci of this research span the northeast (Connecticut, Maryland, Massachusetts, New Hampshire, New Jersey, New York and Pennsylvania); the northwest (Alaska, Colorado and Oregon); the midwest (Illinois, Indiana, Iowa, Michigan, Missouri and Ohio); the south (Alabama, Florida, Louisiana, North Carolina, Tennessee, and Virginia); and the west-southwest (Arizona, California, Nevada, New Mexico, and Texas).

Site Visits to Judicial Units

Forty judicial units were selected by the author for comprehensive site visits during this study. Twenty of these were selected at random, and twenty were chosen purposefully. The judicial units that were selected at random received slightly greater attention during their respective site visits than did some of the other units. The average length of time that any individual field investigator including the author spent visiting any given jurisdiction was three work-days. On a number of occasions, however, two or even three investigators visited a single jurisdiction. In this way, the total person-days devoted to some jurisdictional site visits exceeded five person-days of work. Although a few purposefully selected jurisdictions were visited for only one person-day, several larger jurisdictions that were selected at random were visited by two or more field investigators with each investigator remaining on-site for about one full week. Hence, the total person-days during which some jurisdictions were visited exceeded two work-weeks (ten person-days).

An effort was made during every field visit to have at least one field investigator interview a judge, a prosecutor, and a public defense counsel. In most of the randomly selected judicial units and in many of the other jurisdictions, several judges, prosecutors, and defense counsel were interviewed. Whenever time permitted, an effort was made to have each field investigator (if there was more than one on the visit) interview separately at least one judge, one prosecutor, and one defense counsel, in order to reduce interviewer bias. Naturally, in the course of field visits to forty jurisdictions, a field investigator averaged interviews with more than one judge, more than one prosecutor, and more than one defense counsel per field visit. The author visited most of the randomly selected jurisdictions and many of the others, and tried during each site visit to interview at least two judges, two prosecutors and two defense counsel. Whenever possible, the author tried to interview an administrative judge and a judge who routinely accepted guilty pleas; the district attorney himself, or his deputy, in addition to an assistant prosecutor who routinely participated in guilty plea discussions; and an attorney at law engaged in private criminal law practice in addition to personnel in the public defender's office.

Similarly, the author tried to conduct separate, private interviews with judges, prosecutors and defense counsel at least for a few minutes, often to be joined by other local personalities midway through an interview. Other field investigators were instructed to do the same whenever feasible. In this way, interviewee responses could be triangulated for accuracy, bias, and point of view. It was enlightening quite often to observe the difference both in terms of candor and content of response when the same respondent was interviewed first alone and subsequently in the presence of one or more other persons who worked in the locality. The reverse process was frustrating almost invariably, and almost without exception an interviewee who was interviewed first in the presence of someone else from the locality and subsequently alone did not "open up" during the private interview. For this reason, after the pretests, the preferred order of private interview followed by group session was followed as much as possible.

Usually, field visits began early in the working day, which in turn was early in a working week, after the investigators arrived in the locality the evening before. Arrival the evening before was considered important, in the author's opinion, so that an investigator might become familiar with at least one city (usually the county seat) in the jurisdiction prior to the interview. A skillful investigator could rent an auto, drive around town, spot different neighborhoods and their obvious demographic variations, pinpoint blatant vice attractions and observe local police in action. Such a knowledge was utilized on many occasions not only to stimulate conversation and reduce resistance during interviews, but to tactfully impeach interviewees who tried to mislead an investigator into believing the community that was being studied was free of crime. Interviews were scheduled early in the day to enable field investigators to prod interviewees into inviting the investigators to accompany them during proceedings later in the day; and to accommodate executive-level interviewees who were willing to turn the interview over to their subordinates (who, in turn, were likely to do the same thing one level down still later in the day or on the following day). Interviews were scheduled early in the week, if possible, to enable more interviews to be scheduled on-site, since initial interviews had been scheduled by mail or telephone from long-distance. Moreover, interviews were scheduled early in the week to permit the field investigators to follow cases at least part-way through the system, such as from a plea agreement in the corridor to its consummation in chambers or in open court.

Lunches were excellent opportunities for field investigators to begin to socialize with key actors in the judicial process, allowing them to talk with these interviewees outside of their offices. Interviewers tried to obtain information relating to respondents' salaries, fringe benefits, job satisfaction, and other "gripes," in order to assess their working conditions. Lunches were arranged more easily and consequently more often with prosecutors and defense counsel than with judges, and with bottom-level rather than top-level lawyers. Frequently, the author was invited back to dinner, this time with higher-ranking personalities. The author devoted ample attention to secretaries and other support personnel who worked in the offices of key actors in the judicial process, in an effort to confirm or refute impressions gained by the author during earlier interviews or observations of proceedings.

At the beginning of most field visits, the investigators made contact with data processing personnel, particularly within the courts and prosecutors' offices, in an effort to obtain marginal runs, internal summaries, and other unpublished or not yet published statistics relating to the disposition of criminal cases in the locality. Almost always, this process required two or more days, and in every jurisdiction visited an abundance of such information was ready for an investigator to take with him upon his departure or to be transmitted to him within one or two days thereafter.

The author attempted to become involved in observing as many proceedings as possible within each judicial unit that he visited. Sometimes, he had to be content with wandering from one courtroom to the next, sitting in the gallery as a common spectator. More often than not, however, he was invited to sit with counsel in the courtroom, to accompany counsel into chambers, into jails, and back to their offices. The author made every effort to spend an approximately equal amount of time as the "guest" of both prosecutors and defense counsel, in order not to become biased by either of their roles in a given jurisdiction. Thus, an attempt was made to watch one or several plea discussions either at the prosecutor's office or elsewhere at the invitation of a prosecutor; and then to do the same thing at the office of a defense counsel or elsewhere at his invitation. The allocation of equal time between defense and prosecution was not difficult to do. However, judges tended either to accord the author a great deal of time which out of protocol the author was bound to accept, or to accord him very little time. Most judges who sat on the lower court in a two-tier jurisdiction (having general misdemeanor but only limited felony jurisdiction) tended to make themselves more available to field investigators than did their brethren on superior courts (having general jurisdiction).

Invariably, judges who did devote any significant amount of their time to talking with the author pressured the author for at least a small amount of feedback on the outcome of the field visit to their judicial unit toward the end of the visit. Care was taken not to offend any actors since their continual cooperation would be necessary in terms of providing and updating statistical information. For the most part, prosecutors and defense counsel did not seem to care what impressions the author formed during the visits. Naturally, it was impossible for the author or any field investigator to provide even an inquisitive judge with in-depth feedback at the end of a field visit, since analysis of the gathered data would take weeks if not months, and conclusions could not be reached prior to evaluation of all information obtained including statistical materials and other records.

Interview Schedule

Interviews with judges, lawyers and other personnel alike began usually with open-ended questions and gradually became structured more rigidly to focus on topics of special interest to this study. Most initial interviews were scheduled either for the duration of one hour or one-half hour. Hence the interviewer necessarily had to come right to the point. Judges especially exhibited the tendency to take control over an interview and divert discussion to the topics of their choice. When this happened, it became the task of the interviewers to change the discussion or to reschedule a second or subsequent interview.

Apart from blanket questions that were designed to reduce resistance and to gain some knowledge of each particular interviewee's background, expertise, points of view and temperament, a schedule of predetermined, written questions was followed quite rigidly throughout the interviewing of most judges, prosecutors and defense counsel, particularly in the judicial units that were selected at random. The schedule was relaxed slightly even for these interviewees in other jurisdictions, and was approached much more flexibly in all judicial units during interviews with other persons such as defendants and ancillary court personnel. While many of the same questions were posed to judges, prosecutors and defense counsel alike, a number of questions were considered to be more relevant for judges than for lawyers, for prosecutors rather than either judges or defense counsel, or for defense counsel rather than for either judges or prosecutors. Since in most instances the interviewers were unable to dictate the duration of any given interview and in many cases unable even to predict its length very far in advance of its termination, questions had to be posed to each interviewee in their order of relevance priority, more or less. For this reason, some questions that were put to every judge were not asked of every prosecutor or every defense counsel; some that were put to every prosecutor were not asked of every defense counsel; and vice versa in each situation.

It seems appropriate to itemize the areas of questioning that took place during the majority of interviews, particularly those that occurred within the judicial units that were chosen at random. First, those areas of questioning that were deemed relevant to all judges, prosecutors, and defense counsel alike will be summarized, followed by those areas that were deemed to be of greater relevance to one type rather than to the balance of these interviewees. However, this does not mean that interviewees were asked only those questions that pertain to their own respective functions. On the contrary, judges were asked many questions relating to the tasks of prosecutors and defense counsel. Prosecutors were asked about judicial and defense functions. Defense attorneys were asked about prosecution and judicial functions. In this way, the responses from different classes of interviewees could be triangulated both within and across jurisdictional boundaries to reflect the degree to which both perceptions and assessments of individual respondents are shared or disputed by judges, prosecutors, and defense lawyers generally compared with each other.

Judges, prosecutors and defense counsel were asked questions that pertain to the following areas of concern and interest:

Judicial Role in Criminal Case Disposition

A judge's role in the disposition of criminal cases overlaps three major areas and several additional areas that are less critical. The major areas are:

Judicial supervision of dispositional negotiations

Judicial participation in dispositional negotiations

Judicial sentencing practices

A judge is supposed to thoroughly supervise dispositional negotiations including the consummation of the resulting agreement in the form of a defendant's tender of a guilty plea. A judge is expected to make certain that each defendent knows the nature and elementsof the crimes with which he has been charged; that each defendant understands the sentence possibilities for each charge; that each defendant is aware of collateral consequences of conviction including civil disability; that a defendant makes a knowing, intelligent, and voluntary waiver of his right to trial and other constitutionally protected rights prior to acceptance of a guilty plea; that there is a factual basis for the guilty plea which a defendant is about to enter; and that the details of each proceeding are adequately reflected on record.

A judge is not supposed to participate actively in bargaining that leads to disposition of criminal cases by means of the guilty plea, nor is a judge expected to ratify each agreement reached by prosecutors and defense counsel automatically without scrutinizing its content to ensure that justice is served. A judge should avoid even the appearance of impropriety that may accompany judicial comments to a defendant on the advisibility of a guilty plea or the alternative impact that conviction after trial may have upon sentence.

Judicial sentence practices include differential sentencing of defendants convicted by guilty plea compared with those convicted after trial; predictability of a given jurist's sentences for certain crimes; judicial use of presentence investigation reports; similarity of sentencing practices among different judges in the same judicial unit towards similarly situated offenders; attitudes and rationales of judges toward plea bargaining, withdrawal of a plea before and after sentencing, and fulfillment of both judicial and prosecutorial promises related to dispositional agreements with defendants or their counsel.

In addition, several less critical areas of interest were reflected in questions posed to judges. They were asked to indicate the method (for example, election, temporary or permanent appointment) by which they were selected for a judicial appointment and the political constraints, if any, under which they feel they have to operate. Judges were asked to describe briefly their legal experience prior to ascending to the bench, and their judicial trial experience, particularly of criminal cases. Judges were asked about their social relationships with other jurists and with the lawyers who practice before them in court. Finally, judges were asked to enumerate their own personal recommendations and priorities for implementing these, if they had any, for improvement in the judicial process in their locality and elsewhere. When time permitted, prosecutors and defense counsel were asked similar questions about the *judge's* political constraints, experience, social relationships, and usefulness as a change agent.

Prosecutor's Role in Criminal
Case Disposition

A prosecutor's role in the disposition of criminal cases overlaps the following major areas of concern plus several additional less critical areas:

> Prosecutorial discretion generally
>
> Prosecutor's policy toward negotiations
>
> Prosecutor's willingness to reduce charges
>
> Prosecutor's willingness to make sentence recommendations
>
> Equal opportunities for similarly-situated defendants

Prosecutorial discretion involves each prosecutor's subjective responsibility for launching formal criminal charges against suspects believed to be guilty but for screening-out charges that cannot be proven or that need not be or should not be brought in the interest of justice. Prosecutorial discretion includes use and misuse of the *nolle prosecqui*; a prosecutor's influence over decisions by a grand jury; the relationship between a prosecutor's staff and police complainants; the tendency for some prosecutors to resort to "overcharging"; and the leeway allocated by a district attorney to each of his deputies and assistants.

Some prosecutors have formulated verbal or written policies in favor of or against certain kinds of dispositional negotiations, including guilty pleas, dismissals, charge reductions, and other concessions including sentence recommendations. It is a prosecutor's right to limit the scope of negotiations or case dispositions for certain classes of offenders based upon their case histories, the nature of their crimes, or other input such as the wishes of victims or of the police.

Criminal charges may be disposed of through negotiations that result in several forms of agreement between defendants and a prosecutor. Multiple charges pending against a defendant may be dismissed in return for the defendant's guilty plea to one or two of them. Serious charges may be reduced in magnitude to lesser included or to lesser related offenses. A prosecutor may make or abstain from making sentence recommendations to the court, and if made, such recommendations may be very general or quite explicit. Naturally, when made, sentence recommendations may be followed by the court completely, partially, or not at all, in each situation always or sometimes.

Similarly situated offenders are supposed to receive equal access to dispositional negotiations and to the fruits of the same under the American Bar Association's Standards. This is not the case always in some jurisdictions, where dispositional outcome in a given case may depend upon the defendant's social status or that of his lawyer or victim. Some prosecutors get tougher at least with highly visible criminal offenders during some seasons of the year or during election years in order to mollify or impress the public.

In addition, several less critical areas of interest were reflected in questions posed to prosecutors. They were asked to indicate the method (for example, election, temporary or permanent appointment) by which they were selected as prosecutors or as deputy or assistant prosecutors and the political constraints, if any, under which they feel they have to operate. Prosecutors at all levels were asked to describe briefly their legal experience prior to working in the district attorney's office, and their trial experience particularly in criminal cases. They were asked about their social relationships with members of the bench and bar, the training they received, if any, since beginning to work in the district attorney's office, and their career objectives for the future. Finally, each was asked to enumerate his own personal recommendations and priorities for implementing these, if he had any, for improvement of the judicial process both locally and generally. When time permitted, judges and defense counsel were asked similar questions about the *prosecutor's* political constraints, experience, social relationships, training, career objectives, and usefulness as a change agent.

Defense Counsel's Role in Criminal
Case Disposition

Defense counsel's role in the disposition of criminal cases overlaps the following major areas of concern plus several additional but less critical areas:

Effectiveness of representation

Attitude toward negotiations

Client satisfaction with dispositions

Sufficiency and significance of fees

Defense strategies and tactics

In addition, each defense counsel was asked to indicate how these and other questions vary according to the method by which defense counsel are selected (for example, privately retained, court appointment of attorney in private practice, public defender, and so on).

To be effective in representing a client, a defense lawyer has to be competent and knowledgeable in both the substantive and the adjective (procedural) criminal law, as well as in related legal areas and in advocacy skills. Counsel must be truthful with a client, and be able to ascertain the truth from the client. A defense attorney should be energetic but not abrasive, must resist conflicts of interest and favoritism of one client over others. More than anything else, a defense lawyer must achieve and retain the confidence of his client, or he will cease to be effective.

Different lawyers can be expected to share different attitudes toward the negotiation process generally, but particularly to the practice whereby defendants who are charged with crimes plead guilty and avoid going to trial. Some lawyers feel they are more proficient in the courtroom than others do. Usually, skill as an advocate develops with experience at trials, hearings, and other adversarial proceedings. A defense attorney's attitude toward dispositional negotiations may be shaped by his impression of the fairness of their outcome, the flexibility of the court and the prosecutor, and the ultimate satisfaction of his client with the dispositions reached. Criminal offenders may castigate the system outwardly to impress their peers in jail and on the street, but do offenders who have pled guilty or otherwise disposed of criminal charges by negotiations and without trial feel inwardly satisfied that justice has been done? Do they feel they got a raw deal or got away with something? The person who is in the best position to know is the defense attorney.

A person cannot do the best job in any walk of life unless he is paid the fair value of his services at reasonable intervals. Some lawyers are paid more than others are, and this may affect the services they provide to their clients. Some clients pay the same lawyer more than his other clients pay him, and this may enable them to receive better, swifter, or more personalized representation. The distinction between the kind and amount of consultation and representation received by indigents compared with paying clients is of crucial importance, since too wide a variance in this regard will destroy the mandate of Gideon v. Wainwright (1963).[25] The amount of financial resources on which a defense lawyer can draw may affect the quality and the quantity of the investigation he can do or have done to learn the true facts surrounding the crimes of which his client has been accused.

Defense lawyers can utilize a variety of strategies and tactics to accelerate or delay criminal proceedings and to manipulate the court and the prosecutor into making errors that may be deemed prejudicial by higher courts in the future. Defense attorneys can coerce their own clients as well and in many instances convince a defendant that a negotiated disposition is in his best interests when in fact it is not. Strategies and tactics that defense counsel use inside and outside of the courtroom give considerable indication of whether justice is served or games are played. Contrary to popular impression, in some legal circles, high standards of professional responsibility (ethical considerations) should be in the best interest of the client as well as the lawyer.

Each defense counsel who was interviewed was asked questions relating to other areas of interest, such as how clients are referred to them; the extent to which politics influences their relationship with judges and prosecutors as well as other defense lawyers, if it does at all; their legal experience and especially their trial experience in criminal cases; their social relationships with members of the bench and bar; and their personal recommendations and priorities for implementing changes in the judicial process both locally and in general. When time permitted, judges and prosecutors were asked similar questions about the *defense* lawyer's client referrals, political influences, legal and trial experience; social relationships; and usefulness as a change agent.

Defendant's Role in Criminal
Case Disposition

A defendant's role in the dispositon of criminal charges pending against him overlaps the following major areas of concern together with several other areas:

Reasons for avoiding trial

Confidence in defense counsel

Satisfaction with disposition at time of disposition and after sentence is imposed

Defendants may be expected to agree to pleading guilty to criminal charges and avoiding trial for several reasons, such as to minimize publicity, secure a speedy disposition, insure certainty of sanction, reduce legal expenses, or to accommodate the wishes of others such as the judge, the prosecutor, or the defense counsel. The willingness of a defendant to follow the recommendations of his lawyer as these pertain to the disposition of criminal charges should be a testament to the client's confidence in the competence and integrity of his attorney. A defendant may never be satisfied with the way in which charges against him reach a disposition or with the disposition itself, or he may be satisfied at the time of disposition but become dissatisfied later on, or he may be dissatisfied at the time of disposition but feel contented in retrospect.

Defendants who were interviewed were asked to express their opinions on other areas of concern as well. They were asked when willing to do so to assess the evidence against them in terms of its strength and persuasiveness. (Defendants were asked to comment on the merits of their criminal charges only when being interviewed by attorneys at law, in order that any statements made by a defendant would be subject to the attorney-client privilege.) In addition, defendants were asked to explain their own participation in negotiations if they participated at all, the extent to which defense counsel communicated to them the details of negotiations in which he participated but they did not, and their attitudes toward bargaining and impressions of its utility both generally and in their individual cases.

Defendants were asked to comment on the effect which they believed their personal characteristics such as race, sex, and socioeconomic status had on the likely disposition of charges pending against them, as well as similar effects of their criminal record if they had one, their pretrial custody status (confined or released), and their sophistication in terms of the knowledge which each had amassed about the criminal justice system and especially the judicial process as a result of earlier arrests, convictions, and confinements.

When time permitted, defendants were asked to assess the roles of judges, prosecutors, and defense counsel as they interfaced during the process by which criminal case dispositions are negotiated. Defendants were asked to discuss their perceptions of political constraints, experience and training, social interrelationships, and general class values against which judges, prosecutors and defense counsel alike function throughout the judicial process. Defendants were asked to make any suggestions they might have for improvement in the judicial process, together with their priorities for implementing these changes.

Notes

1. Howard, Criminal Justice in England 321 (1931).

2. Aschuler, The Prosecutor's Role in Plea Bargaining, 36 U. Chi. L. Rev. 50, 106 (1968).

3. 404 U.S. 257,261 (1971).

4. Address before the American Bar Association, 1975.

5. Dash, Cracks in the Foundation of Criminal Justice, 46 Ill. L. Rev. 385 (1951).

6. See supra, note 2. See, also, Davis, Sentences for Sale—A New Look at Plea Bargaining in England and America, Part 1, 1971 Crim. L. Rev. 150 (1971) and Part 2, 1971 Crim. L. Rev. 218 (1971).

7. Berger, The Case Against Plea Bargaining, 62 A.B.A. J. 621,622 (1976).

8. Baker, The Prosecutor—Initiation of Prosecution, 23 J.A. Inst. Crim. L. & C. 770,786 (1932).

9. Cooper, Plea Bargaining: A Comparative Analysis, 5 Intl. L. & Pol. 427,446 (1972).

10. Alschuler, The Defense Attorney's Role in Plea Bargaining, 84 Yale L.J. 1179 (1975) and The Prosecutor's Role in Plea Bargaining, 36 U. Chi. L. Rev. 50 (1968).

11. United States Department of Justice, Law Enforcement Assistance Administration, Criminal Victimization in the United States; 1975 A National Crime Survey Report (1976).

12. Gottfredson, Neithercutt, Nuffield and O'Leary, Four Thousand Lifetimes: A Study of Time Served and Parole Outcomes (1974).

13. Conducted by Georgetown University Law Center, Washington, D.C.

14. For citations, see sources to table 4-1, chapter 4.

15. United States Department of Justice, Federal Bureau of Investigation, Uniform Crime Reports for the United States, 1975 (1976); Id., 1976 (1977); Id., 1977 (1978).

16. For citations, see sources to tables 4-5 and 5-4 in chapters 4 and 5 respectively.

17. For citations, see sources to table 5-4, chapter 5.

18. Id.

19. For citations, see sources for tables 5-1, 5-2, and 5-3 in chapter 5.

20. Reliability is a problem that is especially difficult to control in household survey research on the general population. Even when recall periods are short, respondents tend to "telescope" or confuse *when* different crimes took place. To control for this potential error, bounding procedures are used, and the random group method is a technique that can reduce potential variances among different samples taken of a national population. See United States Department of Justice, Law Enforcement Assistance Administration, Criminal Victimization in the United States, 1975: A National Survey Report 108 (1976).

21. In some instances, the author supervised research that was conducted in the judicial unit studied without being present physically. This was true in fewer than 10 percent of the cases.

22. When a superior court and one or more inferior courts exercise concurrent jurisdiction over the same geographic territory (for example, a county), the location is deemed to be a single judicial unit. In 1975, there were 2,460 county-level governmental units with populations under 50,000; and 338 such units with populations in excess of 100,000. See 1975 World Almanac 183 (1976).

23. Id.

24. In 1975, there were 88 federal judicial districts situated within the United States. Every state has at least one federal judicial district situated within its boundaries, and the District of Columbia is a separate federal judicial district. In addition, three states (California, New York and Texas) had *four* federal districts each in 1975; nine states (Alabama, Florida, Georgia, Illinois, Louisiana, North Carolina, Oklahoma, Pennsylvania and Tennessee) had *three* federal judicial districts each in 1975; and eleven states (Arkansas, Indiana, Iowa, Michigan, Mississippi, Missouri, Ohio, Virginia, Washington, West Virginia, and Wisconsin) had *two* federal districts each in 1975. See 28 U.S.C. 133.

25. 372 U.S. 335.

3 Crime and Punishment in the United States: 1975

An estimated 40.5 million serious crimes took place within the United States during 1975, according to the National Crime Survey conducted by the United States Bureau of the Census and sponsored by the United States Department of Justice.[1] This was only an estimate. The estimate included most major crimes that have specific and identifiable victims, but it excluded "victimless" crimes, numerous offenses that are difficult either to discover or to document, and many crimes in which the victim may have participated.[2] Thus, it seems fair to say that in 1975 there were *at least* 40 million crimes that Americans were able to report, and probably many more.

Not all of the crimes which Americans were able to report were actually reported to the police. According to the National Crime Survey, victims attributed their failure to notify the police most often to two beliefs: Nothing could have been done by the police, and the crime was not important enough to warrant being reported.[3] Of those crimes that were reported to the police, only a fraction were cleared by the arrest of a suspect. Among persons who were charged with committing one or more crimes, fewer than two-thirds (much fewer for those accused of committing some of the most serious offenses) were ultimately convicted in court. By far, most of the convicted criminal offenders received light prison sentences if they received any prison sentence at all.

The significance and the value of the present study are dependent upon the reader's appreciation of the volume and characteristics of the major crimes that were committed in the United States during the mid-1970s, as well as of the aftermath of these offenses in terms of police detection and prosecution in the courts. Six groups of data seem critical to an understanding of the background to the present study. These include the volume of crime and of specific crimes that are believed to have occurred in a given time and place; the overall crime rate and crime-specific crime rates per 1,000 population; the percentages of crimes reported to the police; the percentage of reported crimes cleared by arrest; the percentage of arrests resulting in conviction; and the punishment imposed on convicted criminal offenders.

Volume of Crime

According to the National Crime Survey, 21.4 million crimes against the person of individual victims took place in 1975, of which one-fourth (5.5 million) were crimes of violence. An estimated 17.25 million household crimes occurred during the same year, as did an estimated 1.8 million commercial crimes.[4] Personal and household larcenies (thefts) accounted for an estimated 62 percent of the total criminal victimizations in the United States during 1975, while more serious offenses such as assault, personal and commercial robbery, and rape made up an estimated 14 percent of the crimes.[5] However, the National Crime Survey noted that among the measured crimes, the least frequent was rape, and that the less serious forms of personal robbery (those without injury) and assault (simple rather than aggravated) out-numbered the more serious forms of these crimes. (See table 3-1.)

The National Crime Survey estimated that 64 percent of violent crimes were perpetrated by a lone offender, while 32 percent were committed by two or more conspirators. Crimes of violence involving nonstrangers were far more likely to have been perpetrated by a single offender[6] than those committed by strangers. In addition, the National Crime Survey estimated that 37 percent of personal violent crimes and 71 percent of commercial robberies were carried out by armed offenders. With respect to personal crimes of violence, the Survey found that the proportion of stranger-to-stranger incidents in which the offender used a weapon was greater than that for nonstranger incidents.[7]

Crime Rates

During 1975, there were approximately 167 million persons over twelve years old, 73 million households, and 6.7 million commercial establishments within the United States. As table 3-2 shows, the victimization rate for all crimes of violence combined was estimated by the National Crime Survey at 32.7 per thousand persons over twelve years old, while the victimization rate for crimes of theft was estimated at 95.8 per thousand persons over twelve years old. The survey estimated that for every thousand American households in 1975, there occurred one hundred twenty-five household thefts, over ninety burglaries, and twenty attempted or completed auto thefts. Furthermore, it estimated that for every thousand American businesses almost 230 attempted or completed burglaries and almost forty attempted or completed robberies took place in 1975.

Stranger-to-stranger episodes accounted for about two-thirds of the violent crimes and had an overall estimated rate of 21.3 per thousand population age twelve and over, compared with 11.4 for those by acquaintances or relatives. Males of all races had a higher proportion of violent crimes at the hands of strangers than did females of any race. There was a tendency for the proportion of stranger-to-stranger violent crimes to rise as the level of the victim's affluence increased.[8]

Table 3-1

Personal, Household, and Commercial Crimes: Estimated Number and Percentage
Distribution of Victimizations, by Sector, 1975

Sector and Type of Crime	Estimated Number	Estimated Percentage of Crimes Within Sector	Estimated Percentage of All Crimes
All crimes	40,483,000	–	100.0
Personal sector	21,418,000	100.0	52.9
Crimes of violence	5,448,000	25.4	13.5
Rape	151,000	0.7	0.4
Completed rape	57,000	0.3	0.1
Attempted rape	94,000	0.4	0.2
Robbery	1,121,000	5.2	2.8
Robbery with injury	353,000	1.6	0.9
From serious assault	207,000	1.0	0.5
From minor assault	146,000	0.7	0.4
Robbery without injury	768,000	3.6	1.9
Assault	4,176,000	19.5	10.3
Aggravated assault	1,590,000	7.4	3.9
With injury	543,000	2.5	1.3
Attempted assault with weapon	1,047,000	4.9	2.6
Simple assault	2,586,000	12.1	6.4
With injury	687,000	3.2	1.7
Attempted assault without weapon	1,899,000	8.9	4.7
Crimes of theft	15,970,000	74.6	39.4
Personal larceny with contact	514,000	2.4	1.3
Purse snatching	180,000	0.8	0.4
Completed purse snatching	119,000	0.6	0.3
Attempted purse snatching	61,000	0.3	0.2
Pocket Picking	334,000	1.6	0.8
Personal larceny without contact	15,456,000	72.2	38.2
Total population age 12 and over	166,732,000	–	–
Household sector	17,267,000	100.0	42.7
Burglary	6,689,000	38.7	16.5
Forcible entry	2,252,000	13.0	5.6
Unlawful entry without force	2,960,000	17.1	7.3
Attempted forcible entry	1,477,000	8.6	3.6
Household larceny	9,158,000	53.0	22.6
Less than $50	5,617,000	32.5	13.9
$50 or more	2,708,000	15.7	6.7
Amount not available	278,000	1.6	0.7
Attempted larceny	555,000	3.2	1.4
Motor vehicle theft	1,420,000	8.2	3.5
Completed theft	912,000	5.3	2.3
Attempted theft	508,000	2.9	1.3
Total number of households	73,137,000	–	–
Commercial sector	1,798,000	100.0	4.4
Burglary	1,534,000	85.3	3.8
Completed burglary	1,125,000	62.6	2.8
Attempted burglary	409,000	22.7	1.0
Robbery	264,000	14.7	0.7
Completed robbery	204,000	11.4	0.5
Attempted robbery	60,000	3.3	0.1
Total number of commercial establishments	6,709,000	–	–

Source: United States Department of Justice, National Criminal Justice Information & Statistics
Service, Criminal Victimization in the United States, 1975. Washington: United States Government
Printing Office, 1978, 17.

Table 3-2
Personal, Household, and Commercial Crimes: Estimated Victimization
Rates, by Sector and Type of Crime, 1975

Sector and Type of Crime	Estimated Rate	Base of Rate
Personal sector		
Crimes of violence	32.7	
Rape	0.9	
Completed rape	0.3	
Attempted rape	0.6	Per 1,000
Robbery	6.7	persons age
Robbery with injury	2.1	12 and over
From serious assault	1.2	
From minor assault	0.9	
Robbery without injury	4.6	
Assault	25.1	
Aggravated assault	9.5	
With injury	3.3	
Attempted assault with weapon	6.3	
Simple assault	15.5	
With injury	4.1	
Attempted assault without weapon	11.1	
Crimes of theft	95.8	
Personal larceny with contact	3.1	
Purse snatching	1.1	
Completed purse snatching	0.7	
Attempted purse snatching	0.4	
Pocket picking	2.0	
Personal larceny without contact	2.7	
Household sector		
Burglary	91.5	
Forcible entry	30.8	
Unlawful entry without force	40.5	Per 1,000
Attempted forcible entry	20.2	households
Household larceny	125.2	
Less than $50	76.8	
$50 or more	37.0	
Amount not available	3.8	
Attempted larceny	7.6	
Motor vehicle theft	19.4	
Completed theft	12.5	
Attempted theft	7.0	
Commercial sector		
Burglary	228.6	
Completed burglary	167.6	Per 1,000
Attempted burglary	61.0	commercial
Robbery	39.4	establishments
Completed robbery	30.5	
Attempted robbery	9.0	

Source: United States Department of Justice, National Criminal Justice Information &
Statistics Service, Criminal Victimization in the United States, 1975. Washington, D.C.:
United States Government Printing Office, 1978, 18.

Crimes Reported to Police

Less than one-third of all crimes against the person that were committed in 1975 are believed to have been reported to the police, as table 3-3 indicates. Nearly 40 percent of household crimes and 80 percent of commercial crimes are believed to have been reported to police during the same period, however. The National Crime Survey found no significant difference according to the victim's sex in the overall percentage of personal crimes reported. However, the survey found that females were more likely than males to have reported violent crimes.[9] The survey found that teenagers were least likely to report crimes, and that homeowners were more likely than renters to report crimes, a likelihood that increased in proportion to the value of property lost or harmed.[10]

Known Crimes Cleared by Arrest

It should not be difficult to understand that a crime is unlikely to be cleared by the arrest of a suspect unless that crime has been reported to or detected by the police. In 1975, about 20 percent of all major crimes that became known to the police in most areas of the United States during that year became cleared by arrest. Of course, not all arrests led to the conviction of the suspect. Undoubtedly, some persons who were arrested should not have been in view of the paucity of admissible evidence pointing to their guilt. Moreover, it must be stressed that even known crimes that are not cleared during or within a short while after the end of the year in which they were reported are, for the most part, very unlikely to be cleared by arrest.

Table 3-4 shows that the percentage of known crimes that were cleared by arrest in 1975 varied considerably according to the type of crime. More than three-fourths of known homicides including manslaughter were cleared by arrest in most American jurisdictions, but only half of known forcible rapes and slightly over half of known assaults were cleared during the same time period. Less than half of all known violent crimes combined were cleared by arrest during 1975. Only about one-quarter of known robberies and one-fifth of known burglaries were cleared. In most urban jurisdictions during 1975, less than 15 percent of known auto thefts were cleared by arrest. These percentages remained fairly constant, crime for crime, across jurisdictions of differential size. Percentages of clearance by arrest were slightly better in rural areas and slightly worse in suburban areas compared with urban centers, on the whole.

Arrests Resulting in Conviction

Not everyone who is arrested is formally charged with having committed any crime at all. On the other hand, most persons who are arrested in most

Table 3-3

Personal, Household, and Commercial Crimes: Estimated Percentage of Victimizations Reported to the Police, by Type of Crime, 1975

Type of Crime	Estimated Percent Reported
All personal crimes	31.6
Crimes of violence	47.2
Rape	56.3
Robbery	53.3
Robbery with injury	65.0
From serious assault	66.7
From minor assault	62.5
Robbery without injury	47.9
Assault	45.2
Aggravated assault	55.2
Without injury	65.1
Attempted assault with weapon	50.1
Simple assault	39.1
With injury	47.9
Attempted assault without weapon	35.9
Crimes of theft	26.2
Personal larceny with contact	34.6
Purse snatching	48.7
Pocket picking	26.9
Personal larceny without contact	26.0
All household crimes	39.0
Burglary	48.6
Forcible entry	72.9
Unlawful entry without force	38.0
Attempted forcible entry	32.9
Household larceny	27.1
Completed larceny[a]	27.3
Less than $50	15.4
$50 or more	53.2
Attempted larceny	23.1
Motor vehicle theft	71.1
Completed theft	91.1
Attempted theft	35.3
All commercial crimes	81.1
Burglary	79.6
Robbery	90.2

Source: United States Department of Justice, National Criminal Justice Information & Statistics Service, Criminal Victimization in the United States, 1975. Washington, D.C.: U.S. Government Printing Office, 1978, 73.

[a]Includes data, not shown separately, on larcenies for which the value of loss was not ascertained.

jurisdictions are charged with one crime or another, and some are charged with more than one crime. Table 3-5 indicates that in the major American cities (data is unavailable for other areas), about eighteen persons are charged for every one hundred offenses that are cleared by arrest. The percentage of persons charged is

Table 3-4
Offenses Known to Police and Percentage Cleared by Arrest, by Offense and Size of Place, 1975

Population Group	Total Crime Index	Violent Crime[a]	Property Crime[b]	Criminal Homicide		Forcible Rape	Robbery	Aggravated Assault	Burglary	Larceny-Theft	Motor Vehicle Theft
				Murder and Non-negligent Manslaughter	Manslaughter by Negligence						
Cities 6,449 cities; total population 127,068,000:											
Offenses known	8,198,613	797,688	7,400,925	13,956	4,199	40,168	403,351	340,213	2,237,286	4,367,293	796,346
Percent cleared by arrest	21.0	44.7	18.5	78.3	79.3	51.3	27.0	63.5	17.5	19.7	14.4
Suburban Area[c] 3,584 agencies; total population 59,313,000:											
Offenses known	2,770,490	177,167	2,593,323	3,066	2,582	11,424	55,855	106,822	789,591	1,594,615	209,117
Percent cleared by arrest	19.7	50.0	17.6	77.2	84.0	51.5	29.0	60.1	17.2	17.7	18.6
Rural Area 1,504 agencies; total population 21,198,000:											
Offenses known	483,860	39,923	443,937	1,716	1,538	2,793	5,238	30,176	188,392	230,578	24,967
Percent cleared by arrest	23.6	70.1	19.4	82.7	69.6	68.4	47.3	73.5	19.5	17.5	36.6

Source: United States Department of Justice, Federal Bureau of Investigation, Uniform Crime Reports for the United States, 1975. Washington, D.C.: United States Government Printing Office, 1976, pp. 166, 167.

aViolent crime is offenses of murder, forcible rape, robbery, and aggravated assault.

bProperty crime is offenses of burglary, larceny-theft, and motor vehicle theft.

cIncludes suburban city and county police agencies within metropolitan areas. Excludes core cities. Suburban cities are also included in other city groups.

Table 3-5
Offenses Known to Police and Cleared by Arrest, by Offense and Disposition, 1975
(2,198 cities; 1975 Estimated Population 33,275,000)

	Total Crime Index	Violent Crime[a]	Property Crime[b]	Murder	Forcible Rape	Robbery	Aggravated Assault	Burglary	Larceny Theft
Offenses known	1,936,519	144,644	1,791,875	2,876	8,365	63,078	70,325	505,133	1,103,745
Offenses cleared	405,530	71,986	333,544	2,361	4,379	18,679	46,567	88,893	218,162
Percent cleared	20.9	49.8	18.6	82.1	52.3	29.6	66.2	17.6	19.8
Total arrests	383,351	58,601	324,750	2,818	3,694	20,472	31,617	82,149	218,228
Per 100 offenses	19.8	40.5	18.1	98.0	44.2	32.5	45.0	16.3	19.8
Arrests under 18	179,253	12,451	166,802	214	648	6,388	5,201	45,568	106,429
Per 100 offenses	9.3	8.6	9.3	7.4	7.7	10.1	7.4	9.0	9.6
Persons charged	353,166	55,606	297,560	2,617	3,578	19,123	30,288	76,871	198,126
Per 100 offenses	18.2	38.4	16.6	91.0	42.8	30.3	43.1	15.2	18.0
Persons guilty as charged	106,579	14,476	92,103	780	736	4,489	8,471	15,713	72,935
Per 100 offenses	5.5	10.0	5.1	27.1	8.8	7.1	12.0	3.1	6.6
Persons guilty of lesser offenses	10,963	3,242	7,721	203	210	733	2,096	2,799	4,327
Per 100 offenses	0.6	2.2	0.4	7.1	2.5	1.2	3.0	0.6	0.4
Persons acquitted or dismissed	44,725	11,520	32,205	459	821	2,916	7,324	7,535	23,144
Per 100 offenses	2.3	8.0	1.9	16.0	9.8	4.6	10.4	1.5	2.1
Juveniles referred to juvenile court	121,756	9,213	112,543	135	478	4,746	3,854	34,884	66,260
Per 100 offenses	6.3	6.4	6.3	4.7	5.7	7.5	5.5	6.9	6.0

Source: United States Department of Justice, Federal Bureau of Investigation, Uniform Crime Reports for the United States, 1975. Washington, D.C.: United States Government Printing Office, 1976, p. 176.
aViolent crime is offenses of murder, forcible rape, robbery, and aggravated assault.
bProperty crime is offenses of burglary, larceny-theft, and motor vehicle theft.

highest for homicides followed by other violent crimes, and is lowest for property crimes. Essentially, this is the same pattern as evidenced in table 3-4 regarding percentage of crimes known to the police that are cleared by arrest.[11]

A study of the dispositions of persons who have been formally charged by the police with having committed a crime during 1975 reveals that, on the average, about two-thirds are convicted of at least one crime, which may be the crime (or one of the crimes) charged, or a lesser included offense. Of the other third, half are referred to a juvenile court for adjudication of delinquency, and the other half either are acquitted at trial or manage to obtain dismissal of the charges then pending against them without trial, such as during the pretrial discovery process.[12]

Table 3-6 shows that, with a few exceptions, this overall ratio remains rather consistent among most types of crime. Notable exceptions to this pattern include crimes such as driving a motor vehicle while intoxicated and public drunkenness, where over three-quarters of the persons charged with either offense are convicted. In addition, less than one-quarter of the persons charged with motor vehicle theft are convicted, and just over one-quarter of those charged with vandalism are convicted. One reason for the low conviction rates for persons charged with these crimes is that many such offenders, being youthful, are referred to the juvenile courts for adjudication as juvenile delinquents.

It is crucially important to this study that the reader be cognizant of the fact that not everyone who has been charged with committing any particular offense will be convicted of that offense. A significant proportion of defendants charged with many serious crimes plead guilty to or are found guilty of one or more lesser offenses. As table 3-6 indicates, about 10 percent of the defendants who were charged in 1975 with committing a homicide, a forcible rape, an aggravated assault, embezzlement, or prostitution were convicted of a lesser offense, as were 3 to 5 percent of those charged with most other major offenses.

Finally, and of even more critical importance to the present study, it must be remembered that the Uniform Crime Reports subsume, statistically, less serious crimes into more serious crimes when a person has been charged with more than one offense. Thus, a person who is charged with the rape and murder of a victim will be reported to have been charged only with a homicide, since rape is considered less serious than homicide. If convicted of both homicide and rape, the person would be reported to have been convicted only of homicide. If convicted of rape, the person in this example would be reported to have been convicted of a lesser offense, even though there were not necessarily any mitigating circumstances.

Punishment Imposed for Crime

For years, it was extremely difficult to estimate the actual length of time in prison that a person who was convicted of any given crime would be likely to

Table 3-6

Disposition of Persons Formally Charged by the Police, by Offense, 1975

Offense	Number of Persons Charged (Held for Prosecution)	Percent of Persons Charged			
		Guilty		Acquitted or Dismissed	Referred to Juvenile Court
		Offense Charged	Lesser Offense		
Total	1,556,071	60.7	3.8	16.5	19.0
Criminal homicide:					
Murder and nonnegligent manslaughter	1,734	48.1	12.7	30.3	8.9
Manslaughter by negligence	330	51.2	9.1	24.2	15.5
Forcible rape	2,449	33.0	9.9	36.5	20.7
Robbery	13,916	35.6	5.8	22.2	36.3
Aggravated assault	25,188	41.4	9.7	31.9	17.0
Burglary	69,831	26.7	4.8	12.1	56.5
Larceny theft	190,329	44.2	2.8	13.7	39.2
Motor vehicle theft	19,815	20.0	3.6	13.8	62.5
Violent crime	43,287	39.3	8.6	29.0	23.1
Property crime	279,975	38.1	3.4	13.3	45.2
Subtotal for above offenses	323,592	38.3	4.1	15.4	42.2
Other assaults	64,574	47.7	2.8	36.1	13.4
Arson	2,224	22.8	3.3	15.6	58.3
Forgery and counterfeiting	8,853	53.4	6.3	22.6	17.8
Fraud	23,321	60.6	3.4	32.4	3.7
Embezzlement	727	43.7	9.8	29.3	17.2
Stolen property; buying, receiving, possessing	13,421	38.0	4.9	26.8	30.3
Vandalism	29,219	28.7	1.9	19.9	49.6
Weapons, carrying, possessing, etc.	24,646	60.7	4.0	23.5	11.8
Prostitution and commercialized vice	7,434	51.4	9.8	31.9	6.8
Sex offenses (except forcible rape and prostitution)	8,110	50.0	7.3	25.4	17.3

Narcotic drug laws	70,395	45.8	4.3	25.1	24.9
Gambling	10,301	75.9	2.8	18.4	2.9
Offenses against family and children	6,613	51.7	3.8	27.1	17.5
Driving under the influence	180,197	74.8	15.5	8.3	1.4
Liquor laws	70,464	65.4	0.9	9.6	24.1
Drunkenness	317,367	87.6	0.6	9.7	2.0
Disorderly conduct	157,240	67.8	1.0	20.7	10.5
Vagrancy	5,935	53.5	2.4	24.9	19.2
All other offenses	231,438	52.4	1.6	19.5	26.5

Source: United States Department of Justice, Federal Bureau of Investigation, Uniform Crime Reports for the United States, 1975. Washington, D.C.: United States Government Printing Office, 1976, pp. 166, 167.

serve. It is still somewhat arduous to make this prediction in many states. However, the National Council on Crime and Delinquency conducted a national survey of offenders across the nation who were incarcerated between 1965 and 1970. Their results indicate that even those offenders who have been convicted of the most serious crimes—homicide, forcible rape, and armed robbery—seldom serve much more than five years in prison on the average. Of course, a small minority of offenders spend all or the better part of the remainder of their lives in custody.

Table 3-7 indicates that persons who were convicted of a homicide tended to serve the longest actual time in prison, about five years. Sixty percent of these offenders served between two and ten years. Persons convicted of forcible rape tended to serve the next-longest time in prison, about four years. Sixty percent of these offenders served between 1.5 and nine years. Then there appears to have been a big jump in length of time actually served by an offender in prison. Persons convicted of armed robbery served an average of 2.75 years in prison. Sixty percent served between 1.5 and five years. An even bigger jump was observed between these three offenses and most other offenses, for each of which the average convicted offender served two years or less (and considerably less, in the case of burglary, fraud, and theft offenses, for instance).

One inequitability that emerged from the NCCD study may be summarized

Table 3-7
Median Months Served by Offense Categories; Mean, Standard Deviation, and Range of Time Served by Mid-60 Percent for Each Category

Offense	Median Time Served	Range in Months of Mid-60 Percent of Cases	Standard Deviation	Mean
Homicide	58.6	23-121	72.3	79.3
Forcible rape	49.5	20-106	63.9	68.7
Armed robbery	33.1	17-62	40.2	44.4
Other sex offenses	25.4	12-47	32.6	34.4
Unarmed robbery	24.8	13-43	29.3	32.1
Statutory rape	22.6	11-51	36.0	34.9
Manslaughter	20.8	11-42	27.2	29.3
Narcotics offenses	19.9	10-40	23.3	27.3
Burglary	16.2	9-29	23.0	22.3
Aggravated assault	15.4	7-30	24.4	22.7
Check fraud	14.7	9-24	15.4	18.9
Vehicle theft	13.8	8-23	16.2	18.0
Other theft (larceny)	12.8	8-22	16.9	17.3
Other fraud	12.2	8-21	13.6	16.0

Source: D. Gottfredson, M. Neithercutt, J. Nuffield, and V. O'Leary, Four Thousand Lifetimes: A Study of Time Served and Parole Outcomes. Davis, Calif.: Research Center, National Council on Crime and Delinquency. Above estimates are based on sample of over 100,000 cases from the fifty states and the District of Columbia between the years 1965-1970.

as follows. About one-fifth of those convicted of burglary, aggravated assault, narcotics offenses, and auto theft ended up spending as long or longer in prison than one-fifth of those convicted of homicide and forcible rape. While characteristics of an offender's background, among other factors, might explain these differential sentences, a number of the variations seem to be grounds for concern.

Chances of Punishment

Based upon the aggregate of information that has been presented in this chapter up to this juncture, it should be obvious that a large proportion of most types of crime believed to have been committed during a given year (in this case, 1975) are never reported to the police and therefore never cleared by arrest that in turn precludes conviction of the offender. Among those crimes that are reported, a similarly large proportion are never cleared by the arrest of a suspect and therefore will not result in the conviction of an offender, either. Finally, even among those crimes that are committed, reported, and cleared by a bona fide arrest (some arrests do not result in formal criminal charges being filed, for various reasons[13]) that results in a formal criminal accusation being filed against a suspected offender, the defendant may be acquitted, have the charges against him dismissed, or plead or be found guilty of a lesser offense rather than of the offense charged. With all these strikes against justice, exactly what is the likelihood that one will be convicted of any given crime that one decides to perpetrate?

By computing a rather simple equation, we may learn the rough answer to this gruelling question, as table 3-8 demonstrates. The equation operates as follows: Starting with the estimated number of criminal victimizations that are believed to have occurred during the time period in question (in this case, during 1975, according to the National Crime Survey), in column (a) of the table, one calculates the estimated number of charges per one hundred victimizations (column (e)) by multiplying the estimated percent of crimes reported to police during that time period (column (b), taken from table 3-3) with the estimated percentage of reported crimes cleared by arrest (column (c), taken from table 3-4) adjusted by a factor representing that proportion of each crime-type-specific arrest rate that accounts for arrest "washouts") (arrests not leading to the filing of formal charges, as estimated by means of table 3-5 through subtracting for each respective crime type the "persons charged per 100 offenses" from the "total arrests per 100 offenses"). This estimated number of charges per one hundred victimizations may then be multiplied by the estimated conviction rate of persons who have been charged with each specific type of crime (column (f), taken from table 1-6), which in turn will yield the estimated chances of conviction per one hundred estimated victimizations according to

Table 3-8

Estimated Number of Victimizations, Percentage of Crimes Reported to Police, Percentage of Crimes Reported Crimes Cleared by Arrest, Charges per 100 Reported Crimes and per 100 Victimizations, Chances of Conviction per Charge and Chances of Conviction per 100 Victimizations, According to Type of Crime: United States, 1975

Type of Crime	Estimated Number of Victimizations (a)	Estimated Percent of Crimes Reported to Police (b)	Estimated Percent of Reported Crimes Cleared by Arrest (c)	Estimated Charges per 100 Crimes Reported to Police (d)	Estimated Charges per 100 Victimizations (e)	Estimated Percent Convicted of Persons Charged (f)	Estimated Chances of Conviction per 100 Victimizations (g)
All violent crime	5,752,000	49.2	44.7	42.6	21.0	47.9	10.1
Rape	151,000	56.3	51.3	49.9	28.1	42.9	12.1
Robbery	1,385,000	60.3	27.0	24.8	15.0	41.4	6.2
Aggravated assault	1,590,000	55.2	63.5	61.6	34.0	51.1	17.4
All property crime	34,771,000	34.9	18.6	17.1	6.0	41.5	2.5
Larceny (theft)	25,128,000	26.5	19.7	17.9	4.7	47.0	2.2
Burglary	8,223,000	54.4	17.5	16.4	8.9	31.5	2.8
Motor vehicle theft	1,420,000	71.1	14.4	13.4	9.5	23.6	2.2

type of crime, as shown in column (g) of table 3-8. Of course, all of these estimates are subject to sampling error and are of differential reliability.[14] The author believes that the data presented here is the best known to be available at the present time, and that undoubtedly the data is more accurate than not as it pertains to the nation as a whole during the mid-1970s.

Based upon table 3-8 and the supporting documentation from the previous tables in this chapter, it may be predicted that an average criminal offender who perpetrates any given violent crime thereupon will incur approximately a 10 percent chance of ever being arrested, prosecuted, and convicted of committing that particular crime itself. Thus, such an offender may expect reasonably to be punished for *one* violent crime out of about every *ten* violent crimes that he commits. However, chances of arrest, prosecution, and conviction on any given crime are greater for the rapist than for the robber. The rapist is predicted to have about a 12 percent chance of being arrested, prosecuted and convicted for any given rape, while the robber is predicted to have only about a 6 percent chance of being arrested, prosecuted and convicted for any given robbery. Thus, the average rapist may plan to be convicted for every eight rapes that he perpetrates, and the average robber may plan to be convicted for every sixteen robberies that he commits. On the other hand, one who commits an aggravated assault is predicted to have around a 17 percent chance of being arrested, prosecuted, and convicted of any given crime of this sort, and so an average offender who commits any given aggravated assault may plan to be convicted once for every six aggravated assaults that he commits. Naturally, these expectations pertain to the "average" offender nationwide, and may vary according to a plethora of factors including, but not being limited to, the degree of sophistication and sheer luck of the particular offender himself, the tenacity of any given victim, and the efficiency of any given police department or judicial system.

The average offender who perpetrates a nonviolent property crime is predicted to incur only about a 2 percent chance of being arrested, prosecuted and convicted for any given offense of this kind—a much less chance of arrest or of conviction than if violence occurred. Hence, a nonviolent property offender may expect to be convicted once for every *thirty to fifty* such crimes that he perpetrates. The average burglar is likely to get away with slightly fewer burglaries than is the average thief to get away with thefts. The burglar may plan to be convicted once for every thirty such offenses, more or less, while the thief may plan to be convicted once for every forty or more such offenses. Obviously, the statistical odds are strongly in favor of both offenders.

Assuming that a persistent offender does perpetrate ten violent crimes or about fifty nonviolent property offenses, and that eventually he is convicted of one such respective offense, what will be the projected cost to him in terms of the overall punishment that he may expect to receive? Table 3-8 seems to answer this question with as much reliability as can be achieved. Upon conviction, a rapist may expect to spend about four years in prison as punishment for the one rape of which he has been convicted. However, if he was successful in getting away with seven rapes for every rape that he is not, as table 3-8 suggests he should be with a little luck, then this kind of an offender is likely to end up spending an average of *six months* in prison for each of these eight rapes. The robber who followed the same course with the same degree of success will be likely to spend 2.5 years in prison each time he is convicted of robbery, or about *two months* for each of the fifteen robberies he got away with in addition to the one at which he was caught and convicted. The burglar in the same situation will be likely to spend two years in prison upon being convicted for burglary, or about *six weeks* for each of his thirty-five such crimes. The thief will be likely to spend about 1.5 years in prison upon conviction, or about *two to three weeks* for each of his forty-five criminal transactions of this nature.

Clearly, *crime does pay*. Apparently, the fact that crime does pay is one explanation for why crime has become a big business in the United States. As table 3-8 has illustrated, the greater the volume of crime in which each offender participates, the greater the profits from crime. Not only will the large-volume criminal offender *gross* more rewards from crime, he will *net* more rewards in terms of his after-taxes profits, also. The question is not so much "Does crime pay?" Since we know that crime does pay, the vital concern should be "How *much* does crime pay?" To answer this question, one needs to look briefly at what it costs an offender to do business as a criminal, and then to take a long, hard look at the weaknesses of the American criminal justice system.

In a capitalist society such as ours, we presume that the ultimate difference between success and failure in any business is the difference between profit and loss over time. It should not come as a surprise to anyone that success in crime is a function of profit and loss also, at least in large measure. Profit is the aggregate reward derived from any business, licit or illicit, after deducting expenses (notably operating costs) and taxes from gross income. Profit from crime is no different, essentially, except that most criminal offenders do not pay any direct income taxes to federal, state, or municipal governments on their illegally garnered profits. However, one might view an offender's punishment, particularly if it consists of imprisonment or a significant fine, as being a type of tax levied on profits from crime.

With this in mind, an offender who wants to maximize his profits from crime must specialize by engaging in those criminal pursuits that he knows how to do best (that is, those wherein he runs the least risk of being caught, or at least caught very often) and do so both regularly and systematically. The test of crime's profitability for any given offender lies in the total number of criminal episodes which the offender can get away with in between stints of punishment, coupled of course with the total value of all such episodes (ten robberies yielding an aggregate of $100,000 gross more profit than ten yielding an aggregate of $10,000) in relation to the overall punishment that is imposed (imprisonment for one year per $100,000 grossed is preferable to imprisonment for ten years per $100,000 grossed). Punishments in relation to most criminal episodes "average-out" just as do most business losses when deducted from business profits. However, as in legitimate industry, transportation, retailing, or any other lawful business, crime tends to pay higher returns in proportion to its volume. When sales decline at General Motors, other factors being equal, its profits diminish as well. When a thief reduces the number of criminal transactions that he perpetrates per day, week, month, or year, other factors being equal, he runs the risk of being punished more severely per crime that he does commit if he gets caught, prosecuted, and convicted for any of these crimes at all, as he is likely to do in the long run. Like a farmer, the criminal must "make hay while the sun shines."

The criminal justice system is a thorn in the side of a professional criminal, but it is hardly a barrier. The judicial process, especially, is only a movable obstacle which the criminal can pivot to his satisfaction most of the time. It may be helpful to compare a criminal in the courthouse with an automobile racer in the pit. The racer has to complete so many laps in order to end the race, and he must do so in as short a time interval as possible in order to win the race. The time that the racer spends having his car's engine, tires, or body overhauled in the pit is time lost during a race. Thus, if part of his car breaks down in the middle of a race, it must be made mobile again as quickly as possible even if this is done at the expense of fuel economy, safety, or the vehicle's upkeep. The racer needs to get back on the track rapidly after a breakdown and take his chances that the repair will last throughout the duration of the race. If he wins the gamble, he may win the race. If he loses, he may lose his life.

The situation of a professional criminal is very much analogous to that of an automobile racer. The criminal wants to stay on the street as much as possible just as the racer wants to stay on the track. Hours spent in court and days spent in jail constitute time in the pit. When he is arrested, therefore, a professional criminal wants to get out of jail and back on the street as soon as possible in order not to lose valuable opportunities for crime. It is better for him to plead guilty, get a short sentence, begin to serve it, and get back onto the street than to sit around in pretrial confinement awaiting a trial that itself will consume time and only lead to a sentence that will be at least as long or longer than the pretrial confinement. If he is going to go to prison anyway, it might as well be now to get it over with and be free again sooner. If he has committed twenty auto thefts and stands charged with two, he will breathe a sigh of relief that he has gotten away with eighteen. When he is free once more, he will work all the harder and faster so that next time when he is charged with two auto thefts he will have gotten away with twenty-five.

Notes

1. United States Department of Justice, Law Enforcement Assistance Administration, Criminal Victimization in the United States, 1975: A National Crime Survey Report 5 (1976).

2. Id., at 1.
3. Id., at 9.
4. Id., at 5.
5. Id.
6. Id., at 8.
7. Id.
8. Id., at 7.
9. Id., at 9.
10. Id.

11. After a number of months have elapsed since a crime has been reported, unless the crime is of the most seriousness and sometimes even then, the likelihood of clearance diminishes geometrically until that likelihood almost abates. Reasons include diminution in citizen (including victim) and police interest, lack of evidence because it was not found at the crime scene or if found it was not preserved properly, and other reasons.

12. A magistrate or a judge who is presiding over a preliminary hearing must dismiss charges against a defendant unless the prosecutor meets his burden of showing the existence of "probable cause" to believe the defendant committed the crime(s) charged.

13. A prosecutor retains absolute discretion over the charging process, including over the decisions *whether* any, and if so, *what* charges should be brought against a suspect. Normally, this decision including the determination to *nolle prosecqui* is not reviewable in the courts. See Rule 48(a), Fed.R.Cr.P. See also United States v. Cox, 342 F.2d 167 (5th Cir. 1965).

14. For a discussion of reliability, see supra, Report, footnote 1 at 108.

4

The Disposition of Criminal Cases in the United States During the Mid-1970s

Bargaining with the Law

Throughout America today, most persons who are arrested and formally accused of having committed a crime are not put on trial in front of a judge or a jury to determine their legal guilt or innocence. Far more often than not, criminal charges become the subject matter of negotiations between the prosecutor and the lawyers representing the accused person. The accused, known as the defendant, is likely to plead guilty to one or two criminal charges pursuant to a "plea bargain" with the prosecutor, regardless of whether the defendant has been accused of committing a few crimes or a few dozen crimes, and regardless of the seriousness of the majority of these crimes. As will be developed more thoroughly later in this chapter, a plea bargain is the most common method used to obtain a conviction against the average criminal defendant in virtually every jurisdiction of the United States, whether the defendant is represented by privately retained counsel or by a public defender. Based upon the "bargain," the defendant will waive his constitutional right to a trial on each separate charge, and consent to being convicted without trial on the charges to which he pleads guilty. In return, the prosecutor will dismiss all or most other charges against the defendant that remain outstanding at the time within the same judicial unit. In many instances, the prosecutor will recommend to the court that the defendant receive a lenient sentence as a reward for the defendant's cooperation in making a trial unnecessary. If a prosecutor is unwilling to recommend leniency at sentencing, in situations where a defendant has pleaded guilty and avoided trial the prosecutor is likely at least to remain silent and abstain from recommending to the sentencing judge that a severe sentence should be imposed. Most judges seem to interpret prosecutorial silence at time of sentencing to indicate indifference or even a tacit recommendation for mercy. Consequently, unless a prosecutor demands a severe sentence, most judges will not impose one on the ordinary defendant, regardless of the nature of his crimes.

In the case of Santobello v. New York (1971),[1] the United States Supreme Court held that a prosecutor must fulfill any promises that have induced a defendant to plead guilty to a criminal charge. A prosecutor has little, if any, control over the actual sentence that will follow conviction resulting from a defendant's guilty plea, since in most jurisdictions a judge is not legally bound to follow a prosecutor's sentence recommendation. However, on those infrequent occasions when a judge feels unable to follow the gist of a prosecutor's sentence recommendation that has been negotiated in return for a defendant's plea of guilty, the court generally will permit and even encourage the defendant to withdraw his guilty plea. Trial does not follow necessarily, and the whole negotiation process is likely to begin anew.

One prominent judge in Brooklyn, New York, Hon. Milton Mollen, has become famous for his slogan that typifies both the attitude and the practice of most American jurists toward guilty pleas by criminal defendants: "A defendant who pleads guilty receives mercy; a defendant who is convicted after trial receives justice." Thus, one who exercises his constitutional right to trial but who loses and is convicted following trial receives no mercy. Does this defendant receive justice? Certainly it would seem that a defendant's sentence should be predicated upon the characteristics of his crime and his history of committing crimes rather than on the manner in which he is convicted. Judge Mollen has spoken of a colleague who has systematized his sentencing practices. This judge imposes on a defendant who has pleaded guilty a much lighter sentence than he imposes on a defendant who has been convicted of a crime at trial. A defendant who pleads guilty receives the *minimum* sentence possible under the law, while a defendant who is convicted at trial receives the *maximum* sentence permissible. Thus, an armed robber who pleads guilty in this judge's courtroom may receive a significantly lighter sentence than an auto thief who has the tendency to take his case to trial and lose. The intended effect of these judicial practices is to limit trials, and virtually to eliminate jury trials.

Trials and particularly jury trials are a rarity indeed today in most judicial units throughout the United States. The actual number of trials that are conducted annually in every judicial unit throughout America is not known. Some jurisdictions seem to be reluctant to publish this kind of data. However, this and related information is known as it pertains to judicial units that are located within at least twenty states and the District of Columbia. This data is summarized, beginning with table 4-1.

The disposition of criminal cases may consist of dismissal of the charges; acquittal of the defendant by a jury or by a judge with or without a jury; conviction of the defendant after trial in front of a jury or in front of a judge sitting at a "bench trial" without a jury; or conviction of the defendant without trial by the defendant's plea of guilty or of *nolo contendere*. These dispositional patterns, measured alone and as they interface with each other, reflect the characteristics of the judicial processing of criminal charges from one jurisdiction to another across the nation.

In the tables that are presented within this chapter, five columns of criminal case attrition data are presented. The first column of data indicates the number of defendants or charges that were terminated in a given state or territory during the specific time interval being measured. This column shows the size (the statistical number of cases, known as the "N") of the caseload that is being examined. However, no significance at all should be attached to the fact that caseloads of some jurisdictions (particularly, the more populous states) are greater than those of others. The data being summarized is not represented to be exhaustive of any state's caseload for the period under study. Instead, it reflects simply the amount of case dispositions for which sufficient variable characteristics were available that reflect criminal case attritions during the mid-1970s.

Dismissal Rates

The second column in the tables shows the percentage of the total number of terminated criminal cases that were terminated by dismissal. More simply stated, this column shows dismissal rates. This percentage is derived from computing the number of cases disposed of by dismissal, divided by the total number of criminal cases that were terminated in any fashion, multiplied by one hundred. Throughout these tables, the word "cases" is used instead of more precise words such as "charges" or "defendants." This is done, with accompanying relative inaccuracy, because some judicial units base their dispositional data on the number of charges filed against all defendants regardless of the number of defendants against whom charges have been filed, while other judicial units base their dispositional data on the number of defendants against whom any charges have been filed regardless of the number of charges that have been filed against any given defendant. In the long run, this study assumes that these variations will offset each other. The number of judicial units that calculate their criminal case attrition data based on individual defendants is thought to be about equal to the number of units that calculate this data based on separate charges. This is believed to remain true among judicial units that are located within most states. If these data variations affect any of the information presented within the charts of this chapter, they will affect dismissal rates more than the other rates, since in most jurisdictions throughout the United States defendants tend to plead guilty to and be convicted on a single criminal charge, or to proceed to trial once again on a single major charge.

Dismissal rates indicate the proportion of cases that "wash out" of the criminal justice system following the filing of formal criminal charges but without any formal determination being made on the merits of the defendant's guilt or innocence. As this percentage increases, alongside the limitations noted in the last paragraph, an inference may be drawn either that too many weak cases are accepted for prosecution or that prosecutors are permitting too many strong cases to be dropped without even trying to obtain convictions. Weak cases should be screened out by prosecutors before charges are filed, in order to save unwarranted embarrassment and the expense of a defense to the defendant against whom little or no proof exists that can point to his guilt. Strong cases should not be dropped arbitrarily or capriciously by prosecutors, since to do so may endanger the safety of the community by allowing the guilty to avoid conviction and punishment and to remain free in society.

Table 4-1

Disposition of Defendants or Charges[a] in Courts of General Criminal Jurisdiction,[b] Twenty-one Selected States and the District of Columbia: Most Recent Year Available

| | | Percentage | | | | |
| | Number of Defendants or Charges | Terminated by | Terminated by | Trials Ending in Conviction | | Convictions Obtained |
State	Terminated	Dismissal	Conviction	Jury	Bench	Without Trial
Alaska	13,032	25.5	69.4	52	69	85.7
California	49,827	9.1	85.6	76	53	84.4
Colorado	7,616	40.0	56.8	72		92.0
Connecticut	5,805	14.5	49.5	67	42	~97.1
Delaware	6,253	52.8	26.0	81	74	73.9
District of Columbia	17,232	46.9	33.6	48	54	85.2
Illinois	37,152	37.0	46.8	68	57	90.9
Kansas	6,636	26.2	69.4	77		78.4
Louisiana	7,453	34.1	60.9	84		79.1
Minnesota	5,948	18.5	80.3	85	96	87.8
New Jersey	24,434	29.3	63.2	59	39	88.7
New York	33,138	20.0	80.9	65		93.5
Upstate	12,513	13.1	84.5	67		94.2
New York City	20,625	24.3	78.8	63		93.1
North Carolina	44,700	42.1	≤57.9	–		≥86.4
North Dakota	532	18.4	≤81.4	–		≥91.2
Ohio	19,746	24.8	69.0	76	88	85.9
Oklahoma	15,340	47.0	≤57.5	–		≥82.0
Pennsylvania	76,102	27.6	47.9	65	54	66.5
South Carolina	19,933	19.8	78.7	72		95.1
South Dakota	16,836	17.0	82.3	50		97.7
Texas	67,963	39.8	64.5	80	59	80.6
Vermont	15,686	16.1	≤75.5	–		≥97.9
Wyoming	1,217	48.0	49.5	85		71.0

Sources: **Alaska:** 1975 Ann. Rep. for the Alaska Court System, pp. 87-89 (tables 4-8) and 119-121 (tables 34-35) (1976). **California:** Adult Pros. in California, 1973, p. 14 (table 6) (1976). **Colorado:** Anal. of Crim. Cases Filed in Colo. Dist. Courts, 1972-72 (1974). **Delaware:** Fifth Ann. Rep. of the Judiciary, 1975, pp. 41-46 (1976). **District of Columbia:** 1974 Ann. Rev. of Operation, Superior Court, 20-21 (tables 2-3) (1975). **Illinois:** 1973 Ann. Rep. to the Supreme Court of Ill., Admin. Office of the Ill. Courts, 130-131 (1974). **Kansas:** State Rep. on the Dist. Courts of Kansas, 1974-1975, 12 (1975). **Louisiana:** Rep. of the Attorney General, Crime Stats., 1974, xxxiii (table F) (1975). **Minnesota:** Eleventh Ann. Rep. of the Minn. Courts, 1974, 25 (1974). **New Jersey:** Ann. Rep. of the Admin. Dir. of the Courts, 1973-74, 89 (table D-13) (1975). **New York:** Twentieth Ann. Rep. of the Admin. Board of the Jud. Conf., 1973-1974, 40 (table 9), 44-45 (table 13), 50 (table 19) (1974). **North Carolina:** Tenth Ann. Rep. of the Admin. Officer of the Courts, 26 (1975). **North Dakota:** N.D. Jud. Council Stat. Comp. and Rep., July-Dec. 1974, 38-39 (tables 15-16) (1975). **Ohio:** 1973 Ohio Jud. Crim. Stats., 28-29 (table 9) (1975). **Oklahoma:** Rep. on the Jud., 1974, 243-248 (1975). **Pennsylvania:** PA. Crim. Court Dispositions, 1973, 20-21 (table 4) (1974). **South Carolina:** Ann. Rep. of the Attorney General, Crim. Stats., 1974, 77 (1976). **South Dakota:** S.D. Comp. of Circuit Court

Table 4-1 continued

Caseloads, 1974 (Chart II) (unpub. worksheet 1975); S.D. Comp. of Dist. Court Caseloads, 1974 (Chart I) (unpub. worksheet 1975). **Texas:** Forty-sixth Ann. Rep., Texas Jud. Council, 1974, 138 (1975). **Vermont:** Jud. Stats., State of Vt., 1974 (tables DC-2 and SC-6) (1975).

aSome jurisdictions base case statistics on the number of defendants while others base them on the number of charges terminated at disposition.

bData pertains to courts of general criminal jurisdiction, excluding in most instances companion data for courts of inferior (limited) jurisdiction, such as those without full felony jurisdiction.

Total Conviction Rates

The third column in the tables in this chapter shows the percentage of the total number of terminated criminal cases that were terminated by conviction. More simply stated, this column shows conviction rates. This percentage is derived from computing the number of cases terminated by conviction (whether obtained by trial or by guilty plea), divided by the total number of cases disposed of in any manner, multiplied by one hundred.

A total conviction rate is an indicator of overall success by prosecutors in obtaining convictions of defendants who have been formally charged with committing a crime. A high total conviction rate may indicate good screening that informally disposes of weak cases, just as a high dismissal rate may reflect poor early screening. Or, a high total conviction rate may be the outcome of successful efforts to obtain guilty pleas from a large proportion of defendants, regardless of whether or not the evidence against them is strong, weak, or even in existence.

Trial Conviction Rates

The fourth column in the tables of this chapter reflects the percentage of trials ending in conviction in relation to those ending in acquittal. More simply stated, this column shows trial conviction rates. Whenever possible, this column is subdivided to display separately the percentage of jury trials from the percentage of nonjury court (bench) trials that have ended in conviction. These percentages are derived from computing the number of cases terminated by conviction following a completed trial, divided by the total number of trials completed that ended in either an acquittal or a conviction, multiplied by one hundred. At trial, a defendant may be convicted as charged, or he may be convicted on a reduced charge, such as on a lesser included offense. For statistical purposes, conviction at trial on a reduced charge is considered to be a conviction. In order for a trial to end in an acquittal, the defendant must be found innocent of all charges in jeopardy of which he was placed during the trial. Trials that did not result in completion are not included in this data, whether the trials ended in a mistrial or provoked the defendant to plead guilty prior to the trial's conclusion.

Trial victories are believed to be strong indicators of any lawyer's ability as an advocate. A strong trial conviction rate is a testament not only to a prosecutor's competence in the courtroom, but to the diligence of his staff investigators and to his willingness to commit the necessary financial resources required ordinarily for victory at trial. Defendants and their counsel are cognizant of a prosecutor's trial conviction record, and their perception of a prosecutor's readiness, willingness, and ability to take a case to trial and win it will influence their decision whether to demand a trial or forego trial and plead guilty.

Guilty Plea Rates

The last column in the tables in this chapter reflects the percentage of convictions that have been obtained without trial. More simply stated, this column shows guilty plea rates. This percentage is derived from computing the number of cases terminated by pleas of guilty or of *nolo contendere*, divided by the total number of cases terminated by conviction whether by guilty plea or trial, multiplied by one hundred.

Guilty plea rates indicate the frequency at which defendants are convicted of criminal charges without trial. As the guilty plea rate for a jurisdiction approaches 100 percent, doubt is cast on the readiness, willingness or ability of either prosecutors or defense counsel to take even a marginal case to trial. Indeed, in judicial units where guilty plea rates approach 100 percent, it is doubtful that courts possess the capacity to conduct more than a few "token" criminal trials even if counsel demanded them, and coercion of defendants into pleading guilty becomes ever likelier through the concerted efforts of judges, prosecutors, and defense counsel.

Dispositional Variations

The variables through which criminal case dispositions may be measured can be expected to vary when viewed across jurisdictional boundaries, among different offenders and offenses, and over time. However, the amount and the type of dispositional variations tend to offer substantial insight into the way in which criminal justice is administered across the United States at the present time. For this reason, some of the dispositional variations will be studied in detail.

Variations by State

Based upon data obtained from twenty-one states and the District of Columbia, table 4-1 shows that there is surprisingly little difference in the percentages of convictions obtained throughout trial (guilty plea rates) in most states through-out the nation. Of course, there may well be greater variations among judicial units located within some of these states.

North Dakota, South Dakota, and Vermont have the highest guilty plea rates among jurisdictions listed in table 4-1, although these states are relatively small both in terms of geographic size and population. Alaska, California, Minnesota, and Ohio together with the District of Columbia share very similar guilty plea rates that in turn seem to reflect the national average of around 85 percent. Pennsylvania seems to have the lowest guilty plea rate of the states listed in table 4-1, followed closely by Delaware and Wyoming. Yet rates even for these states are not so low, since all approach or exceed 70 percent. Higher than average guilty plea rates are noticed for Connecticut, Illinois, New Jersey, and New York, states that have substantial rural as well as urban areas. On this point, note that guilty plea rates are almost identical for New York City and for the balance of New York State.

More than half of the states listed in table 4-1 obtain more than 90 percent of their criminal convictions by means of the guilty plea, while less than one-fourth of them obtain fewer than 80 percent of their criminal convictions in this manner. There seems to be a spread of about 21 percentage points (67-98 percent) in the guilty plea rates among the jurisdictions reported in table 4-1. In most of these jurisdictions, however, the spread is less than 10 percentage points (88-98 percent), and so the consistency of guilty plea rates among jurisdictions remains extremely high.

Approaching this data from a slightly different vantage point, one notices that convictions are not obtained by means of any kind of a trial very often. In the average of these jurisdictions, convictions stem from trial in fewer than 15 percent of all cases. In almost all of the jurisdictions, convictions are achieved through trial in fewer than 20 percent of the cases. In about half of the jurisdictions, convictions are the result of trials in fewer than 10 percent of the cases; and in about one-fourth, trials provide less than 5 percent of the convictions.

Of those criminal cases that do go to trial, table 4-1 indicates that a majority are won by the prosecution and result in a conviction of the defendant. Once again, some variation is observed by states for which information is available. Minnesota and Wyoming report a relatively high percentage of trials ending in conviction, while the District of Columbia, New Jersey, and South Dakota report the lowest trial conviction rates among the jurisdictions listed in table 4-1. Separate jury and nonjury trial conviction rates are available for ten of those states and the District of Columbia, out of which seven (California, Connecticut, Delaware, Illinois, New Jersey, Pennsylvania, and Texas) reported a higher conviction rate for jury compared with nonjury trials, while four (Alaska, District of Columbia, Minnesota, and Ohio) reported a higher conviction rate for nonjury compared with jury trials. Of the seven states that reported higher conviction rates for jury trials, the difference between jury and nonjury trial conviction rates was less than 12 percentage points for three: Delaware (7

points), Illinois and Pennsylvania (11 points each). Of the four states that
reported higher conviction rates for nonjury trials, the difference between
nonjury and jury trial conviction rates was 12 percentage points or less for three,
also: District of Columbia (7 points), Minnesota (11 points), and Ohio (12
points). These differences are not traumatic and do not appear to be significant.
Alaska reported a difference of 17 percentage points between lower jury trial
conviction rates and higher bench trial conviction rates. Four states reported
even greater differences between lower bench trial conviction rates and higher
jury trial conviction rates. These states included: California (23 point difference); Connecticut (25 point difference); New Jersey (20 point difference); and
Texas (21 point difference). These wider differences are more significant and
cause for greater concern.

    The smaller variations between a state's jury and nonjury trial conviction
rates (differences of 12 percentage points or less) cannot be accounted for
soundly. In all probability, the differences may be attributable to chance. The
greater differences (17 percentage points and more) cannot be explained by
chance, although these differences may not be explainable sufficiently at all.
Trial conviction rates, and particularly jury trial conviction rates, are likely to be
functions of several or more interacting factors, including the types of cases that
are taken to trial, the personalities of the defendant, defense counsel, and the
prosecutor; the credibility of the victims and other witnesses for both sides; and
the character of public sentiment at the time toward crime generally but
particularly toward the specific crimes of which the defendant has been accused.
Judges are thought by many trial lawyers to be more objective and less
emotional than jurors in reaching a verdict, especially in highly visible criminal
cases involving brutality, death, fear, and sex. While judges should be consistently fair in all judicial units of the nation, it may well be that jurors are more
partial to conviction in certain areas of the country than they are elsewhere. For
instance, in parts of the South, Southwest, and West citizens have expressed
greater respect for "law and order" than they have in some urban sections of the
Northeast and Midwest. However, among the four states where a jury trial is far
more likely to result in a conviction than is a bench trial, two states are located
in the Northeast (Connecticut and New Jersey) and two in the Southwest
(California and Texas). The answer may be in part at least that in these states,
unlike the others listed in table 4-1, defendants who are clearly guilty try to
"snow" jurors but do so unsuccessfully. In other states, perhaps, defendants who
are clearly guilty are more likely to place themselves at the mercy of the court
either by means of a guilty plea or a bench trial. In these other states, perhaps,
criminal offenders share an enhanced respect for a jury of their peers.

    In figure 4-1, the "Johari's Window" model is used to show the interface of
trial conviction rates and guilty plea rates among the jurisdictions listed in table

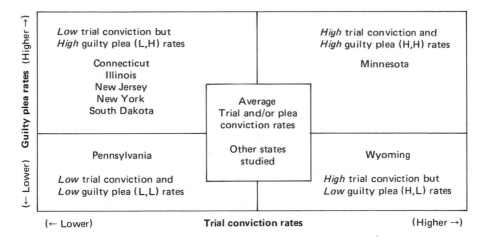

Figure 4-1. The Interface of Trial Conviction and Guilty Plea Rates.

4-1. The Johari's Window is constructed by intersecting an X axis (horizontal) with a Y axis (vertical). As in aeronautical navigation, the X axis acquires higher numbers (ordinarily, 0-10 or more) as it moves from the left to the right, while the Y axis does the same as it moves from the bottom to the top. When the cross that is formed by the intersection of the X and the Y axes is framed, four "windows" appear, one each in the bottom left, bottom right, top left and top right corners. Normally, the bottom left corner is known as window 1,1, since it is low on both the X and the Y axes. The bottom right corner is known as window 9,1, since it is high on the X axis but low on the Y axis. The top left corner is known as window 1,9, since it is low on the X axis but high on the Y axis. The top right corner is known as window 9,9, since it is high on both the X and the Y axes.

Comparing trial conviction rates with guilty plea rates for the jurisdictions that are listed in table 4-1, several patterns emerge, and these patterns are illustrated more vividly in figure 4-1. Trial conviction rates are plotted along the X axis, and guilty plea rates are plotted along the Y axis. Connecticut, Illinois, New Jersey, New York, and South Dakota show relatively low (less than 65 percent) trial conviction rates but relatively high (over 87 percent) guilty plea rates. Therefore, these states are shown in the top left window of figure 4-1, and form pattern 1,9, which is the dominant pattern among the jurisdictions listed within the window. Pennsylvania has shown a relatively low trial conviction rate as well as a relatively low (less than 72 percent) guilty plea rate. Therefore, Pennsylvania occupies the bottom left window and forms pattern 1,1. Wyoming has shown a relatively high (over 80 percent) trial conviction rate but a relatively low guilty plea rate. Therefore, Wyoming occupies the bottom right window and forms pattern 9,1. Minnesota has shown a relatively high trial conviction rate as well as a relatively high guilty plea rate. Therefore, Minnesota occupies the top right window and forms pattern 9,9. The other states that are listed in table 4-1 appear to have either average trial conviction rates, average guilty plea rates, or both. These states occupy the "bifocal lens" of the window, and form pattern 5,5.

Most of the states that are listed within table 4-1 report average rates either of guilty pleas or of trial convictions, and in some cases of both. Hence, pattern 5,5 is the dominant pattern among these twenty-two jurisdictions that compose nearly half of the jurisdictions in the United States. The 5,5 pattern does not differ significantly from chance, since we would expect that most states would have similar guilty plea rates or trial conviction rates. However, eight of these jurisdictions reflect different patterns that need to be explained if this is possible to do. Of these eight jurisdictions, five form a single pattern, labeled 1,9. This is the dominant pattern that differs from chance. It is easy to explain this pattern, since obviously even the most naive defendant can "negotiate" a guilty plea with a prosecutor who has a poor conviction record at trial, simply by threatening to take his case to trial where he should have an even or a better than even chance of being acquitted. This pattern promotes a defendant's market in guilty pleas: The defendant or defense counsel who possesses any reasonable skills at bartering should be able to virtually choose whatever sentence he wants to accept within vague and nominal boundaries. It is easy to explain pattern 9,9, which is the counterpart to pattern 1,9, and which is reflected in data pertaining to Minnesota more than in data pertaining to other states listed in table 4-1. When a prosecutor can demonstrate his effectiveness at trial by obtaining and maintaining consistently high trial conviction rates, only a defendant who is arrogant, innocent, or very foolish is likely to want to take a chance at going to trial. This pattern promotes a prosecutor's market in guilty pleas, and he should be able to name his price for these pleas in terms of the sentences to which he will acquiesce, provided his skills at negotiation resemble his trial skills, as they should undoubtedly do.

The other two patterns are less easily explained with the same degree of confidence. Nevertheless, some insight offers itself toward an analysis of the reasons why these patterns have emerged in at least one state. Pattern 1,1 is reflected in data pertaining to Pennsylvania more than in data pertaining to other states listed in table 4-1. But why is this pattern characteristic of Pennsylvania more so than of these other jurisdictions? The most obvious answer seems to be that, given a low trial conviction rate statewide, a defendant does not need to plead guilty when he can take his case to trial and stand as good a chance, if not a better chance, of being acquitted than of being convicted. This answer is not sufficiently explanatory, however, because while Pennsylvania does not enjoy a very high relative trial conviction rate, its trial conviction rates are no lower than those of at least six other states listed in table 4-1, and its trial conviction rates are higher than similar rates for Connecticut and New Jersey. New Jersey borders Pennsylvania, and Connecticut almost does. The question becomes: Why do criminal defendants in Pennsylvania plead guilty less frequently per one hundred cases than their counterparts do in Connecticut or New Jersey? The answer is by no means readily apparent. Apart from two large cities and a few smaller b t still urban areas, Pennsylvania consists largely of small mining communities, mostly isolated from each other and from the rest of the world. Perhaps, many Pennsylvania defendants prefer to avoid an admission of their guilt in front of their peers who reside with them in small hamlets. Justice may be more personalized in Pennsylvania than in its more densely populated neighboring states. Pennsylvania criminal courts are not as backlogged as their counterparts are elsewhere, and prosecutors do not seem as constrained to avoid trials. Also, sentences for most crimes committed in Pennsylvania appear to be imposed as severely following most guilty pleas as they are following most trials. With the discount for pleading guilty reduced, its attractiveness to the average criminal defendant may diminish.

Pattern 9,1, is reflected in data pertaining to Wyoming more than in data pertaining to other states listed in table 4-1. Why is this so? Why do so few criminal defendants plead guilty when by going to trial they run an 85 percent chance of being convicted? This question is very difficult to answer with certainty. One explanation may have its roots in the history and the legacy of Wyoming, a frontier state that is and has always been inhabited by fiercely independent persons who are used to taking high risks and to making their own decisions. This state may produce the kind of criminal defendants who are willing to take their chances at trial, notwithstanding high odds that favor conviction, rather than to admit guilt. In the Plains states, and in Wyoming particularly, prosecutors may be confronted with traditions and community norms that mandate the involvement of lay citizens (jurors) in the determination of guilt or innocence. Certainly Wyoming cannot be distinguished from other states solely by reason of its sparse population. Vermont, North Dakota, and South Dakota have sparse populations but they have also among the highest guilty plea rates in the nation.

One must keep in mind that while the patterns that are illustrated within figure 4-1 are characteristic of several states generally, they do not necessarily typify each and every judicial unit that is located within any of those states. Some judicial units that are located within Connecticut, Illinois, New Jersey, New York, or South Dakota may not possess low trial conviction or high guilty plea rates. Some judicial units located within Minnesota may not have high rates of both trial convictions and guilty pleas. Some judicial units located within Pennsylvania may not have low rates of both trial convictions and guilty pleas. Some judicial units located within Wyoming may not possess high trial conviction rates or low guilty plea rates. Indeed, any given state may contain judicial units that are characteristic of all five patterns described by figure 4-1. Statewide patterns are useful to observe and consider in relation to other characteristics that are known about each state. Naturally, one would prefer to assemble the same patterns based on data obtained from each judicial unit across the nation. This is not yet possible to do, since many judicial units still do not have automated data processing or any other means of generating the kinds or the amounts of data that are necessary to support a pattern analysis such as that on which figure 4-1 is based.

Total conviction rates that include convictions obtained by means of guilty pleas as well as trials display some additional variations by states, as do dismissal rates. Often, but not always, total conviction rates stand in inverse relation to dismissal rates for a given jurisdiction. For instance, as table 4-1 illuminates, six states (Colorado, Delaware, Illinois, North Carolina, Oklahoma, and Wyoming) and the District of Columbia have relatively low (65 percent or lower) total conviction rates but relatively high (35 percent or higher) dismissal rates. These jurisdictions in turn reported rather average guilty plea rates, as has been mentioned previously. On the contrary, at least four states (California, Minnesota, New York and South Dakota) have relatively high (80 percent or higher) total conviction rates but relatively low (20 percent or lower) dismissal rates. Of these states, New York and South Dakota show fairly low trial conviction rates but fairly high guilty plea rates. Illinois and Pennsylvania show relatively low rates for both total convictions and dismissals, and both of these states report fairly low trial conviction rates. However, while Pennsylvania reports a relatively low guilty plea rate, this rate is relatively high for Illinois. Connecticut, North Dakota, South Carolina, and Vermont show relatively low dismissal rates but average total conviction rates. Other states listed in table 4-1 tend to reflect average dismissal as well as average total conviction rates.

The relationship between total conviction rates and dismissal rates may become complicated, especially when the relationship is confounded by the intervention of additional variables including the interface of guilty plea rates and trial conviction rates. Dismissal rates that are either inordinately high or low may reflect problems in the administration of criminal justice. Relatively high dismissal rates may be evidence of prosecutorial overcharging, although this does not have to be the case at all. Instead, relatively high dismissal rates may indicate overzealous charging practices by the police or even by citizen complainants. Such charges may be dismissed in the courts when they cannot be supported by admissible evidence. Relatively low dismissal rates should be interpreted as being "red flags" that signal potentially abusive guilty plea bargaining practices. Defendants may be encouraged to plead guilty to a number of criminal charges upon the promise that all sentences will be imposed concurrently. This practice falsely increases a prosecutor's conviction rate, which he may sport in campaign advertising when he runs for reelection. Of course, low dismissal rates may be indicative of good early screening by prosecutors who try not to file charges against defendants unless sufficient evidence exists to support a finding of the defendant's guilt. Jurisdictions that have relatively low conviction rates alongside relatively high dismissal rates may be dismissing charges that could result in convictions if properly brought to trial. Jurisdictions that have relatively low dismissal rates but relatively high total conviction rates may be transforming many charges that should be dismissed into guilty pleas by ignorant defendants that would result in acquittals if properly brought to trial.

Variations by Seriousness of Charge

Although table 4-2 contains data from only four states (Alaska, Louisiana, South Dakota, and Wyoming) plus the District of Columbia and New York City, it is based upon an abundance (almost three hundred thousand) of criminal case dispositions. To be sure, only little more than 10 percent (about thirty five thousand) of these are felony dispositions. However, the data reflects remarkable consistencies not only in the disposition of both felony and misdemeanor cases within the same jurisdiction during the same period of time, but also in the disposition of felony and misdemeanor cases respectively across jurisdictional boundaries for the most part. It is not a good practice to use the end to justify the means, but it should be noted that when the total number of observations is too small, false variations rather than false consistencies tend to result as a rule.

Far more misdemeanor than felony cases are terminated each year within the jurisdictions (other than Wyoming) listed in table 4-2, but this is known to be the normal pattern throughout the United States. Among the jurisdictions listed in table 4-2, however, guilty plea rates are higher for misdemeanors than for felonies in four of the five instances, Louisiana being the exception. However, the differences between felony and misdemeanor rates within each specific jurisdiction are small, the largest difference being 10.5 percentage points (for Wyoming) and the average difference being about 5 percentage points.

In the District of Columbia and in New York City, unlike the more rural states, trial conviction rates are higher for felony than for misdemeanor cases, although this characteristic was true also for bench trials in Alaska. In the District of Columbia and in New York City, also, as in Wyoming, dismissal rates are higher for misdemeanors than for felonies. The reverse is true for Alaska, Louisiana, and South Dakota. It appears likely although not certain that during the mid-1970s in Alaska, Louisiana, and South Dakota as in similar jurisdictions elsewhere through the nation, felony charges may have been dismissed routinely in consideration of the defendant's guilty plea to misdemeanor charges. This is not to say that the same practice of felony reduction may not have been prevalent in the larger and more urban jurisdictions during the same period of time, also. This cannot be inferred from the data. One reason why such an

Table 4-2
Disposition of Defendants or Cases in Four Selected States, the District of Columbia, and New York City, Most Recent Year Available: Felonies Compared with Misdemeanors

| State | Number of Defendants or Cases Terminated | Percentage | | Trials Ending in Conviction | | Convictions Obtained Without Trial |
		Terminated by Dismissal	Terminated by Conviction	Jury	Bench	
Alaska						
Felonies	673	28.1	49.3	39	73	88.7
Misdemeanors	12,359+	25.3−	73.2+	54+	69−	96.8+
District of Columbia						
Felonies	4,422	16.4	63.9	66	73	81.3
Misdemeanors	12,810+	57.5+	25.0−	42−	54−	82.3+
Louisiana						
Felonies	7,453	34.1	60.9	84		79.1
Misdemeanors	26,374+	21.4−	74.5+	86+		75.9−
South Dakota						
Felonies	1,378	24.0	69.7	69	−*	92.7
Misdemeanors	15,458+	16.4−	83.4+			98.1+
Wyoming						
Felonies	635	40.2	55.7	82		66.7
Misdemeanors	582−	56.5+	42.4−	90+		77.3+
New York City						
Felonies	20,625	24.3	78.8	63		93.1
Misdemeanors	191,937+	43.6+	39.4−	40−		98.9+

Sources: **Alaska**: Felonies, 1975 Ann. Rep. for the Alaska Court System, pp. 119-121 (tables 34-35), 1976; Misdemeanors, Id. at pp. 87-89 (tables 4-8). **District of Columbia**: Felonies, 1974 Ann. Rev. of Operation, Superior Court, p. 20 (table 2), 1975; Misdemeanors, Id. at p. 21 (table 3). **Louisiana**: Felonies, Rep. of the Attorney General, Crime Stats., 1974 xxxiii (table F) (1975); Misdemeanors, Id.; **South Dakota**: Felonies, S.D. Comp. of Circuit Court Caseloads, 1974 (Chart I) (unpub. worksheet 1975); Misdemeanors, S.D. Comp. of District Court Caseloads, 1974 (Chart II) (unpub. worksheet 1975); **Wyoming**: Felonies, Wyoming Comp. Law Enforce. Plan, 1976, v.2, Crim. Just. Data Book-1974, 125 (1976); Misdemeanors, Id. at 154; **New York City**: Felonies, Twentieth Ann. Rep. of the Admin. Board of the Jud. Conf., 1973-74, 40 (table 9) (1974); Misdemeanors, Spec. Six-month Rep. of the Admin. Board of the Jud. Conf. 37 (table 18) (1975).

aComparable data not available.

+Means misdemeanor rates higher than felony rates.

−Means misdemeanor rates lower than felony rates.

inference cannot be made is that the courts of these larger and more urban jurisdictions were clogged with misdemeanor cases, many of which in turn were dismissed. One does wonder what explanation, other than overcharging, may be proposed to account for the inordinately high dismissal rates among misdemeanor cases in the District of Columbia (57.5 percent), Wyoming (56.5 percent), and to a lesser extent New York City (43.6 percent).

Variations by Judicial Unit Population

Many key actors in the criminal justice system continue to presume that a direct correlation exists (many say it *must* exist) between the size of a judicial unit's population and its rate of guilty pleas. In other words, many contend that a populous judicial unit has to have a high percentage of its convictions obtained by pleas of guilty, whereas its guilty plea rate would be reduced if only its population could be shrunk. Table 4-3 refutes this presumption.

In table 4-3, data related to the disposition of criminal cases is broken down according to aggregate population intervals for judicial units (all counties) within eight states for which relevant data was available on a county-specific basis. A remarkable consistency of rates for all four dispositional variables is evidenced across population intervals. Clearly, guilty plea rates for the more populous counties are *not* higher than similar rates for the less populous counties. On the contrary, in these eight states counties with populations exceeding 1 million show the *lowest* guilty plea rates among counties in all population intervals. The average guilty plea rate for counties in these eight states that have populations of less than two hundred fifty thousand is a few percentage points *higher* than the average guilty plea rate for counties in the same states that serve populations of two hundred thousand or over. Therefore, while a judicial unit's population seems to have little effect on its guilty plea rates, if population has any effect at all on these rates, the relationship is slightly inverse.

A somewhat stronger, and this time direct, relationship between judicial unit population and total conviction rates is noticed, although the slope is imperfect. Conviction rates in counties within states listed in table 4-3 tend to decline as populations decline. However, counties in these states that serve populations of between 50,000 and 99,999 show a total conviction rate that exceeds similar the same rate for counties serving larger populations other than counties with populations in excess of 1 million.

A more perfect but once again inverse correlation is observed when county populations are compared with dismissal rates for the eight states listed in table 4-3. Among these counties, dismissal rates tend to increase as populations decrease. Counties with populations in excess of 1 million (the largest counties),

Table 4-3

Disposition of Defendants or Cases in Superior Courts of Eight Reporting States, Most Recent Year Available, by County Population Within State

		Number of	Percentage			
State	Number of Counties	Defendants or Cases Terminated	Terminated by Dismissal	Terminated by Conviction	Trials Ending in Conviction	Convictions Obtained Without Trial
County population over 1,000,000						
Total	16	94,625	22.9	77.1	70.9	82.3
California	5	30,468	9.5	83.7	70.1	80.8
Illinois	1	7,529	25.3	69.3	66.8	84.1
New York	7	24,408	20.8	76.2	62.4	93.5
Ohio	1	2,246	0.2	99.8	100.0	91.0
Texas	2	29,974	39.4	71.4	76.2	73.0
County population 500,000-999,999						
Total	18	33,464	25.3	70.2	65.2	88.7
California	5	7,861	8.2	89.7	78.6	91.2
New Jersey	5	10,574	29.0	63.3	52.9	86.4
New York	2	1,626	15.0	82.8	62.9	95.5
Ohio	4	7,150	25.6	67.2	74.1	88.2
Texas	2	6,253	42.9	57.6	78.1	86.5
County population 250,000-499,999						
Total	28	24,610	25.3	65.3	60.9	88.5
California	6	4,599	7.3	90.0	76.0	90.2
Illinois	6	3,946	36.3	27.9	71.2	85.2
New Jersey	6	8,807	30.0	62.2	51.6	88.3
New York	4	1,529	12.9	84.3	66.4	93.6
Ohio	4	2,685	24.7	70.5	74.7	91.0
Texas	2	3,044	31.6	71.4	46.8	82.4
County population 100,000-249,999						
Total	58	25,875	29.7	63.4	69.6	90.1
California	10	3,821	10.4	86.5	77.5	87.5
Illinois	10	5,096	53.1	26.4	54.6	90.6
New Jersey	5	3,422	28.9	63.2	45.3	92.6
New York	13	2,176	10.7	87.1	72.0	93.4
Ohio	10	2.725	29.1	62.5	93.4	73.2
South Carolina	5	6,025	24.1	74.8	62.2	97.0
Texas	5	2,610	43.3	56.9	69.6	85.6
County population 50,000-99,999						
Total	94	23,678	26.0	71.2	71.4	91.5
California	8	1,718	9.0	87.5	75.1	87.8
Illinois	8	1,525	53.4	32.4	49.5	90.7
New Jersey	5	1,631	29.1	68.3	51.3	96.5
New York	19	1,432	14.8	83.6	72.6	94.9
Ohio	24	2,760	35.8	58.1	77.5	84.2
South Carolina	11	7,604	19.1	79.3	75.6	93.6
Texas	17	6,598	27.7	71.9	64.3	91.6
Wyoming	2	410	56.8	40.2	84.0	61.8

Table 4-3 continued

State	Number of Counties	Number of Defendants or Cases Terminated	Percentage			
			Terminated by Dismissal	Terminated by Conviction	Trials Ending in Conviction	Convictions Obtained Without Trial
County population 25,000-49,999						
Total	127	17,600	33.9	59.4	76.2	92.9
California	7	652	8.6	88.8	83.0	87.4
Illinois	25	2,386	56.3	27.3	57.0	92.5
New York	12	830	11.1	87.2	60.0	97.1
Ohio	30	1,758	27.4	64.7	81.1	81.9
South Carolina	18	4,845	17.0	78.6	73.4	98.7
Texas	33	6,921	44.5	49.7	80.4	90.6
Wyoming	2	208	46.6	52.4	88.9	85.3
County population of 10,000-24,999						
Total	161	10,745	42.1	52.2	65.4	90.4
California	11	632	10.6	84.2	65.6	88.2
Illinois	36	1,267	53.4	31.3	74.7	82.6
New York	4	141	18.4	80.9	80.0	96.5
Ohio	14	422	33.9	65.2	90.1	62.5
South Carolina	10	1,292	16.2	82.0	70.0	94.7
Texas	80	6,719	49.2	45.9	54.8	93.5
Wyoming	6	272	37.5	54.4	75.4	70.9
County population under 10,000						
Total	140	3,090	45.1	51.5	72.7	89.9
California	6	76	3.9	96.1	100.0	80.8
Illinois	16	289	64.0	23.5	50.0	97.1
New York	1	9	–	77.8	50.0	71.4
Ohio	1	–	–	–	–	–
South Carolina	2	167	9.6	85.6	52.9	93.7
Texas	102	2,309	40.1	51.3	67.1	91.9
Wyoming	12	240	47.1	51.3	91.8	63.4

Sources: **California:** Adult Pros. in California, 1973, 14-16 (table 6) (1976); **Illinois:** 1973 Ann. Rep. to the Supreme Court of Ill., Admin. Office of the Illinois Courts, 128-131 (1974); **New Jersey:** Ann. Rep. of the Admin. Dir. of the Courts, 1973-1974, 89 (table D-13) (1975); **New York:** Twentieth Ann. Rep. of the Admin. Board of the Jud. Conf., 1973-1974, 40 (table 9) and 44 (table 13) (1974); **Ohio:** 1973 Ohio Jud. Crim. Stats., 28-29 (table 9) (1975); **South Carolina:** Ann. Rep. of the Attorney General, Crim. Stats., 1974, 77-84 (1976); **Texas:** 46th Ann. Rep., Texas Jud. Council, 1974, 228-481 (1975); **Wyoming:** Wyoming Comp. Law Enforce. Plan, 1976, v.2, Crim. Just. Syst. Data Book–1974, 126-148 (1976).

those with populations of between 50,000 and 249,999 (the medium-sized counties), and those with populations under ten thousand (the smallest counties) show similar trial conviction rates (about 70 percent). The counties located within these eight states that serve populations in other size intervals tend to have either *lower* trial conviction rates by a few percentage points (those counties serving populations between 10,000 and 24,999 and 250,000 and

999,999) or *higher* trial conviction rates by a few percentage points (counties serving populations between 25,000 and 49,999).

Based on this information, it appears that total conviction rates may be expected to decrease while dismissal rates may be expected to increase as the size of a judicial unit's population is reduced. Since trial conviction rates tend to remain constant, but guilty plea rates tend to increase, the smaller the judicial unit's population, it appears that smaller-sized judicial units tend to place greater confidence in the value of the guilty plea as a mechanism for achieving the conviction of criminal offenders. This confidence may be misplaced, however. With both guilty plea rates and dismisal rates increasing as population size decreases, doubt is cast on the efficiency and the effectiveness of many smaller-sized judicial units in administering criminal justice. While no conclusive inference can be made based on data obtained from judicial units situated within only eight states, it seems likely that in the less populated judicial units charges may be brought against a significant proportion of suspected offenders merely to induce them into pleading guilty. If the defendants do not plead guilty, it seems equally likely that the charges must be dropped, since the smaller judicial units do not appear capable of handling any more trials or of winning any larger proportion of the trials they do handle than do their larger jurisdictional counterparts. If any conclusion, however tentative, is warranted by the data summarized in table 4-3, it is that smaller judicial units take even more of a cavalier attitude toward the filing of criminal charges than do the larger judicial units in the same states. Quite evidently, one reason why small judicial units may not be ready, willing, or able to dispose of criminal cases in any better manner than are larger judicial units is that the smaller jurisdictions take on more cases than they can handle and then end up by tossing out those cases that they cannot handle well enough. This criticism would be equally apt if applied to larger jurisdictions as well.

Variations by Type of Offense Charged

Table 4-4 indicates that patterns of criminal case disposition bear a distinct relationship to specific criminal cases. Although only three states (California, Pennsylvania, and Texas) report data that may be broken-down by type of offense that has been charged, these states alone yield information that pertains to almost one hundred thirty thousand criminal cases. Furthermore, table 4-4 is buttressed by table 4-5 that reflects the dispositional characteristics of defendants who were processed in the United States District Courts between 1961 and 1975, excluding 1965, by class of offense charged.

A much lower percentage of convictions is obtained according to this data when defendants are charged with violent crimes compared with nonviolent crimes. Property crimes including forgery, burglary, and theft (in that order)

Table 4-4
Disposition of Defendants or Cases in State Courts of General
Criminal Jurisdiction, Three States, Most Recent Year Available,
by Offense and Method of Disposition

Offense	Number of Defendants or Cases Terminated	Percentage			
		Terminated by Dismissal	Terminated by Conviction	Trials Ending in Conviction	Convictions Obtained Without Trial
Forgery	7,489	24.2	76.2	69.3	91.3
Burglary	28,566	21.9	72.8	67.8	87.0
Larceny (Theft)	19,758	36.2	61.2	64.3	82.0
Auto Theft	4,734	23.9	60.8	58.0	81.6
Narcotics	33,803	24.6	67.2	66.0	80.9
DWI	16,886	9.8	81.4	59.8	79.5
Robbery	10,953	21.1	72.0	65.8	75.1
Assault	6,603	21.6	61.1	58.2	74.8
Rape	1,924	28.4	63.0	62.7	65.6
Homicide	3,645	18.8	70.2	71.7	55.5

Sources: **California:** Adult Pros. in California, 1973, 13 (table 5) (1976); **Pennsylvania:** PA Crim. Court Dispositions, 1973, 20-21 (table 4) (1974). **Texas:** Forty-sixth Ann. Rep., Texas Jud. Council, 1974, 138 (1975).

seem to be disposed of by means of a guilty plea most frequently, followed closely by serious public order crimes such as narcotics violations and the driving of a motor vehicle while under the influence of alcohol or another drug (driving while intoxicated, or DWI). Guilty pleas appear to be entered considerably less often for violent crimes such as robbery, assault, rape, and homicide (listed in descending order of guilty plea rates). Thus, guilty plea rates seem to be lower as the violent crime becomes more serious in character.

There is less variation by type of offense for the other dispositional variables that are contained within table 4-4. Less than 10 percent of DWI charges were terminated by dismissal in California, Pennsylvania, and Texas during the time periods that are reflected in that table, and more than 80 percent of these charges were terminated by conviction in one way or another. For the other offense categories, variations are still less noticeable. Larceny (theft) offenses, excluding auto thefts, seem to have a fairly high dismissal rate and a relatively low conviction rate. Homicides ended in trial convictions most often, followed by forgery and burglary. Auto thefts, assaults, and DWI offenses that were completed at trial ended in conviction least often.

Most variations by types of offense that were observed through table 4-4 are validated in substance by table 4-5. As with the state offenses, violent federal crimes seem to be terminated by guilty pleas less frequently than are property crimes or public order offenses. Property crimes are terminated by guilty pleas most often. Embezzlement and forgery head the list of federal offenses that are

Table 4-5

Disposition of Defendants in Federal District Courts, by Class of Offense, Fiscal Years 1961-1975 (Excluding 1965)

		Percentage				
				Trials Ending in Conviction		Convictions Obtained
Offense	Number of Defendants Terminated	Terminated by Dismissal	Terminated by Conviction	Jury	Bench	Without Trial
Embezzle-ment	25,104	8.3	88.9	64.0	70.9	94.0
Forgery/counter-feiting	58,238	11.8	85.6	77.2	74.9	89.9
Auto theft	57,648	9.9	87.9	77.6	86.1	87.5
Larceny/theft	49,346	13.5	82.5	70.7	75.4	87.4
Federal statutes (misc.)	77,783	27.6	67.7	63.8	69.4	85.8
Fraud	41,142	20.7	73.9	70.6	58.5	85.0
Burglary	4,316	13.4	83.5	78.4	85.6	83.8
Narcotics offenses	65,056	21.2	75.4	84.5	79.7	80.9
Robbery	16,476	14.5	82.1	86.4	80.8	74.9
Assault	5,628	19.2	71.6	67.7	74.8	70.1
Homicide	1,024	19.3	67.7	63.3	52.5	69.4
Sex offenses	2,525	21.3	67.7	73.2	56.1	63.2

Sources: [1975] Dir. of the Admin. Office of the United States Courts, Ann. Rep. 420-422 (table 000) (1976); [1974] Id. at 470-472 (1975); [1973] Id. at 402-405 (1974); [1972] Id. at 381-383 (1973); [1971-70] Id. at 340-342 (data for 1971) and 337-339 (data for 1970) (1972); [1969] Id. at 273-275 (1970); [1968] Id. at 261-263 (1969); [1967] Id. at 260-262 (1968); [1966] Id. at 220-222 (1967); [1964] Id. at 256-257 (1965); [1963] Id. at 240-241 (1964); [1962] Id. at 234-235 (1963); [1961] Id. at 280-282 (1962).

disposed of by guilty pleas. Unlike the state offenses noticed in table 4-4, however, larceny (theft) and auto theft seem to be terminated by guilty pleas more often than burglary in the federal courts.

Dismissal rates show less consistency in table 4-5 than in table 4-4. Embezzlement has the lowest dismissal rate in federal courts, followed by auto theft, burglary, larceny and robbery. Miscellaneous federal statutory offenses show the highest dismissal rates in the federal courts, followed by sex, narcotics and fraud offenses. Total conviction rates are more consistent than dismissal rates among specific offenses that have been disposed of in the federal courts between 1961 and 1975. Offenses that involve actual offender-victim physical contact, such as homicide, sexual, and other assaultive offenses, together with miscellaneous federal statutory offenses appear to be terminated by conviction at a lower rate than are other offenses processed through the federal courts.

Forgery and counterfeiting offenses, robbery, homicides and sex, narcotics, and fraud offenses are more likely to end in a conviction following a jury trial rather than a bench trial in the federal courts. Embezzlement, larceny, assault, burglary and miscellaneous federal statutory offenses are more likely to end in a conviction after a bench rather than a jury trial. Cases taken to trial in the federal courts appear to be terminated by a conviction of one form or another more often than cases involving similar offenses that are taken to trial in state courts, however, as is indicated by a comparison between tables 4-4 and 4-5.

Other Considerations

What factors inspire a person to waive the right to trial and plead guilty to a criminal charge? Is it because if they pleaded innocent and went to trial they would be convicted anyway? In most jurisdictions, trial conviction rates are not that high. In nearly all jurisdictions, a person who stands trial on a criminal charge enjoys a 50 percent chance (in some, as high as a 60 percent chance) of being acquitted. A few states such as Minnesota seem to have an extraordinarily high rate of convictions obtained at trial, but comparable data available from other states tends to reflect at least a 20 percent chance of acquittal at trial.

Every criminal case is different, and in some instances a person accused of committing a crime may realize fully that the evidence is stacked against him. However, if, as in the ordinary situation, at least a 20 percent chance of acquittal does exist, why is any person so foolish as to throw away the opportunity to be found innocent by a judge or a jury at trial? What does an accused person get out of a plea bargain?

By means of plea bargaining, persons who are accused of committing crimes are able to negotiate not only the number of separate charges of which they will be convicted, but also the seriousness of these charges and the sentence which is likely to be imposed. More than anything else, the accused achieves certainty in the type of disposition to be anticipated. Certainty of outcome holds true whether the accused is a naive, first offender or a sophisticated repeater; and whether he is alleged to have committed one minor violation of the law or several serious crimes.

Plea bargaining is most beneficial to the offender who has committed multiple crimes on numerous different occasions. In the legal language, the notion of a criminal *transaction* is little more than a sequence of crimes committed virtually in the same place at the same time. For example, a person may break into another's house and steal jewelry found there. The breaking and the unlawful entry into the house may constitute the crime of burglary; stealing the jewelry may constitute the crime of larceny or theft; and a third offense, that of criminal trespass, may be perpetrated when the offender walks across the victim's real estate without permission. In many jurisdictions, however, these three crimes would be viewed as constituting a single criminal transaction. And, in most such jurisdictions, the offender would be permitted to plead guilty to one of the three crimes whereupon the two other offenses would be dismissed. Of course, the point to be made is obvious: Commit as many crimes as possible during each separate transaction, since after the first crime, most others will be forgiven upon a guilty plea to one crime.

The same discounting practice takes place in most jurisdictions when an offender is alleged to have perpetrated multiple criminal transactions, each transaction consisting generally of multiple offenses. Upon pleading guilty to one or two offenses arising out of one or two (out of perhaps as many as a dozen) transactions, an offender will not be prosecuted for the remaining transactions. Another point is obvious: Commit as many transactions as possible before being apprehended for any given one, since after the first, most other criminal transactions will be forgiven and "washed out" upon a guilty plea to one or two crimes committed during one or two transactions.

The plea bargaining practice by which companion crimes are dismissed when the offender pleads guilty to one or two charges is known technically as "horizontal charge reduction." The meaning of this phrase can be made clear by thinking of the offender lining up in a row all the crimes of which he stands accused and picking out two or three to which he wishes to plead guilty. The rest are thrown away and forgotten.

Another plea bargaining practice is known as "vertical charge reduction." This technique is applicable whether the offender is charged with multiple offenses or with only one offense. Here, the seriousness of the offenses to which a person pleads guilty beomes the primary consideration, whereas before the number of offenses was of primary significance. Seldom does an offender want to plead guilty to the most serious offense of which he has been accused. This is true no matter how many offenses or transactions have been charged. Thus, in the previous example the offender charged with burglary, theft, and trespass would prefer to plead guilty to trespass (the least serious offense) and would prefer not to plead guilty to burglary (the most serious offense). He might end by pleading guilty to theft as a compromise with the prosecutor.

It is important to an understanding of plea bargaining to realize that a person may plead guilty to a criminal offense that he has not been accused of committing. This happens every day, and in fact is more the rule than the exception. For instance, a person who is charged with committing rape may plead guilty to assault; one charged with arson (unlawfully setting fire to a building) may plead guilty to trespass. Some prosecutors attempt at least to prevent accused persons from pleading guilty to offenses which are unrelated to the crimes charged. For instance, theft has no legal relationship to rape or arson; but assault is related to rape, since rape is a peculiar and serious form of an assault. An offense which is committed whenever a more serious offense is perpetrated is called a "lesser included offense." Thus, assault is a lesser included offense to rape. Whenever a rape is committed the victim is assaulted. The reverse is not true, however, since whenever a person is assaulted (such as by being punched in the nose) the person need not have been raped. Many offenders plead guilty to lesser included offenses instead of to the more serious offenses that were charged originally. Many offenders plead guilty to lesser but nonincluded offenses, also, such as to disorderly conduct when charged with child molesting.

What does a prosecutor get out of a plea bargain? He will avoid the necessity for a trial, primarily, and to most prosecutors this alone is worth the price of negotiating with those accused of committing crimes. A trial requires time (at least one full day, usually two or three days, and often many more); expense (the cost of transporting witnesses sometimes over long distances; the salaries of the judge, the prosecuting attorney, and perhaps a public defender), and delay (pretrial motions and the difficulty of scheduling a courtroom prevent most trials from beginning less than six months following arrest of the accused). In addition, a trial means publicity and substantial news media coverage which may be or seem harmful to the victims and even to witnesses of the crimes. As mentioned previously, there is at least one chance out of four or five that any trial may result in the acquittal of the accused. If the community is antagonized over the crime, the prosecutor may be blamed for losing the case at trial, and prosecutors are elected to office by the citizenry in most jurisdictions.

The prosecutor cannot take every person who is accused of committing a crime to trial. That is an impossibility in every jurisdiction in the nation. Most communities have only one courthouse with two or three courtrooms. This means that only that many trials can take place at a time. Since an average trial requires the bulk of two days or more, and since there are only about two hundred forty working days per year, the average prosecutor can only handle two hundred or so trials per year. Yet, the average judicial unit (county) in America is likely to charge more than ten times as many persons with committing a crime as it could bring to trial. Ninety percent of these accused persons must be processed through the criminal justice system without receiving a trial. The alternatives are simple and clear: The average person who is accused of a crime must plead guilty or the charges must be dismissed. Since the first option is preferable to a prosecutor, he does his best to negotiate a guilty plea bargain with most persons who have been accused of criminal behavior.

Plea bargaining involves more than the negotiation of criminal charges to which an accused person proposes to plead guilty. Since a plea of guilty will result automatically in a criminal conviction, following the plea a sentence must be imposed by the court. It is the sentence and not the charges which most offenders perceive as being of paramount importance. A first offender may express concern over the stigma of a felony conviction on his record. Once this record "virginity" is lost, however, subsequent felony convictions alone mean very little and the penalty which follows becomes the object of negotiation. Most plea bargaining involves considerable emphasis on the probable sentence that will be imposed upon the accused person following conviction by plea. Some prosecutors refer to sentence bargaining as a perversion of the plea bargaining practice. The fact remains, however, that even if the sentence is not discussed directly during negotiations, charge bargaining involves sentence bargaining since most charges (offenses) are punishable by imprisonment for a maximum length of time specified by statute. Thus, the more serious the charge, the longer may be the sentence. If the charge can be reduced by negotiation, the sentence is reduced implicitly.

Actually, it is the sentence which influences the number and type of charges to which an accused individual will be permitted to plead guilty. Most judges are reluctant to impose consecutive sentences even when an offender is convicted (by guilty plea or after trial) of multiple offenses. A consecutive sentence means that the second sentence does not begin until after the first sentence has been served completely. As a rule, an offender who pleads guilty to more than one criminal charge is likely to be sentenced concurrently on all charges. Thus, he will serve the sentence imposed for the most serious charge of which he has been convicted, and upon the completion thereof he will be considered punished in full for that charge and any other convictions, also. No matter how many offenses to which an offender may plead guilty, therefore, he wants to negotiate with the prosecutor the maximum length of time which he will be compelled to serve in prison. He wants to have a ceiling placed on his punishment.

A very successful offender-negotiator may be able to place a ceiling of one year on his punishment in one of two ways. He may plead guilty to a misdemeanor and have any felony charges against him dismissed (since most misdemeanors in most jurisdictions are punishable by one year or less of imprisonment); or he may plead guilty either to a felony or a misdemeanor but before a court which has authority only to sentence offenders to one year of imprisonment or less. Variations of these techniques are known. In states such as New York where each crime is "classified" for purposes of punishment, an offender who pleads guilty to a class D felony may not be sentenced to more than seven years in prison, for example, although one who pleads guilty to a class C felony may be sentenced to prison for up to fifteen years. Thus, by negotiating a reduction of the charge from a class C to a class D felony in New York, an offender can automatically reduce the maximum sentence for which he will be liable from fifteen to seven years—a savings of eight years.

In many states, persons who are convicted of crimes do not necessarily have to serve the maximum sentence prescribed by law. The judge may possess authority in his discretion to reduce this statutory maximum to a lesser sentence. In the above example, therefore, a judge might be persuaded to lower an individual's maximum sentence upon conviction for a class D felony from seven to four years. Judges tend to be persuaded toward leniency in sentence as a result of intervention by the prosecutor. Prior to sentencing, most judges request the prosecutor to make a sentence recommendation to the court. If a prosecutor recommends a light sentence, the judge is likely to follow the recommendation substantially. For instance, a recommendation for a sentence of two years imprisonment might result in the imposition of no more than a three year sentence. If a prosecutor recommends a severe sentence, a judge is likely to give weight to this recommendation and to impose consequently a longer sentence than would have been imposed without such a recommendation. An offender who is going to plead guilty will opt therefore to have the prosecutor make a recommendation for a light sentence; and if the prosecutor refuses to do this, the offender will opt to have the prosecutor make no recommendation at all. Silence by a prosecutor is preferable to a harsh sentence recommendation.

In a number of jurisdictions, the place of confinement has become a topic for negotiation. Repeat offenders seem to enjoy returning to maximum security prisons where they have friends and exert influence. Unsophisticated offenders prefer generally to be confined near their family and, if possible, at a reformatory, county jail, or other facility which may be less regimented than a prison. In some states, likelihood of early release on parole may vary according to the institution or type of institution to which an offender is sentenced.

The ultimate choice relating to sentence which a judge must make is whether to sentence an offender to confinement at all, as opposed to releasing him on probation. In many courts, the offender who has pleaded guilty even to a serious crime involving violence may be sentenced to probation without much hesitation. Some judges acknowledge that by pleading guilty and admitting their wrongdoing, offenders have taken that vital and initial step toward rehabilitating themselves. Not every benefit derived from the guilty plea has been explicitly negotiated in every instance. Some benefits may be implicitly assumed by offenders and by prosecutors. An example of an implicit benefit may be the favor with which a particular judge views an offender's guilty plea and admission of blame. In addition, parole boards may look favorably upon this step taken by an offender, and in turn the offender who has pleaded guilty may serve a lesser proportion of whatever sentence is imposed than will a counterpart offender who was convicted after trial. If both are sentenced to a maximum of ten years, for example, the one who pleaded guilty may be released after two years, while his counterpart is not released until after five years.

Does plea bargaining result in justice being done? This question survives most guilty pleas and especially those that have been bargained. The possibility exists that an innocent defendant may be coerced into pleading guilty to avoid what he fears may be a more severe penalty following conviction at trial. The Supreme Court has held that a guilty plea is valid even though the defendant surrendered his right to a trial solely to forego the possibility of a death sentence. Not only the shadow of a severe penalty, but the influence of a defendant's own lawyer may induce him to plead guilty. Trials are expensive. If the client is wealthy, a trial is expensive to him. If the client is indigent and unable to afford to hire his attorney, a trial is expensive to the state and also to the lawyer, since attorneys receive a lower salary for appointed cases than for those paid by the client. In most cities, a group of lawyers "hustle" cases by hanging around the courts. These lawyers make money by turning over a large volume of cases, and do not endeavor to take most cases to trial. Thus, from the prosecutor to the judge and even to the defendant's own lawyer those who purport to administer justice have a vested interest in the practice of plea bargaining.

The average citizen understands very little about the criminal justice system generally, and less about plea bargaining specifically. To most people, plea bargaining is a controversy without much substantive meaning. The police castigate this practice in most communities, but the courts seem to condone it and lawyers tend to praise it as being a necessity albeit perhaps a necessary evil, since they argue that it saves money for the taxpayer. Plea bargaining has come to resemble a candidate running for public office—one public official says it is good while another says it is bad. Who is right?

The truth about plea bargaining may be ascertainable only in the eyes of the beholder. Even so, the average citizen deserves to be familiarized with enough facts to permit him to draw a reasonable conclusion on this issue. Toward this objective the following chapters are oriented. The purpose of this book is to present to the public as many facts as are available, and to interpret these facts in language which can be understood rather than in legal jargon. Moral points of view will be avoided, but abuses of the plea bargaining process will be illuminated. A balance of arguments for and against plea bargaining will be presented to the reader for judgment, together with evidence in support of both arguments.

This book endeavors to interpret the role of each participant in the plea bargaining practice—the prosecutor, the defendant, the defense attorney, and the judge. Different critical stages in the criminal justice process must be described in relation to the plea bargaining which may take place thereupon.

Plea bargaining is a widespread practice which takes place on a daily basis within more than thirty-one hundred state judicial units across the land and within several hundred additional federal judicial units. Techniques for plea bargaining vary according to local custom. The author has visited or otherwise studied these practices in more than half of the states in preparation for this book. To the fullest extent feasible, unusual aspects of plea bargaining in specific localities will be noted in order that the reader may not infer that a trend exists when it does not. When appropriate, individual officials who have spoken out in favor or against plea bargaining may be named. Similarly, interesting stories about guilty pleas which are known to the participants within certain localities will be summarized. An effort is made, however, not to publicize information which will embarrass any identifiable public official or which may compromise the privacy of any defendant. Such is not the purpose of this book.

Throughout the chapters which follow an emphasis upon alternatives to any plea bargaining practices—whether good or bad—may be noted. In the final chapter of this book a few suggestions will be made to expose the reader's mind to options which may be exercised by those professionals who administer justice and which if selected and implemented might improve the functioning of the criminal justice system. In considering the issues which emerge within the chapters that follow, a reader should think critically but creatively. Attention might be better focused upon remedies rather than blame for negative aspects of the plea bargaining practice.

Note

1. 404 U.S. 257.

5

The Disposition of Criminal Cases in the United States Historically

The per capita rate of reported crimes has increased about 175 percent over the past decade, and the same rate of index crimes (those used by the Federal Bureau of Investigation as indicators of serious crime trends) that have been reported to the police has increased at least 120 percent over the same ten year period of time.[1] Thus, the rate at which serious crimes are perpetrated (if the rate at which they are reported can be used as a measure, and it is likely to reflect the conservative estimate of serious crime) seems to increase at an average of at least 12 percent per annum—similar to the rate of economic inflation during the same interval of time.

The National Advisory Commission on Criminal Justice Standards and Goals cited two major factors as contributing to the increase in serious crime: (1) Criminal methods have become more sophisticated, highly mobile, and possess advanced electronic monitoring and communications equipment; and (2) courts have applied more stringent standards for admitting evidence without adequately explaining their reasoning for doing so and often without providing sufficient guidelines for obtaining sufficiently admissible evidence.[2]

Whatever may be the reasons serious crime rates continue to escalate, many judges, prosecutors, other legal practitioners, and even scholars have contended that rising crime rates in turn are responsible for the practice of plea bargaining in the courts. They have alleged that if the rate of serious crime were to decline significantly, then the practice of plea bargaining would decline, also. Of course, since the rates at which most serious crimes are reported have not declined in recent years, it is impossible for their hypothesis to be tested directly. On the other hand, the historical data that is presented within this chapter casts substantial doubt on the argument that plea bargaining is a function of the crime rate. Although the rate of serious crime has increased progressively for nearly thirty years, the rates of most dispositional variables (dismissal rates, total conviction rates, trial conviction rates, and above all, guilty plea rates) have remained virtually constant for at least forty and presumably for more than seventy years. (See tables 5-1-5-4.)

To begin with, it must be conceded that compatible data is unavailable to reflect the characteristics of criminal case dispositions throughout state courts across the United States during the entirety of the century. However, excellent dispositional information is available for twenty-eight reporting states and the District of Columbia for the year 1937 (more than forty years ago), and for approximately thirty states (one or two different states failed to report during

69

Table 5-1

Disposition of Defendants by Courts of General Jurisdiction Who Were Charged with Major Offenses, Twenty-Eight Reporting States[a] and the District of Columbia 1937, by State

State	Number of Defendants Terminated	Percentage		Trials Ending in Conviction		Convictions Obtained Without Trial
		Terminated by Dismissal	Terminated by Conviction	Jury	Bench	
Arizona	835	25.9	67.4	56.3	–	88.1
California	4,330	10.8	82.8	62.4	74.0	84.8
Colorado	1,567	18.6	75.2	64.4	55.6	85.3
Connecticut	1,168	13.9	84.8	92.9	80.0	90.7
Dist. of Columbia	1,720	17.8	76.0	65.7	–	84.6
Idaho	432	9.0	87.3	75.4	91.7	84.9
Indiana	5,068	37.3	57.3	66.8	77.3	72.4
Iowa	1,572	20.1	77.9	63.4	92.9	93.6
Kansas	1,793	22.0	74.8	74.4	87.0	86.8
Massa- chusetts	3,044	10.0	83.1	69.1	–	84.2
Michigan	4,723	11.1	82.6	71.7	76.8	79.3
Minnesota	1,908	9.2	87.8	62.1	88.9	94.2
Montana	586	18.1	77.1	77.1	–	83.8
Nebraska	1,034	10.9	84.6	55.3	83.3	90.1
New Hampshire	422	14.0	84.6	79.3	–	92.7
New Jersey	5,260	11.8	79.7	52.6	58.7	86.5
New Mexico	838	17.7	75.5	60.1	–	83.4
New York	10,316	16.1	75.2	48.8	–	89.0
North Dakota	536	17.5	79.7	65.1	–	92.7
Ohio	6,010	14.4	80.8	71.9	69.9	85.5
Oregon	832	7.9	87.9	55.1	–	93.4
Pennsylvania	22,603	13.1	70.4	61.1	75.9	61.6
Rhode Island	568	0.7	98.6	42.9	–	99.5
South Dakota	526	13.5	83.8	66.7	90.0	92.1
Utah	377	13.0	78.5	68.0	90.0	74.7
Vermont	649	20.8	77.8	70.4	–	96.2
Washington	1,579	14.9	81.6	73.3	90.0	87.5
Wisconsin	3,024	13.1	84.3	68.0	82.3	89.3
Wyoming	328	15.9	81.1	58.3	–	90.6

Source: United States Bureau of the Census, Judicial Crim. Stats., 1937, 9-64 (table 2 for each State) (1939).

one or two of these years) for the decade between 1936 and 1945. (See tables 5-1-5-2.) Furthermore, equally excellent dispositional data is available for all United States District Courts (excluding the District of Columbia) for most of the seventy years since 1908 with the exception of a seven year period starting

Table 5-2
Disposition of Defendants by Courts of General Jurisdiction Who Were
Charged with Major Offenses: Thirty Reporting States,[a] 1936-1945

		Percentage				
Year	Number of Defendants Terminated	Terminated by Dismissal	Terminated by Conviction	Trials Ending in Conviction		Convictions Obtained Without Trial
				Jury	Bench	
1936	75,682	16.0	73.8	63	74	77.3
1937	83,648	15.2	76.1	62	73	80.1
1938	84,153	14.0	77.7	65	66	80.0
1939	70,265	14.2	78.2	57	65	85.9
1940	76,543	16.0	77.1	53	66	85.7
1941	61,868	15.6	77.1	55	67	84.3
1942	57,641	17.5	75.2	55	70	82.3
1943	48,719	17.4	75.5	58	69	82.1
1944	47,697	15.5	77.5	56	72	82.8
1945	57,426	18.5	75.4	63	72	81.4
		Average (Mean)				
Total	663,642	15.8	76.4	60	69	82.0

Sources: **1936:** United States Bureau of the Census, Jud. Crim. Stats., 1936, p. 9 (table 3), p. 10 (table 5), and p. 12 (table 8) (1938). **1937:** Id., 1937 3 (tables 1-2) and 4 (tables 3-4) (1939); **1938:** Id., 1938 3 (table 1), 4 (table 2), and 5 (table 3) (1940); **1939:** Id., 1939 3 (table 1), 4 (table 2), and 5 (table 3) (1941); **1940:** Id., 1940 3 (table 1), 4 (table 2), and 5 (table 3) (1942); **1941:** Id., 1941 v (table 1), vi (table 2), and vii (table 3) (1943); **1942:** Id., 1942 3 (tables 1-2) and 4 (table 3) (1944); **1943:** Id., 1943 3 (table 2), 4 (table 3), and 5 (table 4) (1945); **1944:** Id., 1944 3 (table 2), 4 (table 3), and 5 (table 4) (1946); **1945:** Id., 1945 3 (table 2) and 4 (table 3) (1947).

aThese states include most of those listed in table 5-1. Several of these thirty states did not report during each of the ten years being studied.

with 1938 and ending with 1944. (See table 5-4.) By comparing these the tables presented within this chapter with those that were presented within chapter 4, it should become obvious that criminal cases are terminated today in essentially the same manner as they have been terminated throughout much of this country during most of this century, with very limited exceptions that will be clearly pointed out.

Table 5-1 displays criminal case dispositional information that is available for twenty-eight reporting states plus the District of Columbia for the year 1937. A high degree of consistency is observed not only between 1937 and recent years, but among most of these jurisdictions during 1937. As a matter of fact, a slightly greater degree of consistency is noted for the twenty-nine jurisdictions reporting in 1937 than for the twenty-one states and the District of Columbia for which similar data is available for recent years, as reported in table 4-1. Note particularly that in 1936, as during the mid-1970s, Pennsylvania showed a much lower guilty plea rate than other states did then or do now.

Of the states that are included within either table 4-1 or table 5-1, thirteen (California, Colorado, Connecticut, Kansas, Minnesota, New Jersey, New York,

Table 5-3

Disposition of Defendants in State Courts of General Criminal Jurisdiction, Thirty Reporting States[a] 1936-1939, by Offense and Method of Disposition

		Percentage				
				Trials Ending in Conviction		Convictions Obtained
Offense	Number of Defendants Terminated	Terminated by Dismissal	Terminated by Conviction	Jury	Bench	Without Trial
Forgery	18,530	14.2	83.1	65	77	93.6
Burglary	59,309	9.0	87.0	69	79	89.2
Auto theft	20,717	10.5	84.0	62	74	88.5
Embezzlement and fraud	22,441	28.4	63.1	58	66	86.2
Larceny other than auto	68,643	12.7	80.6	63	74	84.6
Receiving	6,753	20.4	66.1	50	60	77.2
Sex offenses other than rape	20,089	17.6	72.8	64	73	75.3
Rape	12,852	19.2	67.8	61	68	69.7
Robbery	24,697	11.6	77.9	71	67	69.0
Aggravated assault	25,988	20.8	61.1	55	62	62.3
Murder and manslaughter	10,573	18.8	58.5	56	59	52.6

Sources: **1936:** United States Bureau of the Census, Judicial Crim. Stats., 1936, 29 (table 29) (1938); **1937:** Id., 1937, 5 (table 6) and 6 (table 7) (1939); **1938:** Id., 1938, 7 (tables 6-7) (1940); **1939:** Id., 1939, 11 (table 2) (1941).

[a]These states include most of those listed in table 5-1. Several of these states did not report during each of the four years studied.

North Dakota, Ohio, Pennsylvania, South Dakota, Vermont and Wyoming) plus the District of Columbia are included in both tables. Thus, similar data is available for fourteen jurisdictions that will facilitate a comparison between the mid-1930s and the mid-1970s.

When all dispositional variables are compared on a jurisdiction-specific basis for each of these fourteen jurisdictions, the *least* amount of variation is observed for guilty plea rates of the mid-1970s compared with those for the same jurisdictions in the mid-1930s. By comparing the last column of table 5-1 with the last column of table 4-1, the differences may be observed for each respective jurisdiction for the 1970s compared with the 1930s, as table 5-5 illustrates. Notice that in only five jurisdictions did guilty plea rates vary by more than 5 percentage points up or down, and that in only one state (Wyoming) did they vary by more than 10 percentage points. Wyoming's guilty plea rate for the mid-1970s was almost 20 percentage points lower than its guilty plea rate was in the mid-1930s. On the other hand, in at least five other jurisdictions (California, District of Columbia, Ohio, North Dakota, and Vermont guilty plea rates varied by approximately 1 percentage point or less when the two time periods that span forty years are compared.

Evidently, the per capita crime rate which has risen consistently at least since the end of World War II has not exerted a significant impact upon guilty plea rates at least in twelve states and the District of Columbia for which comparable historical data is available. Guilty pleas do not seem to be as affected by rising crime rates as many key actors in the criminal justice system have contended. In the one state for which evidence is available that documents a significant change in guilty plea rates for the mid-1970s compared with the mid-1930s, the guilty plea rate has *declined* sharply rather than having risen. And, indeed, the fourteen jurisdictions listed in both tables 5-1 and 4-1 include states that were densely populated (New Jersey, New York) in the 1930s and in the 1970s; states that were sparsely populated (North Dakota, South Dakota, Vermont) in the 1930s and in the 1970s; and jurisdictions that have become traumatically more densely populated in the years since 1937 (California, District of Columbia). Based on this information, it is incorrect to blame high or rising guilty plea rates on high or rising crime rates. To do so is to accomplish little or nothing more than to reiterate a poor excuse.

A somewhat greater amount of variation is observed for trial conviction rates of the mid-1930s compared with those for the same jurisdictions in the mid-1970s, based once again on jurisdiction-specific comparisons that may be made for the thirteen states plus the District of Columbia that are listed in both tables 5-1 and 4-1. By comparing the fourth (next-to-last) column of table 5-1 with its counterpart on table 4-1, the differences may be seen for each respective jurisdiction for the 1970s compared with the 1930s, as table 5-6 shows. Notice that in four states for which data is available both for the mid-1930s and the mid-1970s, the *bench* trial conviction rates decreased by 20 or more percentage points, although this rate increased by almost the same number of points in Ohio. In most of the states for which data is available, jury trial conviction rates changed less markedly, and showed a tendency to increase. Jury trial conviction rates increased significantly in California and in Minnesota, although Connecticut's jury trial conviction rate decreased by 26 percentage points. In those states for which trial conviction data could not be controlled for type of trial (jury or bench), four states (Colorado, New York, South Dakota and Wyoming) showed trial conviction rate increases of 12 percentage points or more, although the District of Columbia showed a trial conviction rate decrease of 15 percentage points. Finally, it is pointed out that in three of the states that showed bench trial conviction rate decreases in the mid-1970s compared with the mid-1930s, the jury trial conviction rates showed an increase. The lone exception was Connecticut, where both bench and jury trial conviction rates decreased sharply but where bench trial conviction rates decreased significantly more sharply than did jury trial conviction rates.

One reason bench trial conviction rates may have decreased in the mid-

Table 5-4

Disposition of Defendants in Federal District Courts (Excluding the District of Columbia), Fiscal Years 1908-1975[a]

Year	Number of Defendants or Charges Terminated	Percentage				
		Terminated by Dismissal	Terminated by Conviction	Trials Ending in Conviction		Convictions Obtained Without Trial
				Jury	Bench	
1908	12,942	23.9	65.0	74		51.9
1909	11,705	29.3	58.7	66		60.9
1910	15,371	28.8	61.5	77		48.1
1911	14,700	25.8	63.8	77		47.0
1912	15,741	25.9	64.5	76		52.2
1913	16,757	22.6	68.5	77		55.4
1914	18,128	25.0	66.6	80		49.5
1915	19,120	20.9	70.5	80		50.0
1916	20,432	21.9	69.1	68		72.1
1917	17,671	22.4	70.0	70		75.2
1918	30,949	18.6	75.0	68		81.7
1919	35,734	22.3	72.1	66		84.7
1920	34,230	25.0	69.0	66		83.2
1921	47,209	25.4	69.4	63		87.1
1923	68,152	23.6	71.4	67		85.7
1924	73,488	24.2	71.6	67		87.8
1925	92,711	35.4	61.2	65		89.8
1926	76,536	25.9	70.7	70		89.2
1927	67,279	24.9	71.9	77		85.3
1928	88,336	18.7	78.4	74		89.2
1929	85,328	17.7	78.8	74		87.1
1930	82,609	14.9	82.0	73		89.9
1931	91,701	13.2	84.3	74		91.6
1932	96,949	11.4	86.3	74		92.2
1934	45,577	28.4	68.6	73		88.0
1936	52,777	16.4	79.0	–		90.3
1937	52,393	14.1	90.1	–		89.4
1945	41,653	15.3	81.9	72	77	90.3
1946	36,482	15.1	81.9	65	80	91.6
1947	36,635	12.2	84.9	58	76	93.7
1948	34,242	11.5	85.8	59	71	94.7
1949	36,264	9.0	88.4	62	68	94.9
1950	37,675	8.6	88.9	63	69	94.7
1951	41,066	7.7	90.1	66	67	95.3
1952	38,622	7.5	90.1	66	73	94.1
1953	37,762	8.4	88.6	65	66	93.6
1954	42,989	8.3	88.7	68	65	93.2
1955	38,990	9.7	86.8	67	67	92.0
1956	31,811	9.6	86.7	68	69	90.8
1957	29,725	8.0	88.3	67	72	90.9
1958	30,469	8.4	88.0	69	73	90.5
1959	30,729	8.6	88.0	67	70	91.7
1960	30,512	8.5	87.6	67	70	90.7
1961	32,671	8.8	87.6	66	88	86.7
1962	33,110	10.2	86.1	69	84	86.4
1963	34,845	10.7	85.5	71	79	87.0

Table 5-4 continued

				Percentage		
	Number of Defendants or Charges	Terminated by	Terminated by	Trials Ending in Conviction		Convictions Obtained
Year	Terminated	Dismissal	Conviction	Jury	Bench	Without Trial
1964	33,381	8.8	87.4	73	63	90.1
1965	33,718	11.2	85.3	73	68	90.1
1966	31,975	11.2	85.4	75	73	88.3
1967	31,535	13.3	83.5	79	72	87.8
1968	31,843	15.6	80.6	78	71	85.9
1969	32,796	14.8	83.8	80	71	86.7
1970	36,356	18.2	77.5	76	65	85.6
1971	44,615	23.9	72.0	73	67	85.8
1972	49,516	20.6	75.2	73	73	85.2
1973	46,724	20.9	74.9	76	97	82.9
1974	48,014	20.9	75.5	75	78	84.6
1975	49,212	20.9	76.1	79	80	85.0

Sources: **1975** Dir. of the Admin. Office of the United States Courts, Ann. Rep. 420 (table D-4) (1976); **1974:** Id. at 470 (1975); **1973:** Id. at 402 (1974); **1972:** Id. at 381 (1973); **1971-1970:** Id. at 340 (data for 1971) and 337 (data for 1970) (1972); **1969:** Id. at 273 (1970); **1968:** Admin. Office of the United States Courts, Fed. Offenders in the United States District Courts 7 (Figure B) (1969); **1967:** Dir. of the Office of Admin. of the United States Courts, Ann. Rep. 260 (table D-4) (1968); **1966:** Id. at 220 (1967); **1965:** Id. at 000 (1966); **1964:** Id. at 256 (1965); **1963:** Id. at 240 (1964); **1962:** Id. at 234 (1963); **1961:** Id. at 280 (1962); **1960:** Id. at 304 (1961); **1959:** Id. at 236 (1960); **1958:** Id. at 208 (1959); **1957:** Id. at 220 (1958); **1956:** Id. at 256 (1957); **1955:** Id. at 208 (1956); **1954:** Id. at 194 (1955); **1953:** Id. at 184 (1954); **1952:** Id. at 162 (1953); **1951:** Id. at 166 (1952); **1950:** Id. at 178 (1951); **1949:** Id. at 164 (1950); **1948:** Id. at 170 (1940); **1947:** Id. at 144 (1948); **1946:** Id. at 118 (1947); **1945:** Id. at 112 (1946); **1937:** United States Department of Justice, Ann. Rep. of the Attorney General 178 (table 2B) (1938); **1936:** Id. at 168 (1937); **1934.** Id. at 170 (Exhibit No. 2) (1935); **1932:** Id. at 146 (1933); **1931:** Id. at 140 (1932); **1930:** Id. at 106 (1931); **1929:** Id. at 90 (1930); **1928:** Id. at 88 (1929); **1927:** Id. at 80 (1928); **1926:** Id. at 129 (1927); **1925:** Id. at 135 (1926); **1924:** Id. at 117 (1925); **1923:** Id. at 108 (Sum of Bsn., Rev., & Expend. of the Dept. of Just. and the Courts of the United States) (1924); **1922:** Id. at 109 (Exhibit No. 2) (1923); **1921:** Id. at 151 (1922); **1920:** Id. at 201 (1921); **1919:** Id. at 120 (1920); **1918:** Id. at 156 (1919); **1917:** Id. at 125 (1918); **1916:** Id. at 103 (1917); **1915:** Id. at 87 (1916); **1914:** Id. at 89 (1915); **1913:** Id. at 79 (Appendix 2) (1914); **1912:** Id. at 110 (Appendix I) (1913); **1911:** Id. at 98 (1912); **1910:** Id. at 95 (1911); **1909:** Id. at 152 (Exhibit 9) (1910); **1908:** Id. at 185 (Exhibit 7) (1909).

aFiscal years 1922, 1933, 1935, 1938-44 are not reported because comparable data for those years is not available.

1970s compared with the mid-1930s is that we have experienced a general constriction in the willingness of many courts throughout the United States to admit evidence against criminal defendants, particularly if the evidence has been accumulated by means of search and seizure by police. Jury trial conviction rates have not increased significantly in most instances noted, but they have not decreased, either. The citizenry does not seem to have accepted the doubts

Table 5-5
Guilty Plea Rates in Different Jurisdictions,
1970s Compared with 1930s,[a] Selected States

Jurisdiction	Guilty Plea Rate Difference
California	−0.4
Colorado	+7.7
Connecticut	+6.4
District of Columbia	+0.6
Kansas	−8.4
Minnesota	−4.4
New Jersey	+2.2
New York	+4.5
North Dakota	Equal
Ohio	+0.4
Pennsylvania	+4.9
South Dakota	+5.6
Vermont	Equal
Wyoming	−19.6

[a]+ = Percent increase 1970s/1930s; − = percent decrease 1970s/1930s.

about the wisdom of convicting the guilty to the same extent that some judges appear to have done. Yet, neither does the community seem to have overreacted to "law and order" demands to the extent of rendering more guilty verdicts, which tends to confirm that a defendant can still get as fair a trial as ever he could get before jurors of his peers.

Total conviction rates for the thirteen states and the District of Columbia that are listed in both tables 5-1 and 4-1 decrease invariably when these rates for the mid-1970s are compared with similar rates for the mid-1930s. By comparing the third column of table 5-1 with the third column of table 4-1, the differences may be seen for each respective jurisdiction for the 1970s compared with the 1930s, as reflected in table 5-7.

Total conviction rate differences among these fourteen jurisdictions may be classified into three groups. Three of the jurisdictions (Connecticut, District of Columbia, and Wyoming) show total conviction rate decreases in excess of 30 percentage points. Another four states (Colorado, New Jersey, Ohio and Pennsylvania) show total conviction rate decreases in excess of 10 percentage points. The balance show total conviction rate decreases of less than 10 percentage points, including three states (California, New York and Vermont) that show total conviction rate increases of up to 6 percentage points.

Total conviction rates may be affected by many variables, including guilty plea rates and trial conviction rates. However, since we have already found that guilty plea rates did not change significantly in most of these fourteen jurisdictions when mid-1970s data is compared with mid-1930s data, we must look elsewhere for an explanation of the declining total conviction rates. Bench

Table 5-6
Trial Conviction Rates in Different Jurisdictions, 1970s
Compared with 1930s,[a] Selected States

| Jurisdiction | Trial Conviction Rate Differences | | |
	Jury Trial	Bench Trial	Both
California	+14	−21	*
Colorado	*	*	+12
Connecticut	−26	−38	
District of Columbia	*	*	−15
Kansas	*	*	+3
Minnesota	+23	+7	*
New Jersey	+6	−20	*
New York	*	*	+16
North Dakota	*	*	*
Ohio	+4	+18	*
Pennsylvania	+4	−22	*
South Dakota	*	*	+18+
Vermont	*	*	*
Wyoming	*	*	+27

*Means data unavailable.
a+ = Percent increase 1970s/1930s; − = percent decrease 1970s/1930s.

trial conviction rates declined, but in most of these jurisdictions the volume of bench trials was not large enough during either the mid-1930s or the mid-1970s to account for the decreases in total conviction rates that are observable for at least seven of the fourteen jurisdictions being compared. Often, total conviction rates vary inversely with dismissal rates, since charges that are filed but not disposed of by conviction or acquittal must be dismissed in order to be terminated.

Dismissal rates for the thirteen states plus the District of Columbia that are listed in both tables 5-1 and 4-1 increase invariably when these rates for the mid-1970s are compared with similar rates for the mid-1930s. By comparing the second columns of both table 5-1 and table 4-1, the differences may be seen for each respective jurisdiction for the 1970s compared with the 1930s, as table 5-8 illustrates. Dismissal rates decreased in the mid-1970s compared with the mid-1930s in only two of the fourteen jurisdictions being compared (California and Vermont), and then only insignificantly. Among the other twelve jurisdictions, dismissal rates increased more than 10 percentage points in six (Colorado, District of Columbia, New Jersey, Ohio, Pennsylvania and Wyoming) but considerably less than 10 percentage points in most of the others.

Dismissal rate increases do seem to bear some responsibility for total conviction rate decreases observed for many of these fourteen jurisdictions when mid-1970s data is compared with mid-1930s data. In all of the jurisdictions that showed dismissal rate increases in excess of 10 percentage points, their respective

Table 5-7
Total Conviction Difference Rates in Different Jurisdictions,
1970s Compared with 1930s,[a] Selected States

Jurisdiction	Total Conviction Rate Differences
California	+2.8
Colorado	−18.4
Connecticut	−35.3
District of Columbia	−42.4
Kansas	−5.4
Minnesota	−7.5
New Jersey	−16.5
New York	+5.7
North Dakota	Equal
Ohio	−11.8
Pennsylvania	−22.5
South Dakota	−1.5
Vermont	+2.3
Wyoming	−31.6

[a]+ = Percent increase 1970s/1930s; − = percent decrease 1970s/1930s.

total conviction rates decreased, often by about the same number of percentage points. Similarly, in California and Vermont where dismissal rates decreased slightly total conviction rates increased slightly. Total conviction rates did not increase or decrease significantly in states such as New York, North Dakota, and South Dakota where dismissal rates did not increase or decrease significantly, either. One exception to this overall pattern is noticed in Connecticut, where the dismissal rate did not increase by more than a fraction of 1 percentage point but where the total conviction rate decreased by 35 percentage points. However, in Connecticut's case the sharp decrease in its total conviction rate was caused by a sharp decrease in both bench and jury trial conviction rates.

In the states mentioned where dismissal rates increased enormously in the mid-1970s compared with the mid-1930s, the explanation must be simply that these states tended to lodge formal charges against defendants without being ready, willing or able to support the charges with admissible evidence in many instances. The mid-1970s tend to show a greater eagerness by prosecutors in these states to accuse persons of having committed crimes when the likelihood of conviction at trial is small. This does not mean that more innocent defendants, necessarily, were hurled into the criminal justice processes during the mid-1970s than during the mid-1930s. It may indicate a greater propensity for dismissal bargaining, the practice by which a defendant pleads guilty to one charge and in return secures the dismissal of one or several companion charges. It may indicate hasty charging practices coupled with inadequate screening procedures. Finally, it may reflect a greater tendency by judges in the mid-1970s to toss out criminal charges when the evidence appears at all tenuous.

Table 5-8
Dismissal Rates in Different Jurisdictions, 1970s Compared
with 1930s,[a] Selected States

Jurisdiction	Dismissal Rate Differences
California	−1.7
Colorado	+21.4
Connecticut	+0.6
District of Columbia	+29.1
Kansas	+4.2
Minnesota	+9.3
New Jersey	+17.5
New York	+3.9
North Dakota	+0.9
Ohio	+10.4
Pennsylvania	+14.5
South Dakota	+3.5
Vermont	−4.7
Wyoming	+32.1

[a]+ = Percent increase 1970s/1930s; − = percent decrease 1970s/1930s.

A brief look at table 5-2 confirms the implications that have been drawn from studying table 5-1. In table 5-2, dispositional data is presented for an average of thirty states (a few reported during some years but not during others) for the decade that began in 1936 and ended in 1945. Notice that most guilty plea rates for this decade exceeded 80 percent. Most trial conviction rates fell between 55 and 70 percent. However, bench trial conviction rates in most states were slightly higher than jury trial conviction rates for the same respective states between 1936-1945. The opposite is true for most jurisdictions for which similar data is available for the mid-1970s, as table 4-1 revealed. Table 5-2 shows, also, that dismissal rates tend to be inverse predictors of total conviction rates, and that both dismissal rates and total conviction rates remained stable during the period between 1936-1945. Once again, by comparing table 5-2 with table 4-1, one notices that the total conviction rates for the second-half of the 1930s and the first-half of the 1940s is about one third higher (about 25 percentage points higher) than the total conviction rates are for the mid-1970s. In addition, the same comparison of tables reveals that in the mid-1970s the dismissal rates are between two and three times higher (close to 20 percentage points higher) and much less consistent among different states than are dismissal rates for the 1930s and the 1940s. Times have changed, dismissal and conviction trends have changed, but guilty plea trends have *not* changed measurably.

Table 5-3 reflects the disposition of defendants in state courts of general criminal jurisdiction for approximately thirty states (a few reported during some years but not during others) during the last four years of the 1930s (1936-1939), a type of offense charged. This table may be compared with table 4-4 which reflects similar dispositional information for three states during the mid-1970s, and with table 4-5 which reflects the same dispositional information for United States District Courts during the years 1961-1975, excluding 1965.

Table 5-3 confirms the observations that have been made earlier in this chapter with respect to guilty plea rates, trial conviction rates, total conviction rates, and dismissal rates. In both tables 5-3 and 4-4, forgery has the highest guilty plea rate; and in both of these tables burglary has the second-highest guilty plea rate. Violent fatal and nonfatal crimes have the lowest guilty plea rates in both of these tables, also. Trial conviction rates for most offenses are similar in tables 5-3 and 4-4, except that the trial conviction rate for homicides is higher (71.7 percent) for the three states listed in table 4-4 than for the thirty states (56 percent jury trials; 59 percent bench trials) listed in table 5-3. Although some distortion in variations may be anticipated when data pertaining to three states is compared with data pertaining to thirty states, it may be true that homicide trials in the mid-1970s stood a greater chance of ending in conviction than did homicide trials in the 1930s. If true, the reason for this could be that since 1940 crime laboratory analysis techniques have been improved and expert testimony on matters such as fingerprint identification has become acceptable to more judges and jurors. In addition, burglarly dismissal rates have begun to conform more to the dismissal rates for other crimes in the mid-1970s as table 4-4 demonstrates, whereas in the 1930s burglary had the lowest dismissal rate (9 percent) of all reported crimes in table 5-3. It may be that burglary was viewed as being a much more serious crime in the 1930s than it has come to be viewed forty years later. More likely, it may be that criminal offenders in the mid-1970s, unlike their counterparts in the 1930s are able to have burglary charges dismissed when they plead guilty to other charges such as to crimes of violence. This in turn may indicate that the sanctity of enclosed property has declined since 1940, and that prosecutors who echo the sentiments of the community may be more eager to obtain convictions in cases of violent street crime than in cases of burglary.

Table 5-4 summarizes the disposition of defendants in the United States district courts, excluding the District of Columbia, during the years since 1908 excluding 1922, 1933, 1935 and 1938 to 1944 for which comparable data is not available. Perusal of this table confirms most of the trends that have been noted previously in this chapter and in chapter 4. Several additional observations may be worth discussion, however.

The number of criminal cases that are processed annually through the federal courts has increased substantially over the years since 1908. Less than thirteen thousand criminal cases were heard in that year. Of course, there were fewer states then, and fewer people lived in most states. It is interesting to discover that the number of criminal cases processed through the federal courts peaked with 96,949 cases in 1932. Since the Depression, the federal courts have not handled much more than half that number of criminal cases in any given year. The number of cases processed has alternately increased and decreased from year to year. Table 5-4 summarizes dispositional information for all the years except eight since 1908 (seventy years ago). More than one third of those years have witnessed a decrease rather than an increase in the number of terminated criminal cases. Overall, however, criminal cases terminated in the federal district courts appear to have increased at an average rate of about 3 percent per annum. Drastic increases in case dispositions occurred between 1917 and 1918 and between 1920 and 1921, when criminal case dispositions in each of those two fiscal years increased by about thirteen thousand. Even more drastic increases occurred between 1924 and 1925 and between 1927 and 1928, when criminal case dispositions increased by about 19,000 and 21,000 cases respectively. Each of these traumatic increases may be attributable to the prohibition experiment.

Table 5-4 indicates that guilty plea rates in the federal courts have remained rather constant in the vicinity of 80-90 percent in the years since 1918. Prior to 1918, guilty plea rates were between 10 and 30 percentage points lower. It is likely that the types of criminal offenses that are processed through the federal courts changed during and after World War I. New regulatory statutes were enacted, and the federal courts began to hear criminal cases involving contraband substances, embezzlement in federal banks, and other nonviolent crimes. Prior to World War I, many federal courts took criminal jurisdiction over defendants who had been accused mostly of violent crimes perpetrated on federal territories in the West. Naturally, when these territories became subject to state regulations, federal jurisdiction over traditional crimes stopped.

Guilty plea rates in the federal courts have fluctuated between 80 and 90 percent in the years since 1918, however, and some patterns may be observable. In the years since 1960, guilty plea rates have hovered around 85 percent with the exception of 1964 and 1965 when they reached 90 percent in both years. For about fifteen years prior to 1960s, guilty plea rates were never less than 90 percent and approached or reached 95 percent during the five year period between 1947 and 1952. On the other hand, federal guilty plea rates remained around the 85 percent level between 1918 and 1930, similar to the level at which they have remained in the years since 1960. Guilty plea rates increased to the 90 percent level during the 1930s.

Even in the federal courts, guilty plea rates do not seem to be a function of caseloads. Between 1928 and 1932 when federal criminal case terminations peaked higher than they have at any time in history guilty plea rates fluctuated between 87 and 92 percent—the same spread that federal guilty plea rates have followed during many other years when the number of criminal case terminations have been little more than half as many as during peak years. For example, every year between 1945 and 1960 guilty plea rates exceeded the 90 percent level, even though during those years the highest federal criminal caseload (in 1954) was 42,989—was less than half of what it was during the peak year of

1932 (96,949). Moreover, federal guilty plea rates approached or exceeded the 95 percent level for five straight years between 1947 and 1952, and during that period the highest federal criminal caseload (for 1951) was 41,066.

It is possible, however, that federal guilty plea rates may rise from the 85 percent level to the 90 percent level or from the 90 to the 95 percent level during times when there are not enough sitting federal judges, but that when new judges are appointed the guilty plea rates shrink back to the 90 or 85 percent levels. This possibility is not at all likely, and except for it there does not seem to be any concrete link between federal criminal caseload size and federal guilty plea rates.

Trial conviction rates in the federal courts have not been quick to change during most parts of this century. Federal trial conviction rates did not reach 80 percent until 1914, and slipped back into the 60 percent level for most of the period between 1916-1925. Between 1925 and 1934 trial conviction rates stabilized at the mid-70 percent level, but data is not available for the World War II period. In 1945, federal trial conviction rates were at the 80 percent level but fell back to the mid-60 percent level for jury trials through 1962 and for bench trials through 1956. Since those years, jury and bench trial conviction rates respectively have remained at the mid-70 percent level for the most part, with fluctuations into the 60 and into the 80 percent levels during brief intervals. Between 1945 and 1963, bench trial conviction rates exceeded jury trial conviction rates by 3 to 8 percentage points in all but two years (1954 and 1955). Between 1964 and 1972, however, jury trial conviction rates exceeded bench trial conviction rates by about the same percentage points in every year. These trial conviction rates were exactly even for 1973, and in 1974 bench trial conviction rates began to exceed jury trial conviction rates again.

Total conviction rates in the federal courts rose slowly but steadily from 1908 to 1969, from about 60 percent to almost 85 percent. Beginning in 1970, total conviction rates in federal courts fell back to the 75 percent level, a drop of about 10 percentage points. This decline is attributable to the "criminal law revolution" and its aftermath that began when the United States Supreme Court under then-Chief Justice Earl Warren started to constrict the rules relating to the admissibility of evidence at criminal trials, particularly evidence that was obtained through searches and seizures by law enforcement officers. Bench trial conviction rates became lower than jury trial conviction rates in the aftermath of the criminal law revolution, also, perhaps because judges began to fear appellate reversal of their convictions. The criminal law revolution seems to have exerted a delayed statistical impact upon both bench trial conviction rates and total conviction rates, presumably because at that time in the federal courts trials were delayed until several years elapsed since the criminal conduct occurred, and negotiated dispositions tended to take place at time of trial.

Between 1908 and 1918, dismissal rates in the federal courts declined from one year to the next five out of ten times. Dismissal rates were lower in 1915 and 1919 than they had been in 1908. During all but three of the years between 1908 and 1918, total conviction rates rose steadily, however. Except for the period between 1916 and 1917 when both total conviction rates and dismissal rates rose by less than 1 percentage point each, total conviction rate increases occurred in proportion to dismissal rate decreases, establishing each as an inverse predictor of the other. This trend has continued for the most part as total conviction rates and dismissal rates both have risen and fallen in the federal courts.

Between 1920 and 1927, total conviction rates and dismissal rates for the federal courts remained fairly constant as illustrated by figure 5-1, each fluctuating up and then down by less than 5 percentage points. At the end of that period, total conviction rates started to increase and dismissal rates began to decrease both dramatically and in proportion to one another. Between 1928 and 1951, total conviction rates rose and dismissal rates sunk continuously in the federal courts, except for 1934, when dismissal rates increased and total conviction rates decreased each by about 17 percentage points, and except for the years 1938 to 1944 for which information is unavailable. In 1952, total conviction rates peaked and dismissal rates bottomed out, then the former declined while the latter increased gradually but again proportionately through 1970 where each ended at their respective 1929 levels. Since 1970, for the most part, both of these rates have remained constant at points equal to the mean of their spread over more than half a century. These rates have documented the statistical principle known as regression toward the mean.

It seems much more likely that dismissal rates constitute the independent variable of which total conviction rates are a dependent function, than that the obverse is true, because dismissals encompass a single type of case termination whereas total conviction rates are the aggregate of dismissal rates, bench and jury trial conviction rates, and guilty plea rates. This observation gains credence in the fact that guilty plea rates remain rather constant over vast periods of time in both the federal and state courts. Thus, the rates which fluctuate most widely are the dismissal rates.

Why do dismissal rates vary so widely, not necessarily from one year to the next, although this happens, but across the span of one or two decades? Dismissals tend to be characteristic of the number of separate charges filed against each individual offender, primarily, and secondarily they tend to be characteristic of the difference between the seriousness of the conduct of which the defendant has been accused and the severity of the penalty which the community demands as payment for the crime. During some periods in history, law enforcement agencies, particularly at the federal level, have insisted upon launching a separate charge against defendants for each separate violation of the law. Judges have become more and more inclined over the years to impose concurrent sentences for multiple crimes committed by the same offender. In turn, when judges show a pattern of imposing concurrent rather than consecu-

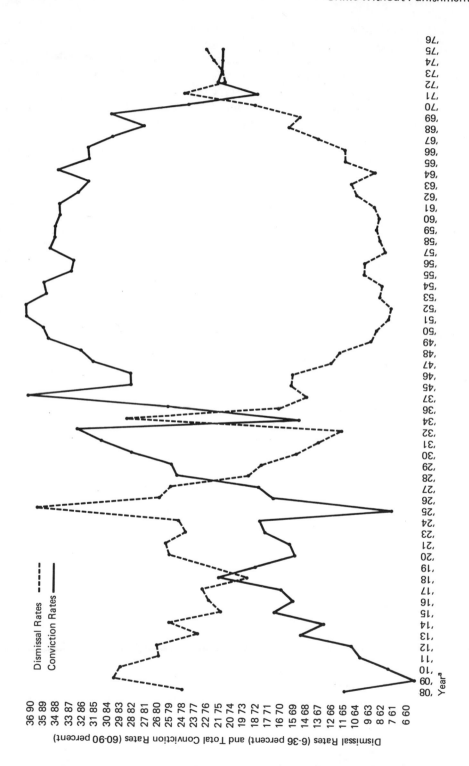

Figure 5-1. Dismissal Rates and Total Conviction Rates of Criminal Cases in the Federal Courts, 1908-1978, by Percentage.

tive sentences, prosecutors have little to gain by obtaining multiple convictions against defendants who are willing to plead guilty to at least one charge, and so become increasingly more willing to dismiss companion charges. This was the trend throughout the 1950s and 1960s. Finally, as prisons have become increasingly overcrowded and proportionately more offenders are convicted of federal crimes, the average convicted offender actually serves a progressively shorter time in prison. For this reason, the average offender will not spend any longer in prison whether he is convicted of the crime that reflects the offense he committed or of a reduced offense. Knowing this, many prosecutors agree to charge reductions and dismiss more serious charges when a defendant pleads guilty to lesser included or lesser related offenses.

Notes

1. See United States Department of Justice, Federal Bureau of Investigation, Uniform Crime Reports for the United States, 1976 (1977) compared with Id., 1966 (1967). See also National Advisory Commission on Criminal Justice Standards and Goals, *Report on Police* 146 (1973).

2. National Advisory Commission on Criminal Justice Standards and Goals, *Report on Police* 206 (1973).

The Mechanics of
Guilty Plea
Negotiations

As soon as a criminal charge or a group of charges has been filed against a person accused of criminal behavior, or even before this juncture, negotiations that are intended to dispose of the charges without need for trial are likely to begin. It is extremely difficult for a person who is himself accused of criminal conduct to negotiate away his charges. The old maxim seems to apply here: A lawyer who represents himself has a fool for a client. That statement applies even more disasterously to a defendant who is not a lawyer but who tries to pretend that he is by representing himself either in the courtroom at trial or outside the courtroom in plea negotiations with the prosecutor. He lacks clout, may lack coolness, and undoubtedly does not possess the finesse that is necessary at any bargaining table.

The sooner a lawyer does appear to represent a criminal defendant, the earlier the plea negotiation process may begin and in turn the easier it may be to strike a bargain that will be acceptable to the prosecutor and the defendant. For this reason, a person who learns that he has been or is about to be charged with a criminal offense should retain an attorney at once if he can afford to do so. An indigent defendant can look forward to having an attorney appointed by the court to represent him free of charge, but the appointment may well be delayed until weeks after the charges have been filed. Delay in the assignment of a court-appointed legal counsel may make a substantial difference in the kind of negotiations which take place and in their outcome.

The characteristics of plea negotiations vary at different stages of the criminal justice process. Two early stages which are of immense importance to plea negotiations are (1) the charging stage and (2) the screening stage, each of which needs to be described in detail alongside of the negotiation process taking place at the same time.

The Charging Stage

One may be accused of having committed a crime in different ways and on more than one occasion for the same offense. When a person is arrested at the scene of a crime or shortly thereafter, the arrest is likely to be made by police officers who "collar" the offender during or in flight from the criminal act. As soon as an apprehended offender is arrested by police and brought to the station for "booking," a *complaint* is drafted by the police and filed with the court. A complaint is nothing more than a written document alleging the accused offender's criminal conduct at a specified time and place, plus a list of appropriate statutes or ordinances which the accused offender is alleged to have violated.

If the accused offender was not apprehended at the scene of the crime or if he was arrested by a citizen and not by the police, someone other than a police officer may sign the complaint. Whoever does sign the complaint is known as the complainant. The truth of a complaint (or at least the complainant's belief in its truth) must be verified by the complainant under oath and on penalty of perjury. In this way, frivolous or malicious complaints are discouraged. As a practical matter, a complaint is filed generally by the police or by the victim of the offense complained of. Once drafted, signed, and sworn to, a complaint becomes filed when it is delivered to the clerk of an appropriate court. Usually, a complaint is filed with the clerk of a lower court of limited jurisdiction. The name of such a court varies from one jurisdiction to another. Common names include Justice's Court, City Court, Municipal Court, or Court of Common Pleas.

Very little opportunity for negotiation is afforded to an accused person until the complaint against him has been filed. Indeed, until the complaint has been filed the accused may not know for certain the specific crimes with which he is charged. Some persons who possess both a guilty conscience and a lawyer who has been retained to defend them on an ongoing basis may exert an initial advantage by asking the lawyer to determine the contents of the complaint even before it is filed. It is possible, although infrequent, for the accused or his lawyer to learn of the contents of a complaint and persuade the complainant to withdraw the document even before it is filed. To accomplish this task, legal dexterity is required, since at least the appearance of a bribe or a threat may be perceived by the complainant if approached to withdraw the complaint before filing. Even more remote, but still a possibility, is the chance that the accused or his lawyer may persuade the prosecutor to abstain from filing one or two particularly serious charges in the complaint in return for a promise by the accused to plead guilty to less serious charges as soon as they are filed. The difficulty with this type of an "embryonic" plea bargain is that in most jurisdictions no prosecutor becomes assigned to a criminal case until after a complaint has been filed with a court.

Within a very short period of time after a complaint is filed, the person accused in the complaint must be brought before a judge or a magistrate for what is known generally as an "initial appearance." At this first appearance in court, the accused individual becomes known as a defendant for the first time. The complaint must be read to the defendant verbally by the judge or the magistrate during the initial appearance, unless this reading is waived by the defendant. If the defendant is represented by an attorney at this proceeding, the reading of the complaint will nearly always be waived. However, at this early proceeding few defendants and particularly few indigent defendants (those unable to afford a lawyer) are represented by counsel. Without the presence of an attorney to advise the defendant, many judges and magistrates are reluctant to permit a defendant to waive reading of the complaint. Thus, an initial appearance may become a time-consuming event to say the least.

Once the complaint has been read to the defendant, the defendant must be warned of his right to remain silent and be apprised of his constitutional rights. Particularly, he must be advised of his right to be represented by an attorney at each subsequent court proceeding, and of his right to demand a jury trial to determine his guilt or innocence. The formal role of a judge or a magistrate presiding at an initial appearance is to determine if the complaint is sufficient to charge the defendant with a crime. If deemed insufficient, the defendant must be released and the complaint must be dismissed. Bear in mind, however, that evidence will not be evaluated at this proceeding, and no testimony will be taken. The complaint will not be dismissed as a rule unless it charges the defendant with conduct which does not constitute any crime.

One other important issue may, customarily, be determined at the initial appearance. This is the matter of the defendant's pretrial release. The judge or magistrate may exercise one of several options. The defendant may be released without bond upon his own personal recognizance by pledging to the court that he will return voluntarily upon being notified of further scheduled proceedings. This option is available to defendants who are charged with trivial offenses only as a matter of practice, although a person who has been charged with a serious offense for the first time in his life and who has lived in the community for a long time may be offered this opportunity. On the other hand, the defendant may be ordered held in custody without being eligible for bail at all. A defendant who is charged with having committed a very serious crime, particularly one of violence such as murder or one for which the death penalty may be imposed upon conviction, may be denied eligibility for pretrial release. Most defendants are provided an opportunity to enjoy pretrial release but only if they can afford to make bail. The federal Constitution states that bail should not be unreasonable. For many defendants who are destitute, however, five dollars may be unreasonable.

The purpose of bail is to insure a defendant's return for subsequent proceedings and especially for trial. Hence, the amount of bail required by a court should be commensurate with the defendant's likelihood of absconding. Many judges and magistrates view the purpose of bail as being somewhat different, however. They tend to look toward the likelihood that the defendant may commit additional crimes in the interim period if he is released on bail. Under this latter view, a defendant may be denied pretrial release and bail may be set at an amount that he cannot afford for the sole purpose of incapacitating him until the charges reach a disposition. This situation is a frequent occurrence with offenders who have a long history of repeated offenses but who have always returned to court to face proceedings when required to do so.

The availability of pretrial release exerts a drastic impact upon the progress of negotiations leading to a guilty plea. When the defendant is free on pretrial release, there is no need for his lawyer to rush into a plea bargain. Quite the contrary, a defendant who is out on bail may benefit if the charges against him remain pending for months or even for years, since the strength of the evidence against him may be expected to diminish over time. Evidentiary strength will be the subject of a future chapter. The defendant who must remain in confinement before charges against him are resolved may feel continuous pressure to plead guilty to some charges if for no reason other than to have the length of his confinement defined. Generally, a defendant who is able to achieve pretrial release will be able also to negotiate a more advantageous plea bargain than will his counterpart who must remain in jail during the entire negotiation process. This discrepancy seems to be unfair on its face, but since many aspects of the criminal justice system are unfair, the question becomes what to do about it. Answers to this question will be considered from time to time throughout this book.

A complaint is one form of an accusatory instrument by means of which a person may be formally charged with having committed a criminal offense. Instead of or even in addition to a complaint, other accusatory instruments may be used for the same purpose. These include principally the prosecutor's information and the grand jury indictment. These documents are similar in form and content to the complaint. Each must be sworn to under oath and on penalty of perjury. Instead of being sworn to by a police officer or by the victim of a crime, as in the case of a complaint, the information and the indictment must be sworn to by the district attorney or another person serving as a prosecutor. An indictment must be sworn to by the foreman of the grand jury which handed down the indictment. The role of the grand jury and of the prosecutor will be noted in greater detail when the screening stage is explained in this chapter.

The information is used as an accusatory instrument to bring criminal charges before a trial level court. It is a frequent tool used to bring misdemeanor charges beyond the initial appearance. A misdemeanor is a criminal offense in most jurisdictions that may be punished by imprisonment up to one year. It is less serious than a felony, which in turn is a criminal offense for which more than one year of imprisonment may be imposed in most states. In many states, felony charges must be prosecuted by a grand jury indictment unless this is waived by the defendant. In Pennsylvania, a defendant cannot be brought to trial for either a felony or a misdemeanor except by indictment. In several western states, an information alone is sufficient to compel a person to stand trial for either a felony or a misdemeanor.

The Screening Stage

Once a complaint has been filed, the accusations contained therein may undergo initial and ongoing evaluation to determine the wisdom and value of bringing each defendant to trial as charged. Screening may take place by the prosecutor acting alone, or with the prosecutor acting in concert with a grand jury, or by the court. In many prosecutors' offices across the nation, a systematic process known as "early screening" takes place routinely as soon as each complaint becomes filed. Following filing of the complaint and possibly of the information, also, a defendant may demand a preliminary hearing before a judge to determine whether probable cause exists to bind his case over for grand jury action. A preliminary hearing, which is available only for felony charges in most jurisdictions, is an example of judicial screening of criminal charges. Ordinarily, a preliminary hearing is forfeited unless it is demanded and received prior to the handing-up of a grand jury indictment. The role of a grand jury is to screen criminal charges which have been complained of by police or other persons. While the prosecutor may present evidence of wrongdoing to a grand jury, the latter may refuse to indict an individual in which case the complaint against him must be dismissed.

Early Screening by a Prosecutor

Since neither police nor victims of crime tend to be experts on the prosecution of criminal charges, complaints may be and are frequently filed even though likelihood of a successful prosecution is slim. Often times, a person who has been accused of committing a crime may raise or have available to him a technical defense. Most crimes, for example, must be prosecuted within a time period (such as three years) specified by a law referred to as the "statute of limitations." Most serious crimes must be committed intentionally rather than inadvertently in order for punishment to be appropriate. Complainants may not be familiar with the statute of limitations, the requirement of a criminal intent, or with other legal technicalities. What is more, the ordinary complainant is as a rule not familiar with the amount of evidence necessary to convict a person of the crimes charged or the quality of evidence which is available at the time. If a prosecution is going to be unsuccessful, prosecutors prefer to predict this in advance and as early as possible, in order to dismiss the charges quietly and without undue burden on the accused, the victims, or witnesses.

Toward this objective, several prosecutors in major cities across the country, New Orleans and San Diego, for example, have established early screening units. The major duty of these specialized units is to examine in detail and from the start each charge on which a complaint has been filed. Personnel in these units are generally experienced prosecutors who know how to evaluate a criminal charge objectively and without personal bias. The person accused in the complaint may be a vicious individual and may deserve punishment, but if the charges specified cannot be proven, to prosecute on the charges would be a waste of the taxpayers' money. In these and other jurisdictions, when a complaint is rejected by the screening unit it must be returned to the complainant together with an explanation of the reasons supporting the rejection. The complainant is advised whether the charges may be prosecuted at some future time if additional evidence can be gathered. Usually, a complainant may appeal to the district attorney himself the decision of the screening unit not to prosecute if the complainant is that persistent.

Most charges which are dropped at the time of early screening are abandoned at the initiative of the prosecutor. Very little negotiation takes place at this stage in the ordinary course of events. Once again, as with filing of the complaint, the accused person is unlikely to be aware specifically of the charges against him or of evidence to support the charges at this stage of the proceedings. Now and then an attorney, usually retained rather than appointed, may appear before the early screening unit in the office of a prosecutor in an effort to persuade screening personnel to reject a case. At this point in time, a case against a defendant will not be rejected as part of a deal with the offender. If rejected, the charges will be disgarded entirely and the defendant will not be asked to plead guilty to any charge in return. It is safe to conclude that when a charge is thrown out at this stage, following arrival of defense counsel at the screening unit, the charge would have been thrown out even in the absence of the lawyer. The defense attorney may visit a screening unit for a purpose other than to have the charges against his client dismissed then and there, however. He may be preparing for the preliminary hearing to come.

Preliminary Hearing

Unless a grand jury has already handed up an indictment against the defendant, in most jurisdictions the defendant is entitled to a preliminary hearing upon demand. At a preliminary hearing the opportunity for judicial screening of criminal charges exists, perhaps for the second time but for the first time in any depth. During the initial appearance the judge or magistrate exercised an opportunity to scrutinize the complaint, but only for the limited purpose of deciding whether a crime had been charged. Evidence was not presented or considered at the initial appearance, but evidence becomes the subject matter to be evaluated at the preliminary hearing. At this proceeding, the prosecutor is obligated to show to the satisfaction of the court that probable cause exists to believe the defendant committed the offenses charged.

Since at the preliminary hearing a prosecutor has only to show probable cause and does not have to prove the defendant's guilt as would have to be done at trial, the cautious prosecutor will introduce only so much evidence at this hearing as will be necessary to have the court find probable cause. The prosecutor is not eager at this stage to reveal to the defendant and defense attorney all the evidence which points to the defendant's guilt. Usually, a police officer will be a witness at this proceeding, to place the accused at the scene of the crime if this is possible to do. A victim may testify also, but briefly and only to identify the defendant in court rather than to describe in detail the substance of the offenses. Most judges will make a finding that there is probable cause if any evidence at all exists to support such a finding. As soon as probable cause is shown at the preliminary hearing, plea bargaining is likely to begin in full force.

Both the prosecutor and the defense attorney are eager under most circumstances to strike an acceptable plea bargain as shortly after a preliminary hearing as possible. At the hearing itself, the defense attorney focused attention onto the witnesses whom the prosecution called to testify against the defendant. Were the prosecution witnesses and evidence credible? Not infrequently, a defense lawyer learns for the first time at the preliminary hearing that his client is factually guilty—that the client was at the scene of the crime when it occurred and did participate in criminal behavior. Following a determination of probable cause at the preliminary hearing, a defendant is apt to concede his guilt in discussions with his lawyer, and to begin to consider the minimum length of time he is prepared to spend in prison if his lawyer is able to negotiate a deal with the prosecutor.

The modern trend is for the prosecutor to provide the defense counsel with ample evidence to document the client's guilt—at least once the preliminary hearing is over. A defendant is entitled to some information relating to the prosecutor's case against him and can compel disclosure of this material from the prosecutor. The procedure for obtaining a view of the prosecutor's case is known as "discovery." A defendant is not, however, entitled to the prosecutor's internal working papers nor to specific details of the testimony to be offered by witnesses at trial. He is entitled to advance notice of the results of scientific tests such as ballistics tests conducted on a weapon found at the scene of a crime, or fingerprint tests linking the defendant to a crime scene. If the prosecutor supplies defense counsel with most items of information which the latter has requested without a court order, "informal discovery" has taken place. Quite often informal discovery is used skillfully by a prosecutor to convince a defense attorney that the defendant will lose at trial. Since most defense attorneys do not relish the prospect of having a client convicted at trial, the lawyer who becomes assured of his client's guilt will in turn try to persuade the client to avoid trial by pleading guilty.

It may be advantageous for some defendants to plead guilty as soon after a preliminary hearing as possible if they are planning to plead guilty at all, and many have little choice in the matter. The repeat offender who has committed an attrocious crime can do well by pleading quietly before the news media attracts public attention to the matter. Prosecutors are reluctant to reduce charges substantially or to make favorable sentence recommendations in the face of public alarm. Similarly, a judge may refuse to go along with a prosecutor's charge or sentence recommendation once publicity has been generated and the gory details of a crime have been exposed to public scrutiny. While justice delayed may be justice denied, a "quickie" guilty plea may be of enormous benefit to the offender although arguably not beneficial to the public.

Once probable cause has been determined at a preliminary hearing, the defendant is bound-over for indictment by a grand jury. Several weeks may elapse between the preliminary hearing and indictment. Grand juries do not convene every day, and in many jurisdictions the caseload of charges awaiting presentation to a grand jury may be copious. Since a sufficient opportunity is available for most defendants to plead guilty prior to grand jury action, some prosecutors become reluctant to enter into a plea bargain following grand jury indictment. Indeed, it is true that many prosecutors will not be as generous in the concessions offered to a defendant who wants to plead guilty after indictment compared with an earlier stage of the proceedings.

Grand Jury Indictment

The final formal screening process prior to the trial of a criminal charge involves the grand jury. A grand jury consists of a group of citizens sworn to determine whether there is probable cause to believe that the person accused by the prosecutor actually committed the offenses charged. This jury is distinguished from a trial or petit jury if only in its size: while a trial jury consists of no more than twelve persons, a grand jury numbers at least eighteen and may reach twenty-three. For the most part, a grand jury may be expected to return an indictment against any person for whom the prosecutor desires an indictment. Many prosecutors utilize a grand jury as a screening mechanism to share the blame with him when he wants to abandon prosecution of an individual. Thus, a skillful prosecutor can manipulate the evidence he presents to a grand jury in order to influence their decision to return a "true bill" and indict or a "no bill" and fail to indict.

A defendant may not negotiate with the grand jury itself. In most states, a defendant against whom a complaint has been filed may appear before a grand jury to offer testimony in an effort to thwart an impending indictment. This appearance seldom prevents an indictment altogether, but it may cause the grand jury to return an indictment for a lesser offense than otherwise would have been returned. Indeed, the indictment may be for a lesser offense than that alleged in the complaint by the victim or the police.

Sometimes a date is set on which, every month, grand jury indictments are handed up. As this date draws near, lawyers representing worried clients may intensify negotiations in a last minute effort to avoid the indictment by means of a guilty plea. As soon as an indictment is handed up, a defendant is likely to become unnerved and urge his lawyer to approach the prosecutor immediately with the offer of a guilty plea to some charges which may be less serious than the charges contained in the indictment. An indictment is publicized in the news media as a rule, unless it is a secret indictment handed up by a "blue-ribbon" grand jury which is investigating crime on its own initiative rather than upon a complaint. The publicity dissuades many prosecutors from further guilty plea negotiations until additional time has elapsed. For this reason, as mentioned previously, a defendant may be well advised to strike a guilty plea bargain in advance of an anticipated indictment.

By the time an indictment is returned by a grand jury, most defendants have enjoyed an extensive opportunity for plea bargaining. Why have they waited? Some crimes are so repulsive and visible to the public that no prosecutor would be willing to negotiate the charges. The rape or murder of a child is such an example. These charges must be decided at trial unless the offender is willing to plead guilty as charged but without any bargained concessions, which is not likely. Other defendants are left without a bargain when an indictment is handed up either because they have waited too long and miscalculated, or because they or their attorney may be hoping for a change of events to occur between indictment and trial. A material witness may die or otherwise become unavailable to testify at trial. New evidence may be awaited which if found will cast a doubt on or negate entirely the defendant's guilt. Naturally, the truly innocent person is likely to demand a trial rather than to plead guilty even in the aftermath of a grand jury indictment.

The Discovery Stage

Following the completion of the charging process and after early screening has been unsuccessful in exonerating a defendant, both the prosecution and the defense will want to "discover" as much as possible about the evidence on which the other side will rely at trial if the case ever gets to trial. The accusatory instrument that contained an enumeration of the charges alleged only the conduct and intent of the defendant at a particular time and place (the scene of the crime). It did not share with the defendant any details surrounding the reasons why the prosecutor believes the defendant is guilty of the crimes in question. The task of defense counsel in the discovery stage is to unravel the prosecutor's case as fully as practicable, preferably in the shortest time span possible. Only in this way can the defendant be informed intelligently about the likelihood of his being convicted at trial and about the concessions, if any, that he can expect to receive by pleading guilty to one or more charges.

As part of the discovery process, the defendant will want to learn the details of two fundamental types of evidence that the prosecutor may possess: *direct* evidence, if it exists, and *indirect* or circumstantial evidence. Direct evidence includes "eyewitness" testimony, but the direct evidence that is available in any given case may vary. It may consist of the defendant's "confession" made to the police during interrogation while in confinement following arrest. Or, it may include admissions or other declarations which the defendant is said to have uttered to friends or acquaintances. Indirect evidence is less conclusive than direct evidence on the issue of a defendant's guilt. It may consist of threats that a defendant made on the life or the well-being of the victim of a crime, the inference being that the defendant carried out his threats. It may include the results of ballistics tests showing that a bullet that killed or injured someone was fired from a gun that was owned or possessed by the defendant, or fingerprints that show the defendant was present at a particular place or touched a specific object. Circumstantial evidence cannot prove a defendant's guilt by itself, but it can become highly persuasive when introduced at a trial to buttress direct evidence that would be less impressive standing alone.

In attempting to discover the strength and quality of each other's case, the prosecutor and defense counsel will try to learn about and evaluate three forms of evidence—testimonial, tangible, and judicially noticed evidence. *Testimonial* evidence is oral testimony that will be given by a witness in court while under oath. It may be offered at trial, and it may have been offered prior to trial in front of a grand jury in support of an indictment or in front of a judge or a magistrate at a preliminary hearing. Prior to offering testimony orally in court, a witness may execute in writing a sworn pretrial deposition to confirm the nature of the testimony in advance.

Tangible evidence consists of physical exhibits that will be introduced into evidence at a trial, such as a weapon, counterfeit money, a contraband substance such as cocaine, or a picture of the crime scene. It may include "mock" evidence, also, such as a diagram of the route taken by the perpetrator of a crime to lie in wait for his victim, or an anatomical model of a human skull that depicts the sort of injuries a victim received.

Courts may take *judicial notice* of facts that are within the common knowledge of society and that for this reason do not require formal proof. For example, a judge may take judicial notice that in a given year, May 15th came on a Monday, firearms and fingerprint identification methods are valid, and that slang such as "horse" or "red devils" may refer to contraband substances. However, courts will not take judicial notice that polygraph tests are valid.

In order to evaluate the credibility of any form of evidence, counsel must be informed of its existence. For many years, the exact nature of the most damaging evidence that prosecutors planned to introduce against defendants at criminal trials remained a tightly-guarded secret in most cases. The defendant and his lawyer learned about the evidence at trial when it was too late for them to do much about it. Then, case law and statutes emerged in most jurisdictions requiring the prosecutor to summarize the character of much of the evidence on which he plans to rely at trial, and to provide this summary to defense counsel upon demand by the latter. In many states, however, defense counsel had to file written discovery motions in court and obtain a court order if he wanted to "inspect" physical evidence in the possession of the prosecutor. For a while, prosecutors were required to share most of their evidence with defense counsel, but defense counsel were not required to share much of their evidence with prosecutors. In the last few years, many states have enacted "mutual discovery" statutes whereby prosecutors and defense counsel alike are required to exchange basic evidentiary information on which each plans to rely at trial, and to do so informally without involving the court other than in exceptional instances. The evidence that must be exchanged in criminal cases still falls short of that which must be exchanged prior to trial in civil actions, however. For example, some states mandate that each side to a criminal case supply the other side with the names and addresses of witnesses whom they expect to call at trial, together with an abstract of their projected testimony. Ordinarily witnesses who will testify in a criminal trial cannot be cross-examined before trial or otherwise questioned by the adverse party in advance of trial, as they can be in civil actions.

Once defense counsel has gained access to evidence on which the prosecution will rely in proving the defendant's guilt at trial, the task becomes to analyze this evidence in terms of its admissibility and, if it is admissible, in terms of its value for proof and persuasion. Some evidence is stronger than other evidence. To result in a defendant's conviction, the prosecution's evidence must prove the defendant's guilt beyond a reasonable doubt *and* persuade the fact-finders (judge in a bench trial, jurors in a jury trial) to reach a guilty verdict. A jury especially may be inclined to believe certain kinds of evidence more than other kinds, although all the evidence or none of the evidence points to the defendant's guilt conclusively. Jurors are likely to be impressed by testimony of ordinary citizens who have knowledge of a defendant's guilt, and less likely to be persuaded to convict a defendant primarily upon technical evidence that has been explained to them by "expert" witnesses whom they do not know in the community.

In many states, defense counsel may obtain access to physical evidence possessed by the prosecutor for the purpose of causing it to be studied by experts hired for the defense. Thus, a weapon may be tested by ballistics experts working on behalf of the defendant in addition to those employed by a federal or state crime laboratory. Fingerprints obtained from the scene of a crime may be scrutinized by a defense expert, also. So may blood, hair, skin or tissue samples as well as clothing and other remnants of an altercation that may link a defendant with the victim or the place where a crime took place. However, scientific tests are expensive to perform, and when conducted at the request of the defense these must ordinarily be paid for by the defendant. For this reason, an average defense counsel will concede the validity of most forensic evidence once he has been given the opportunity to read the reports that have been prepared for the prosecutor.

It is much easier for defense counsel to evaluate the quality of tangible evidence that will be introduced against his client at trial than it is for him to assess the quality of testimonial evidence to be delivered at trial by witnesses for the prosecution. One method does exist whereby the defense can catch a preview of the state's "eyewitnesses," if it has any. This is by means of the suppression hearing. By raising issues of illegal search and seizure by the police or issues of improper identification of the defendant by witnesses for the prosecution, defense counsel may be successful in forcing the prosecutor to put one or two witnesses on the stand at a pretrial suppression hearing. The question of the defendant's guilt or innocence will not be decided at this hearing, and the prosecutor will call only witnesses who can testify to the circumstances surrounding identification of the defendant or the factual basis used to support a search warrant for the defendant's property. Nevertheless, even such limited testimony provides the defense counsel with an opportunity to observe how a witness responds to direct examination by the prosecutor, and an occasion to test how the witness reacts to cross-examination. A defense lawyer will assess the physical appearance of each witness in terms of middle-class standards of attentiveness, neatness, and politeness. He will see how clearly the witness recalls events from the past and the precision with which the witness recites answers to questions. Finally, defense counsel will judge how convincing each witness is and how well he can intimidate the witness on cross-examination. A witness whom defense counsel cannot fluster even at a pretrial hearing will be devastating in front of a jury. The suppression hearing is a valuable tool that may prompt defense counsel into urging that his client plead guilty and avoid going to trial.

As soon as a defense counsel has been appointed or retained, he should confer at length with his client to analyze the client's appearance, attitude, and general effectiveness as a witness in court. If he is wise, counsel will want to determine to the best of his ability whether his client is factually guilty of some or all of the charges of which he has been accused. Prominent defense counsel may insist upon a polygraph examination of the client to corroborate protestations of innocence. Any skillful defense attorney will cross-examine his own client privately before the client reaches any decision about denying his guilt at trial and testifying on his own behalf. A defendant may not be compelled to take the stand and testify in his own defense at a trial under his Fifth Amendment privilege against self-incrimination, and in theory the triers of fact (judge or jury) cannot infer his guilt from his silence. In practice, a defendant's refusal to deny his guilt may preclude any possibility of an acquittal, particularly in a jury trial. Counsel will want to learn from his client the details of the crime if committed by the defendant, or the activities of his client at the time of the crime if the defendant maintains his innocence. Some lawyers will retain a private investigator to gather original evidence relating to the crime or the defendant's whereabouts at the time of the crime, but as with private laboratory tests this is expensive. Defense lawyers are prone to unravelling the facts surrounding a crime by conversing verbally with contacts in the police department and with other lawyers who are representing co-defendants. A lawyer learns whether or not he can win his client's case in court by doing his homework weeks, months, or even years ahead of time.

The Negotiation Stage

A defense attorney may commence negotiations with a prosecutor at any time with an eye toward disposing of charges pending against his client without going to trial to do so. However, most defense counsel will not enter into serious plea discussions until all of the material facts surrounding the defendant's involvement in the crimes in question have been learned, documented, and, when possible, corroborated by more than one source. The discovery process takes a longer time in some cases than it does in others. At least two weeks may be required following the filing of misdemeanor charges to complete discovery into evidence of the defendant's factual guilt. At least another month may be required following the filing of felony charges. Scientific testing of tangible evidence itself may consume two weeks. A preliminary hearing may not be scheduled for several weeks after being demanded by the defendant. A suppression hearing may not be scheduled for several weeks after counsel learns of the existence of potentially suppressible evidence. Even in states that have enacted "speedy trial" legislation where trials must be commenced within a specified time period such as ninety days or charges against a defendant must be dismissed, trials cannot be scheduled very far in advance of the deadline date, and frequently the defendant or his counsel waives a "speedy trial" in order to conduct a more exhaustive discovery. As a general rule, serious plea discussions do not get started in most judicial units across the United States until more than three months have elapsed following the filing of criminal charges. In many jurisdictions, negotiations on felony charges do not become serious until more than six months have elapsed, particularly if during that period the defendant has managed to secure pretrial release from custody.

One of the most interesting questions is not when dispositional negotiations begin, but where, how, and by whom they are initiated? Of these questions, the most significant in terms of outcome may be the answer to the question: *By whom* are discussions initiated? Most prosecutors profess publicly that they never initiate guilty plea discussions or otherwise solicit defendants to avoid trial. Their practice in many judicial units does not confirm this. Many prosecutors will approach a defense attorney, sometimes half in jest, and ask, "What deal are you going to be looking for?" A prosecutor is more prone to initiate guilty plea discussions with defense counsel whom he knows personally and with whom he and his family socialize than he is with counsel who are strangers. Prosecutors seem less discrete in acknowledging the availability of clear bargains when charges are trivial rather than serious. Some prosecutors will await the first overture by defense counsel but will take it from there, and from that point onward will even strive for negotiated dispositions.

In at least two of the judicial units that were studied by the author on-site, assistant prosecutors were observed blatantly initiating plea negotiations directly with defendants who were housed in jail and not represented by counsel. In fact, these prosecutors were promising defendants further charge or sentence reductions if they would plead guilty without being represented by counsel. This practice is clearly improper and should be sufficient grounds for subsequent plea withdrawal by the defendant, who could contend that without counsel he did not knowingly or intelligently waive his constitutional rights including the right to a trial. Moreover, the practice by prosecutors of negotiating directly with defendants who are confined in jail raises the appearance of coercion even if it does not document actual coercion, and should be sufficient grounds for subsequent plea withdrawal by the defendant on grounds that he did not voluntarily waive his rights including his right to trial. Most prosecutors do not engage in the practice of initiating plea discussions with defendants. Indeed, most prosecutors will not even respond to a defendant's personal overture to negotiate charges pending against him unless the defendant has waived his right to be represented by counsel first before a judge in open court.

Some prosecutors go to the opposite extreme and pretend that a negotiated disposition is hard or impossible to reach in a criminal case handled by them. They may resort to this technique with defense counsel generally, but far more often a prosecutor does this only with a defense lawyer with whom he enjoys a poor working relationship, based, perhaps, on past differences. Doing this exacerbates whatever tensions existed previously and in effect penalizes a defendant for being represented by the counsel of his choice. Prosecutors who follow this route refuse to accept or to return telephone calls from defense counsel, and vehemently oppose requests by defense attorneys for extensions of time within which to make or to respond to pretrial motions, to schedule pretrial hearings including arraignments, or to docket a case on the court's trial calendar. They pledge to "go to trial or bust." What they really try to do is to scare defendants and inexperienced counsel into tendering a guilty plea "on the nose" as charged without benefit of any charge or sentence concessions as an inducement to pleading guilty. These prosecutors will back off as soon as a jury is impaneled, much as many insurance carriers who put forward a tough image will insist upon a settlement "on the courthouse steps" the day of the trial. A prosecutor who plays tough when he is unprepared to win at trial runs the risk that his challenge will be accepted by defense counsel and that he will be forced into a confrontation that he will lose and that the defense will win. After this happens a few times, a prosecutor's image will be tarnished with the bench, and judges may negotiate with defense counsel directly, acting as surrogate prosecutors and bypassing the district attorney's office.

The general norm seems to be for defense attorneys to set negotiations in gear by asking the prosecutor what concessions their clients will be likely to receive in return for a guilty plea in view of the nature of the crimes charged, the sufficiency of evidence pointing to the defendant's guilt, the defendant's history of previous criminal behavior, and the prosecutor's trial calendar at the moment. Other factors that may have some bearing on dispositional negotiations include the defense attorney's reputation as a trial advocate and the defendant's reputation in the community for honesty, peaceableness, and truthfulness.

Where and *how* negotiations take place vary considerably from one judicial unit to another, and even within a number of these judicial units, for felonies compared with misdemeanors. The setting for the negotiations is either some part of the courthouse or an office building in which judges' chambers or prosecutors' offices are located. However, most negotiations involving the disposition of criminal cases are three-way rather than two-way, and one of the parties functions as a broker. This third party does not serve as an arbitrator, since he has no unilateral power to impose a settlement. However, the broker fulfills the role of a mediator and a conciliator, and in general is responsible for determining both where and how negotiations take place. The balance of this chapter will be concerned with identifying the role of a dispositional broker, the role of the other parties in relation to this broker, and the methods that a broker may employ in order to have the other parties agree to a disposition without trial.

The Brokerage Role

The resolution of criminal charges pending against a defendant has traditionally entailed a sequence of adversarial proceedings under Anglo-American jurisprudence. Criminal trials are adversarial proceedings in every sense of the word, as are preliminary hearings, suppression hearings, and, to a lesser extent perhaps, sentence hearings. In most jurisdictions of the United States, negotiations that are intended to lead to the disposition of criminal charges without a trial have become adversarial as well. In a trial, the prosecution and the defense are adversaries, while the court fulfills the role of an arbitrator by presiding over the proceedings. At a trial, the court maintains decorum throughout the ordeal, rules on questions of law, decides what evidence a jury may consider, and either renders a decision itself in a bench trial or supervises jurors as they reach a verdict in a jury trial and then imposing judgment.

In dispositional negotiations, the judge does not always function as a neutral and detached third party. Instead, he may become an adversary to the defendant, the prosecutor, or to both. When a judge assumes an adversarial role in negotiations, one of the other parties may begin to function as a broker or neither may do this, in which case a three-way skirmish may ensue. It is more common for a prosecutor to function as a broker between the defense and the court than it is for a defense counsel to become a broker between the prosecution and the court.

In identifying who has assumed the role of a broker in dispositional negotiations, one must discern *who convinces whom* that a particular outcome is acceptable. Usually, this means the observer looks to see if the prosecutor convinces the court or if the judge convinces the prosecutor. On occasion, however, an observer may find that instead defense counsel convinces the court or the prosecutor, or that the judge or the prosecutor convinces defense counsel. The person who performs the role of a courier and does the convincing is the broker. A broker receives information from a source and transmits the information to its destination. The person who needs to be convinced that an arrangement is acceptable is the party for whom the information is destined. Subsequently, a broker may convey feedback to the source of the original information and then reconvey additional information to the party who must be convinced. Information may be exchanged within a matter of minutes or during the course of days, weeks, or even months. All of the parties may be present together in the same room, or the broker may meet separately with each of the other two parties who in turn never meet with each other until the time comes to consummate whatever settlement has been worked out.

The Judge as a Broker

Superior courts possess general jurisdiction over felony cases in most states. Therefore, dispositional negotiations that involve felony charges tend to occur under the auspices of superior court judges. Superior court jurists seem to perform the brokerage role in negotiations more often than do their colleagues who sit on lower courts. In felony cases, negotiations seem to involve a superior court judge serving as a broker. Usually, the judge expends effort convincing the prosecutor that a settlement suggested by defense counsel is fair. When defense counsel is particularly recalcitrant, the judge may have to convince counsel that a settlement suggested by the prosecutor is fair and reasonable.

When a judge functions as a broker in the disposition of criminal cases by negotiation, the setting for the discussions is almost always the judge's chambers. Once in a while, open court becomes the setting for these negotiations over which the judge will preside from his bench. Usually, this happens when a settlement has been reached by the parties earlier in chambers, but the defendant refuses to abide by the arrangement when it comes time for him to tender a guilty plea on the record. When this happens, most judges will either return to chambers directly, or schedule additional discussions for sometime in the near future. A few judges will open up the negotiations right in the courtroom. When a judge does this, he is certain to convey the appearance of coercion to public spectators who are present in the courtroom as well as to other defendants who are waiting for their cases to be called.

Judges tend to want both the prosecutor and the defense counsel, but not the defendant, to be present in chambers during negotiations. If one side cannot attend, a judge will adjourn the discussions until a later date or time. When both are present, the judge will ask the prosecutor to summarize for him the material evidence on which the state plans to rely if the case goes to trial. It is in this way, many times, that defense counsel learns of the strength or the weakness of the prosecution's case against a defendant through informal discovery. It is customary for a judge to ask defense counsel to summarize any portions of the state's case that the defendant plans to refute at trial, and to point out to the court and the prosecutor the merits of any defenses or affirmative defenses which the defendant may raise at trial. The judge is looking to decide informally whether the prosecution can prove a prima facie case against the defendant, assuming the evidence is presented the way he says it will be and is found to be admissible. If the court feels the prosecution lacks a prima facie case against the defendant, generally he will ask the prosecutor why he refuses to dismiss the charges. If the court feels that defenses to be raised at trial by the defense will not negative the state's prima facie case, he will ask defense counsel why the latter sees merit in the defenses and point out his own observation of the risks involved to each side in going to trial.

As a matter of course, a judge who is moderating dispositional discussions in his chambers will ask each party in front of the other if they have considered the possibility of a settlement without trial. If they say they have, the judge will ask what the defendant thinks of the arrangement. If counsel represents that the defendant is dissatisfied with the arrangement, the judge is quite likely to express his own views on the reasonableness of the defendant's obstinance. Whether or not counsel have exchanged previous suggestions for a settlement, the judge can be counted on at this point to encourage them to concur on a proposition which defense counsel may then pass on to his client. The judge is quite apt to ask for and receive from the prosecutor or his own probation office a summary of the defendant's social and criminal history, and to make known his observations on this score to counsel. At the end of a negotiation meeting in the judge's chambers, which may have lasted about one half hour, counsel will depart and agree to report to the court and to each other within a specified time period concerning a schedule for the defendant's tender of a guilty plea as protocoled by counsel in chambers, or a need for another meeting with the judge. If another meeting is needed, the judge can be expected to dominate discussions more so than at the earlier one. Each time counsel meet with the judge after the first session, he will express his discouragement and vexation and announce the sentence that he is contemplating for the defendant if the latter takes his case to trial and loses. Invariably, it will be only a matter of time before a prudent defendant who is not completely innocent of the charges pending against him will plead guilty to the charges negotiated by counsel through the judge.

Obviously, when a judge operates as a broker in dispositional negotiations, he may find it necessary to convince the prosecutor to accept the defense counsel's offer or to convince defense counsel to accept the prosecutor's offer. The first time counsel meet with a judge to negotiate a defendant's guilty plea, accompanying charge dismissals, or sentence concessions, the judge will tend to urge the prosecutor to be reasonable by agreeing to dismiss multiple counts, special allegations relating to weapons, or habitual offender accusations. The next time, and any subsequent time when the three meet for the same purpose, the judge will tend to shift the thrust of his influence toward urging the defendant through defense counsel to be reasonable. Once a judge concludes in his own mind that a particular settlement is in the best interests of justice and of a defendant, he seldom changes his mind and in practice can be predicted to impose the same sentence upon the defendant eventually whether the defendant pleads to the first negotiated settlement or to one that looks better on paper because an additional charge has been dismissed or reduced. Skillful counsel and a sophisticated defendant know when to draw the bargaining line, and with a judge as the broker the time is sooner rather than later unless the defendant through counsel convinces the judge that he had a bona fide reason for delay or that he had justification for believing himself to be entitled to some further concessions.

Judges in some superior courts are more pressed for time than are judges in others. A judge who is inundated with pending cases cannot devote the same amount of time to each felony case that comes before his bench. In most of the jurisdictions that have been studied by the author, however, defendants who have been charged with serious felony offenses but who have had the charges disposed of without a trial have done so through the participation of a judge during the negotiations. Some judges participate in the negotiation process much more actively than others do. While a judge who sits in a busy judicial unit may be inclined to urge counsel to be prepared when they enter chambers for plea discussions, the degree to which a superior court judge participates in these negotiations actively or passively does not seem to be a function of his schedule but more of his personality. Judges who sit on the same bench tend to approach the disposition of criminal cases with different attitudes. It is difficult for a judge to avoid fulfilling the brokerage role in the disposition of criminal cases without relinquishing this responsibility to someone else such as the prosecutor, which many judges do not care to do.

The Prosecutor as a Broker

Misdemeanor cases are processed through courts of limited jurisdiction in most states, as are many felony cases during the early pretrial stages. Dispositional negotiations that involve misdemeanor charges tend to occur under the auspices of magistrates (justices of the peace) or judges without, or with only limited, felony jurisdiction. Sometimes these judges and magistrates are attorneys, sometimes they are not. Almost always, they are thoroughly deluged with pending cases so that they could not possibly devote individualized attention to each case. For this reason, apparently as much as for any other reason, lower court judges and magistrates seem to abdicate the brokerage role in most judicial units, relegating this task to assistant prosecutors. Here is where "assembly line justice" really begins.

In most judicial units, assistant prosecutors function as the brokers in the disposition of misdemeanor cases by negotiation. It is not uncommon for them to continue this function in relation to many felony cases as well, primarily those that can be disposed of without trial in front of a lower court judge. In many states, lower court judges do not possess authority to preside over felony trials, to sentence felony offenders to long prison terms, or to invoke the death penalty. However, lower court judges do possess authority to preside over preliminary hearings and even suppression hearings in many felony cases, to hear some felony guilty pleas and to impose prison terms of relatively short duration (often up to five years) upon defendants who have pled guilty to felony charges. Indeed, one reason, and perhaps the primary reason, why many defendants who have been charged with a felony plead guilty before a lower court judge or magistrate is to benefit from the automatic ceiling that has been established by law on the maximum sentence which this judge unlike a superior court judge may impose.

When lower court judges have relinquished their brokerage role in favor of prosecutors, they tend to set boundaries on the discretion of these prosecutors to negotiate unusual case dispositions. In situations where the prosecutor proposes to offer a certain defendant a greater charge reduction or sentence concession than is offered to defendants as a rule under similar circumstances, the judge may require the prosecutor, defense counsel and even the defendant himself to approach the bench or appear in chambers for "questioning" by the court. This activity takes the judge's time on a selective basis, and if the judge finds that a defendant does not merit the leniency requested by the prosecutor, he may subsequently impose an even more severe sentence than the defendant would have received had he pled guilty to a "boiler plate" agreement as most defendants do.

Negotiations, if the discussions can be called that, take place elsewhere than in chambers or the courtroom when the judge is not the broker. In many judicial units, the prosecutor has a temporary office near each misdemeanor courtroom which he uses almost exclusively for "rapid-fire talks" with defense counsel. In most jurisdictions, misdemeanor-level courts are located at different sites throughout a county, whereas felony-level courts are found in the main courthouse at the county seat as a rule. Unlike felony charge negotiations that are scheduled in the chambers of a superior court judge on a case-by-case basis according to the mutual convenience of both counsel, misdemeanor charge negotiations have to take place generally at an appointed time of the day or night and on an appointed day of the week or month. On this periodic occasion, all counsel having misdemeanor (or early pretrial felony) cases in the area are expected to appear, wait in line, and talk with the prosecutor for one to five minutes per case. This constitutes the negotiation process for the most part. If the defense counsel accepts the "marketplace bargain," he will wait in the hallways while the prosecutor finishes talking with other lawyers about their cases and then sit in the courtroom while the prosecutor presents the outcome of his "negotiations" to the court for final approval. If the defense counsel seeks additional relief beyond the "marketplace bargain," he can expect first of all to wait for several hours (usually well into the evening or night) for defendants who are willing to follow the crowd to do just that and tender their commonplace pleas to the court. Finally, after all the routinized cases have been processed and the judge is tired, the court will permit the prosecutor to summarize the reasons why those defendants whose cases have not yet reached a disposition seem to want preferential treatment. They are scolded by the court more often than they are accorded the remedy which they seek. Counsel who are experienced in handling these cases in the lower courts try their best customarily to persuade their clients to deal through the prosecutor as broker rather than to ask for more and deal with the judge directly. Lower court judges have a tendency to hold counsel responsible for delays or avarice on the part of their clients, and to be hostile to lawyers in the future who have "rocked the boat" on behalf of other clients in the past.

Negotiations in the lower courts of most judicial units do not include very much in the way of an exchange of information or of opinion between counsel. Nor does the judge learn or want to learn the reasons why one defendant thinks he is different from the others. Virtually any defendant can expect to receive charge and sentence concessions that are accorded routinely to other defendants, but if that is not good enough for him and he protests, by attracting attention to himself as a person rather than as a case docket number he runs a considerable risk of annoying both the prosecutor and the court. The prosecutor may withdraw as a broker if provoked by the defendant or defense counsel, and the defense counsel is unlikely to be successful as a broker with a lower court judge. The judge will immediately begin to coerce a defendant directly into pleading guilty then and there by delivering abusive comments ranging from the defendant's dress and speech to the defendant's lack of education or of employment, and by sternly admonishing the defendant as to the maximum sentence that could be imposed for the conduct of which he has been accused. Some judges under these conditions will threaten to revoke bail or other pretrial release, summon the sheriff, and order the defendant taken away to jail whereupon many a defendant will decide swiftly to tender a guilty plea at or against the recommendation of counsel.

The Defense Counsel as a Broker

The defense attorney has less opportunity as a rule to function as the broker in negotiations leading to the disposition of criminal cases. There are situations through which he may serve as a broker, however. One is where he is part of a powerful public defender agency to which both judges and prosecutors cower in order to avoid "court busting" or other retaliation. Such a defense attorney may be able to take a settlement proposal alternately between the prosecutor and the judge, pitting each against the other and dictating concessions which his client will receive. Another is where a defense lawyer is a personal friend of the district attorney or a judge, such that he can bypass the wishes of an assistant prosecutor altogether and negotiate directly with the prosecutor at the front office. Finally, a defense attorney may find himself fulfilling a de facto brokerage role between a prosecutor and a superior court judge when, after protracted discussions, the prosecutor refuses to agree to a settlement which the judge deems fair. The judge may be reluctant to direct a prosecutor to agree to an arrangement between defense counsel and the court, and in some states the court does not have authority to approve charge reductions without consent of the prosecutor. Under these conditions, defense counsel may be able to suggest an alternative formula to which the prosecutor will agree and which the court will not oppose, such as a longer sentence in return for a less serious or less stigmatizing charge, or lengthy probation plus restitution instead of a shorter term of imprisonment.

Whenever a defense lawyer becomes the broker in negotiations leading to the disposition of criminal charges, he will have to be discreet enough not to flaunt his role in front of the judge or the prosecutor, and especially not in front of other lawyers or judges. He will have to discharge his role as a rule in chambers, since a prosecutor cannot take the time normally to travel to the offices of private attorneys, and a judge should avoid visiting the offices of either a defense counsel or a prosecutor as much as possible to preclude the appearance of impropriety.

7 Patterns of Negotiation in the Disposition of Criminal Cases

At least a score of qualified observers, in addition to the author of this book, confirm that in the typical American court nearly all criminal cases that are terminated without a completed trial reach a disposition by means of some form of negotiation. It has become well known that most guilty pleas are products of negotiation, but less well known that most dismissals are negotiated, and still less well known that many sentences, or at least many sentence ranges (minimum and maximum boundaries), are negotiated by defendants individually or through counsel. Each of these negotiation outcomes has become labeled as a bargain, the most famous of which is the plea bargain. Apparently for this reason, the process of negotiation leading to the termination of criminal cases short of trial has become known as bargaining, and more commonly but less precisely as plea bargaining.

Few words in the annals of Anglo-American jurisprudence have become euphemized more than the noun "bargain" and the gerund "bargaining." Many criminal defendants, and far too many professionals who administer criminal justice, seem to associate a bargain with a *discount* in the context of criminal case disposition. Indeed, such a bargain is perceived frequently as a discount in a sense not unlike that understood by a shrewd shopper who is looking for a merchandise sale in the bargain basement of a department store. In its traditional meaning, of course, the concept of a bargain has no necessary relationship at all to a discount. It is a term that is used to indicate an agreement involving a definite exchange of equivalents—of a quid pro quo. As it pertains to the disposition of criminal charges, the bargain has become confused with the consideration (value) supporting the exchange, and the consideration underlying many dispositional bargains is lopsided in many jurisdictions. Indeed, not all defendants who avoid trial by negotiating the disposition of criminal charges pending against them get what they bargained for. Some find a better deal than they set out to achieve, while others end up worse than they expected at the start.

The American Bar Association has urged that similarly situated defendants (those with similar criminal histories who stand accused of crimes thought to be of substantially the same seriousness) should enjoy as nearly equal dispositional opportunities as possible, including identical access to negotiations and parallel sentence concessions. The reality does not match the theory all of the time in most judicial units, or even most of the time in some units. A defendant's likelihood of being successful at dispositional bargaining may be influenced by

109

who his lawyer is, what assistant district attorney has been assigned to prosecute him, what judge will hear his case, accept or reject his guilty pleas and impose sentence on him, or other factors that are extraneous to the merits of his case, including the financial resources that are available to him and his ability to secure pretrial release. For this reason, it seems useful to analyze both varieties of bargains and varieties of bargaining as these patterns pertain to representative judicial units around the United States.

Varieties of Bargains

At least four varieties of agreements—known imprecisely as "bargains"—may be identified as stemming from negotiations over the disposition of criminal cases. These include: (1) the guilty plea agreement (plea bargain); (2) the *nolle prosecqui* agreement (dismissal bargain); (3) several types of agreements that relate to the choice of sentence that will be imposed upon a defendant following his conviction (sentence bargain); and (4) several forms of agreements by a prosecutor not to initiate any additional charges against a suspect, a defendant, or a defendant's accomplice (forbearance bargain). Each of these varieties merits a more detailed explanation.

Plea Bargain

A guilty plea agreement (plea bargain) is an understanding between a defendant (usually through his counsel) and a prosecutor (to which the court may or may not have agreed) whereby the prosecutor promises to provide or at least to attempt to secure some concessions for the defendant in exchange for the defendant's promise to waive his right to trial and to enter a plea of guilty or a plea of *nolo contendere* (no contest) to one or more specified criminal charges pending against him. A prosecutor may promise to provide concessions that lie within his power to provide, such as the dismissal of companion charges against the defendant or against the defendant's accomplices. Or, a prosecutor may promise to intervene on behalf of the defendant in an effort (which may not be successful or which may be only partially successful) to have the court impose a more lenient sentence than the defendant could expect to receive otherwise.

Some states do not permit *nolo contendere* pleas at all, and in those that do most judges seem reluctant to accept them unless the underlying criminal conduct resulted in serious personal injury or property damage to the victims for which a major civil tort action will be commenced. A *nolo contendere* plea results in the defendant's conviction of the charge(s) to which he pleads, just as does a guilty plea, upon its acceptance by the court. Unlike a guilty plea, however, a *nolo* plea is not dispositive of the defendant's civil negligence or intentional tort. A guilty plea and a *nolo* plea both include the defendant's admission of his criminal culpability as a rule. In the case of North Carolina v. Alford (1970),[1] on the other hand, the United States Supreme Court held that a judge, in his discretion, may accept either plea when offered by a defendant even though the defendant persists in maintaining his innocence. Most judges seem unwilling to accept *Alford* pleas except under very limited and unusual circumstances, such as where evidence against a defendant is overwhelming, but psychologically the defendant is unable, rather than merely unwilling, to admit his guilt.

Indeed, the defendant's admission of guilt appears to be the major reason why prosecutors and judges alike support plea bargaining. A plea of guilty or *nolo* results automatically in the defendant's conviction of the charges to which he has plead upon acceptance of the plea by the court. If properly offered and accepted, a guilty or a *nolo* plea will preclude direct appeal by the defendant of his conviction in the future. It will ratify the clearance of the underlying crimes by the police who arrested the defendant. In other words, a guilty or a *nolo* plea is a final gesture of contrition by a defendant to confirm publicly the wrongfulness of his conduct, the rightfulness of his arrest and prosecution, and the finality of his conviction. His admission to both factual and legal guilt will absolve the police of potential liability for false arrest, preclude the court from having its preliminary rulings (for example, on probable cause, suppression of evidence, and so on) overturned on appeal, and authenticate the prosecutor's claim to have won still another victory in the ongoing battle against crime. The community may fall asleep thinking that the criminal justice system is in fine shape.

Meanwhile, both the defendant and the prosecutor have avoided the prospect of taking the case against the defendant to trial. It is expensive for both sides to go to trial. At trial, both sides have to call witnesses, pay their transportation costs and, in the case of expert witnesses, pay their fees. Courtroom security costs are high. Many defense lawyers and most prosecutors prefer not to take cases to trial because they do not have what they feel is sufficient experience in trial advocacy, and if they lose at trial the community will learn of this. Rules of evidence admissibility and trial procedure have become confounded by appellate courts in recent years to the point that many judges feel that whatever they do while presiding over a criminal trial will be viewed on appeal as constituting prejudicial error. Trials make lawyers and judges look as if they do not know how to do their jobs.

A criminal defendant is particularly anxious to avoid trial as a rule. The public may learn about the severity of his crimes, his viciousness, or the frequency at which he resorts to criminal behavior. Usually, a defendant does not want visibility in the news media, and trials attract reporters. If a defendant is a situational offender, he wants to save his family from embarrassment and ridicule, and he does not want to deplete his financial resources on the costs of a trial. If he is a professional criminal, he strives to avoid public recognition as such, and so he wants his case over and done with as soon as possible. A defendant who has only a short criminal record or none at all will be induced into pleading guilty to a misdemeanor to avoid the stigma of a felony conviction and its consequential civil disabilities such as loss of the voting franchise and of the right to hold public office. A defendant who has a felony record but who has never spent time in prison will plead guilty even to another felony to avoid the prospect of "hard time." Even a persistent offender with a long record of serious criminal convictions will be eager to plead guilty if in doing so he can avoid accelerated penalties (such as life imprisonment) that may be meted out to habitual offenders who are specifically charged with being such.

The plea bargain is the backbone of the process by which criminal case dispositions are negotiated. Very few defendants who have been charged with committing serious crimes avoid pleading guilty to at least one charge, unless they are ready, willing, and able to withstand a trial, which most are not. On the other hand, many plea bargains are accompanied by other dispositional agreements as well, and these merit an explanation.

Dismissal Bargain

A *nolle prosecqui* agreement (dismissal bargain) is an understanding between a defendant (usually through his counsel) and a prosecutor whereby the prosecutor promises not to prosecute any additional charges then pending against the defendant in exchange for the defendant's promise to waive his right to trial and enter a plea of guilty or *nolo contendere* to one or more specified criminal charges pending against him. Unlike the guilty or *nolo* pleas themselves, which require acceptance by the court in order to be valid, a *nolle prosecqui* is within the range of a prosecutor's exclusive power and does not depend upon ratification by the court. However, a wise prosecutor may make the dismissal bargain conditional upon the court's acceptance of the pleas in return for which the dismissal agreement has been made.

In addition, a *nolle prosecqui* agreement may be reached without need for a defendant to plead guilty or *nolo contendere* to any criminal charge at all in cases where defense counsel convinces a prosecutor that dismissal of all pending charges would be "in the interest of justice." What constitutes the interest of justice is a subjective determination that a prosecutor must make individually. In some judicial units, all pending charges against a defendant may be dismissed upon the defendant's successful completion of a diversion program. Or, a probation agreement may be negotiated under the terms of which criminal charges will be dismissed retroactively if at the end of a specified time period (one, two, or three years) the defendant has not had any further altercation with law enforcement authorities. Some prosecutors will consider the dismissal of charges "in the interest of justice" in unique situations where the offender has been a victim of the crime. An example would be the dismissal of child abuse charges against a mother whose child abuse was the direct result of her husband's spousal abuse (that is, the husband beat the wife, causing her to forget that she left their baby alone in a bathtub where it drowned or was scalded).

More commonly, charges are dismissed against a defendant who has been charged with committing multiple crimes when the defendant pleads guilty or *nolo contendere* to one or two companion charges. This form of the dismissal bargain is known also as the "charge bargain." Under such an arrangement, negotiations tend to involve discussion over which charges will be eliminated by means of the *nolle prosecqui* (dismissal) and which will be retained for pleading. If a defendant has been charged with several crimes that are all of relatively equal seriousness in terms of both the harm caused and the exposure to punishment, the defendant and the prosecutor can agree rapidly for the defendant to plead guilty to one such charge and to have the others dismissed. An exception may be if a defendant has been charged with four or more crimes, in which case he may be required by a prosecutor to plead guilty to at least two charges. Seldom will a defendant be urged to plead guilty to more than two charges of equal seriousness, since judges usually impose concurrent sentences on most offenders, and almost never do they impose consecutive sentences for more than two different crimes.

Negotiations become somewhat more complex when a defendant is charged with multiple crimes that vary in terms of seriousness or type. Normally, a defendant will balk at pleading guilty to the most serious crime with which he has been charged, while the prosecutor will not agree to permit a defendant to plead guilty to the least serious and have all the others dismissed. Similarly, a defendant will resist pleading guilty to the most stigmatizing of the charges pending against him (such as, arson, rape, sodomy), while most prosecutors will not agree to dismissing all stigmatizing charges against a defendant, particularly if there is more than one such charge pending. A likely compromise is for the defendant to plead guilty to an offense (or to two offenses, if four or more have been charged) other than to the least or the most serious as long as all charges are of relatively equal stigma. A wise prosecutor will demand that a defendant plead guilty to at least one crime of violence if any of the charges involve allegations of violence; to at least one sex-related crime if any of the charges are sex-related; or to at least one offense the title of which reflects the offender's primary motive for participating in a criminal transaction that involved a series of crimes. For instance, the purpose behind a burglary may range from the desire to find a free place to sleep for the night to stealing property located inside of a building to burning down the building to raping or killing an occupant of the building. By pleading guilty to attempted theft, a burglar who planned to set the building afire could disguise not only his intrusion but his arson motive as well. Clearly, he should plead guilty at least to attempted arson if not to burglary as well.

The defendant who has been charged with committing multiple crimes possesses a distinct advantage in dismissal bargaining over the defendant who has been charged with only one crime, since the former has more charges to tradeoff. Negotiations become less complex but more perplexing when a defendant is accused of committing a single crime. Why should this defendant plead guilty "on the nose" to the crime as charged? Ordinarily, such a defendant can arrange with the prosecutor to plead guilty to either a less serious charge or a less stigmatizing charge in exchange for the dismissal of the charge that reflects his true crime. Sometimes, a defendant may plead guilty to a "lesser included offense" if such a charge exists in relation to his crime. For instance, rape is a particular form of assault and battery, so assault and battery are lesser included offenses to rape. Manslaughter is a less serious form of homicide than murder, so in most states manslaughter is a lesser included offense to murder. Similarly, unlawful entry is a lesser included offense to burglary; both assault and theft are lesser included offenses to robbery.

At other times, however, a defendant may be charged with a crime that does not have a real lesser included offense, in which case a creative prosecutor will invent a charge to serve this purpose. For example, a man who is charged with consensual sodomy may plead builty to disorderly conduct in return for dismissal of the more serious and more stigmatizing charge of sodomy. If the sodomy was committed peaceably and outside the public view, it bears no logical relation to disorderly conduct at all. Instead, the charge of disorderly conduct is a legal fiction that is contrived to facilitate dismissal of the real charge and a guilty plea to some charge no matter what.

Sentence Bargain

A sentence agreement (sentence bargain) may take different forms from one case to the next even within a judicial unit, and it usually reflects at least slightly different characteristics from one jurisdiction to another. Any given sentence agreement is likely to be a function of the general sentencing statutes that are in effect at the time within the state where sentence is to be imposed. In some states, the sentencing judge is invested with a wide latitude in terms of the actual sentence or sentence range than he may impose upon the typical defendant. In other states, the sentence for each generic crime has been molded more rigidly by the legislature to limit or even to eliminate judicial discretion. Even within the same state and county, some judges will be more flexible than others in imposing sentence from one defendant to the next who has been charged with committing similar crimes. A prosecutor's "boiler plate" sentence agreement should be tailored to the nature of the crimes to which the defendant has agreed to plead guilty as well as to the defendant's personal criminal history.

In most jurisdictions, prosecutors will do little, if anything, more on the record than to make a sentence recommendation or abstain from doing the same thing. As a result of negotiations, a prosecutor might agree to recommend that the sentencing judge be lenient, or he might even agree to ask the judge not to impose a sentence that is any longer than an agreed upon number of years. A prosecutor may request probation for a defendant. In serious cases, a prosecutor may agree to do nothing more than abstain from recommending imposition of a severe sentence. He may remain silent when asked by the court to make a sentence recommendation, and in turn this may provoke the judge into imposing the minimum or a moderate sentence by prearrangement or it may goad the judge into ignoring the wishes of the prosecutor altogether. However, some prosecutors will do more off the record than on the record in terms of trying to secure a sentence for a defendant that will be acceptable to the latter.

A prosecutor may enjoy a kind of symbiotic relationship with one or more judges as a result of political or social ties, for example, whereby the prosecutor can virtually dictate the sentences that will be imposed upon defendants who appear for sentencing before the judges. In this case, the prosecutor will have to maneuver a given defendant's case before the particular judge, and this manipulation (a form of judge shopping) in turn may be a part of the sentence bargain. On the other hand, some judges are very predictable in terms of the sentences they impose against classes of convicted offenders who appear before them for sentencing. Of these judges, more are predictably harsh than predictably lenient. Part of a sentence bargain may involve judge swapping whereby a prosecutor agrees to delay sentencing until a "hanging judge" goes on vacation, is ill, retires, or is rotated to hear noncriminal cases. Then, the defendant can appear before another judge to receive a predictably less severe sentence.

Prosecutors may exert influence over the contents of presentence investigation reports. Thus, a prosecutor may be able to manipulate the sentence or range of sentence that a judge will impose on a defendant by controlling the kind or the amount of information about the defendant and/or the defendant's crimes that the judge will possess prior to time of sentencing. By pleading guilty pursuant to a negotiated agreement, for example, a defendant may persuade the prosecutor not to release to the court the grizzly details surrounding the defendant's criminal behavior. In this way, the sentencing judge may be misled into believing the defendant is nonviolent or that the defendant is a situational offender when in fact the defendant used violence during his crimes or is highly skilled in the arts and sciences of professional crime. Of course, all judges cannot be fooled all of the time. However, many judges do not care really what sentence they impose upon ordinary defendants who plead guilty to invisible crimes so long as the presentence report before them does not contain information that will haunt the judge later for not imposing a more rigorous sentence.

First offenders and others who have very short and nonserious criminal records and who have been charged currently with nonserious crimes are concerned primarily about their prospects for being placed on probation rather than being sent to prison. Whether a sentence of probation or of imprisonment is

imposed, these defendants are concerned only with the *minimum* duration of
the sentence, since almost assuredly they are not destined to serve longer than
their minimum sentence anyway. In rural judicial units, the option between
probation and imprisonment is still the subject of negotiation even for offenders
with short criminal records who have been charged with relatively trivial crimes.
In most urban jurisdictions, first offenders are seldom ever imprisoned and even
seasoned offenders can expect probation as a rule unless their current offenses
involve charges of aggravated violence. Once again, therefore, the emphasis is
upon negotiating the length of their minimum sentence.

Sophisticated offenders who are to be convicted by trial if not by guilty
plea can expect to be incarcerated as a rule. Probation is out of the question. In
addition, they can expect to serve at least their minimum sentence before
becoming eligible for parole. Their greatest concern is over the *maximum*
sentence of imprisonment that will be imposed, since they know they are poor
parole risks and that they may have to serve all or at least a great proportion of
their maximum sentence. As with new and trivial offenders who want to
negotiate the length of their probation, sophisticated and serious offenders want
to negotiate the length of their imprisonment. Each type of defendant will seek
a sentence bargain if one is available.

In cases where incarceration is assured, some defendants will opt to select
the place of confinement by means of a sentence bargain. Defendants who have
never served hard time in a prison may want to remain in jail, avoid a prison
record and be closer to the community and to their families. Some defendants
who have served time in a prison previously are usually eager to get out of jail
and back to prison, since to them prison is a deluxe hotel and jail is a flophouse.
In some states, defendants who know they are headed for prison will try to
negotiate the location of the prison for various reasons. One might have enemies
in a given prison, and want to avoid injury by obtaining confinement elsewhere.
In a few states, such as Massachusetts, a prisoner's chances for parole are better
in some prison facilities than in others. Place of confinement cannot be
negotiated in many states, however, since the court has no control over
placement of prisoners, this being determined by the state correction department.

Forbearance Bargain

In addition to the bargains already mentioned, skilled counsel may be able to
negotiate other features on behalf of criminal suspects, sometimes even before
formal charges have been filed against their clients. A person who has knowledge
that the prosecutor is trying to have him indicted by a grand jury may be able to
persuade the prosecutor to abandon the indictment effort by offering to plead
guilty to a misdemeanor. A person who has been arrested may be able to
convince the police or a prosecutor to release him prior to formal booking, or a
parent may succeed in doing the same thing on behalf of a child. In cases where

two or more persons are suspected of joint criminal behavior as part of the same episode, one of them may agree to plead guilty to some charges in return for which the prosecutor may promise not to file any charges against the other. This practice is most common when two spouses or two lovers are suspected of criminal involvement but one "takes the rap" for both to protect the other.

The prevention of criminal charges from being filed is less important when the suspect has a criminal record already than when the current charges would be the first. Normally, a person who does not have a criminal record does not want to have one and is much better off not having one. Once a person has been charged with any misdemeanor or felony, his fingerprints and photograph are taken by local police and forwarded to the National Criminal Information Center (NCIC) maintained by the Federal Bureau of Investigation. The existence of such a record may exert an adverse effect upon a person's future success in obtaining employment, in being believed under oath, and, of course, in negotiating criminal charges that may arise in the future. A prosecutor may be willing to forbear initiating criminal charges against an ancillary offender such as an accomplice if by doing so he can obtain a conviction against the principal offender in the same criminal transaction. However, to prevent criminal charges from being filed requires considerable influence and skill and, to be successful, one who is about to be so charged must obtain the immediate services of a very competent lawyer.

A prosecutor may abstain from invoking provisions of a state's habitual offender (career criminal) law against a particular recidivist defendant, in exchange for the latter's agreement to plead guilty to a substantive charge. A prosecutor may refrain from accusing a defendant of having been armed during a crime in states where this allegation, if sustained, subjects an offender to a mandatory escalated penalty. A defendant may be charged with criminal conspiracy *or* a substantive crime instead of *both*, in return for his agreement to plead guilty. Other examples of prosecutorial forbearance also exist.

National Bargain Trends

As a result of the on-site study of more than forty judicial units throughout the United States, ten national trends have been observed that are descriptive of agreements reached between prosecutors and defendants after negotiating the disposition of criminal cases in jurisdictions throughout the country. These trends are as follows:

Trend 1

Almost invariably, a defendant who is charged with a single felony or a single misdemeanor count will succeed in having that charge reduced at least one grade pursuant to his agreement to plead guilty to the reduced charge, as long as a charge that begins as a felony ends as one, and to a lesser extent, as long as a charge that begins as a misdemeanor ends as one. In states where crimes are classified (for instance, felony classes A to E; misdemeanor classes A to C), most defendants routinely expect that any given charge will be reduced at least one grade in class (in other words, from a class C felony to a class D felony; from a class A to a class B misdemeanor) in exchange for doing nothing more than simply agreeing to plead guilty to the reduced charge and waive their right to have a trial. In states where crimes are not classified by type or seriousness, defendants routinely expect that most charges will be reduced to either a lesser included or a lesser related offense (from aggravated assault, for instance, to simple assault) in exchange for the same things. Because so many defendants assume that charge concessions will be offered almost as a matter of right, they tend to demand additional benefits from the prosecutor, such as sentence leniency recommendations in return for any cooperation on their part beyond the mere avoidance of trial. Thus, defendants have come to expect additional adjustments on their punishment if they provide the state with information about the location of stolen property or the bodies of murdered victims.

Many prosecutors seem to be loathe to reduce a bona fide felony charge to a misdemeanor or a bona fide misdemeanor charge to a summary offense. Indeed, a number of prosecutors have advised the author that they would prefer to offer additional sentence concessions than to allow an ordinary felony charge to erode into a misdemeanor. Such an obsession seems to be self-contradictory, since the ultimate punishment rather than the paper conviction should be of importance. Some prosecutors have admitted that a criminal case becomes more highly visible in the news media when a charge that started off as a felony ends up as a misdemeanor.

Trend 2

In nearly all judicial units, a defendant who is charged with multiple criminal counts can have these reduced to no more than two charges, and occasionally to one charge, pursuant to his agreement to plead guilty to the reduced charges. The charges to which a defendant pleads guilty are usually not the most serious of the lot. Charges that become dismissed following such a defendant's guilty plea may be and often are charges that arose out of completely separate transactions from those in which the charges arose to which the defendant pleads guilty.

Very few prosecutors seem to be concerned at all about obtaining a conviction on at least one charge relating to each separate criminal episode in which a defendant is known to have participated. This means clearly that during the time interval between commission of a defendant's first serious offense (or his first serious offense since being released from custody earlier) and his sentencing for that offense, as long as he remains at large he is awarded an opportunity to commit virtually as many free crimes as he wants to commit for which he will never receive any additional punishment than he would have received anyway upon conviction of the single charge.

Trend 3

Consecutive sentences are imposed only extremely rarely in most judicial units, even following a defendant's guilty plea to and subsequent conviction of multiple charges stemming from wholly separate criminal transactions. Almost never are more than two sentences imposed consecutively.

Most judges who were interviewed for this study admitted they are reluctant to impose consecutive sentences against most defendants. Many judges excuse their recalcitrance by stressing that institutions of confinement are overcrowded. Other judges point to the policies of parole boards against keeping prisoners in continuous confinement for the full duration of even one sentence, let alone two or more sentences. A judge of a court of general jurisdiction stated to the author confidentially that the highly respected chief justice of his state's highest court (himself a very highly regarded jurist who has been associated prominently with efforts to study and to reform the administration of criminal justice) had directed judges to avoid imposing prison sentences as much as possible and, when absolutely necessary to impose a prison sentence, to impose the shortest one possible due to gross overcrowding in the state's prison system.

Trend 4

In every jurisdiction studied, without exception, it is the practice of prosecutors and defense counsel, and a practice in which judges concur heartily, to incorporate into one monolithic plea bargain, provisions for the disposition of all charges then pending against a defendant. Consequently, the goal of a plea agreement has become to grant the defendant a general absolution and a ceiling on the penalty that may be imposed for all of his known crimes, in return for the defendant's waiver of trial. In this fashion, the backlog of criminal charges that are pending within a judicial unit becomes reduced artificially.

Trend 5

Special allegations that would mandate enhanced punishment for offenders who possess, use, or threaten to use a weapon during commission of a crime are rarely filed by prosecutors. If filed, such charges are dismissed without hesitation pursuant to the defendant's agreement to plead guilty to the substantive charges and waive his right to trial. This is true even though in many states proof that an offender even possessed a weapon during the course of committing a crime compels imposition of a longer and more severe sentence and generally precludes consideration for probation and sometimes for parole as well. This trend indicates that prosecutors negotiate as readily with vicious and dangerous offenders as with those who are less willing to cause death and personal injury to their victims. In fact, this trend actually encourages criminal offenders to be armed during their crimes, since they are unlikely to receive any greater punishment for doing so.

Trend 6

In judicial units where indigent criminal defendants are represented more often by a public defender agency (as opposed to an attorney-at-law in private practice who has been appointed by the court to represent a given defendant in a single case), there is a significant likelihood that on occasion some defendants who are perceived by the agency as being "bad" will be traded-off to the prosecutor and urged to plead guilty in exchange for less valuable concessions in order that other defendants who are perceived by the agency as being "good" may receive a better bargain from the prosecutor. In this way, obviously, the defendant's own lawyer decides what punishment he should receive and then advises the prosecutor of the same.

A public defender agency tends to perceive a client as bad if the client is uncooperative with counsel more than if the client has perpetrated a particularly serious offense. An arrogant defendant, a person with a low intelligence quotient or a low threshold for coping with stress will be perceived as bad when he vacillates or complains over accepting a dispositional arrangement that is suggested by his lawyer. A client who lies to the public defender but whose lie is uncovered may be perceived as being "very bad." A public defender agency tends to perceive a client as good if the client is cooperative, subservient, repentant, and both candid and truthful with his lawyer. Often, but not always, such a client is a youthful, first or early offender, who appears to be naive and comes from a middle-class background. A "good" client is likely to be white, while a "bad" one is more likely to be nonwhite or a member of a minority subculture the communication norms of which hamper discussions with the white, middle-class counsel.

The process known as trading-off, which many public defenders and some attorneys in private practice admit to doing, involves a colloquy between defense counsel and prosecutor during which defense counsel recites the worst aspects (whether these are true, false, or privileged as they are as a rule) of one defendant's background together with the best aspects of another defendant's background in an effort to benefit the latter at the expense of the former. It is common for a defendant who has been traded-off to receive a sentence of commitment rather than of probation (whether he would have anyway even without the trade-off may be problematic), and both his minimum and his maximum sentence will be higher than they would have been otherwise in jurisdictions where indeterminate sentencing is used. On the other hand, the defendant who reaps the benefits of a trade-off is almost assured of probation. Furthermore, the client who is traded-off will be convicted of multiple criminal charges that in turn may diminish his chances for early parole.

Trend 7

In many of these same jurisdictions where public defender agencies control a large proportion of the criminal caseload, public defender lawyers at least appear to negotiate "package deals" with the prosecutor whereby the concessions that pertain to each individual defendant become a function of those relating to the entire public defender agency's caseload that is being processed at the same time. As a result of batch processing, most defendants who are represented by a public defender agency (unless they are singled out by the agency as being uncommonly "good") tend to receive from the prosecutor general concessions based upon the "marketplace value" of the crime at the time rather than upon the merits of each individual defendant's case.

A "package deal" between a public defender and a prosecutor may be any dispositional arrangement involving single or multiple charges against the same or different defendants, but in this context it refers to multiple defendants whether or not each has been charged with a single crime or with multiple crimes. Most public defenders "wash-out" the bulk of their caseloads periodically, such as weekly on a preappointed day or two. During each "washout" day, a public defender may reach a disposition on as many as fifty separate defendants who have been charged with the same crime or with the same set of crimes, such as burglary, robbery, narcotics violations, etc. Many of these defendants are not similarly situated because their criminal histories are different and the aggravating or mitigating circumstances of their offenses are different. Most will be processed as a batch.

Especially in the larger urban judicial units, ordinary criminal offenses tend to develop a "marketplace value" based upon the degree to which the prosecutor witnesses the crimes as being serious or common at the time. The marketplace value is a predictor of the type and length of sentence that will be imposed upon all but the most notorious offenders who plead guilty to the given crime. For instance, probation may be the marketplace value for narcotics possession offenses, but up to three years imprisonment may be the value for possession of narcotics with intent to sell them or to traffick in them. The marketplace value of an armed robbery may be five years imprisonment whether the offender stole $500 or $5,000 and whether he withdrew without abusing the victims or locked the victims up in a dangerous place such as a vault. Seldom does marketplace value take into account a defendant's previous criminal history in perpetrating the same offenses or equally serious and dangerous crimes.

Marketplace value tends to vary not only across jurisdictions but within the same judicial unit from one moment in time to another. Thus, a defendant who is accused of having committed a burglary in June may blend into the crowd, particularly if he pleads guilty as soon as possible and is sentenced along with numerous other spring- or summer-time burglars, when the crime is common and the marketplace value low. A defendant who is accused of having committed a burglary in January when days are shorter, colder, and fewer burglers are operating may encounter a higher marketplace value and receive a more rigorous sentence, as might a June burglar who delayed his guilty plea for so long that he came up for sentencing alongside January burglars.

Trend 8

A few public defender agencies as well as some members of the private criminal defense bar in a few judicial units employ "court busting" techniques to facilitate favorable guilty plea bargains for their clients. The most common example of this methodology is for a coalition of lawyers to threaten to bring their entire aggregate caseloads to trial by jury unless their demands are met. Foremost among their demands will be for a reduction in the marketplace value of selected crimes with which the bulk of their clients have been charged, such as burglary, narcotics offenses, and robbery.

"Court busting" is a label that is associated with efforts by defense lawyers to coerce judges as well as prosecutors into imposing sentence concessions as well as charge concessions (dismissal of companion charges in return for a guilty plea to one or two offenses). In urban judicial units where criminal cases are traumatically backlogged, judges who do not capitulate to court busting can expect a variety of pressures to be launched against them, ranging from poor evaluations from the criminal bar to rotation from a good bench to a poor bench (from imposing sentences, for instance, to handling preliminary motions). Poor evaluations from the bar may hurt a judge's chances for reelection. The bar may even avoid bringing cases before a judge who does not "play hard ball" with them. This happens on occasion in California where each defendant may exercise one preemptory challenge of the judge by right. When the bar conspires to retaliate against a judge who has resisted court busting techniques, the judge may be disgraced in the newspapers.

Court busting was tried successfully by the Legal Aid Society of New York City. This agency represents the large majority of criminal defendants in all five boroughs of New York City. In one familiar case, a municipal judge in New York City who persisted in imposing sentences that were anathema to the Legal Aid Society was transferred within one day following their request to a bench where sentencing would not occur, and subsequently he was not reappointed by the city's mayor to the Criminal Court of New York City. Following that episode, most other judges bent over backwards to please the public defender agency as often and as much as possible.

Trend 9

Other public defender agencies as well as many members of the private bar who have been appointed to represent indigent criminal defendants tend to plead their clients guilty as early as practicable in the criminal justice process, apparently for no reason other than to reduce their caseload and to receive payment for the services that have been rendered. In most judicial units, attorneys in private practice who represent indigent criminal defendants cannot receive payment for their services or reimbursement for their expenses until the case reaches a disposition. This same constraint is imposed upon a few public defender agencies, but much more rarely. It should be obvious that any delay in processing the payment of an attorney's fee and expense voucher may detract from his effective representation of a client.

A lawyer's rush to terminate the charges pending against his client by means of a guilty plea may cause the lawyer to overlook valid defenses or grounds for evidence suppression which, if properly and timely raised, would result in the client's acquittal rather than conviction. Delayed payment of legal fees for appointed legal counsel in criminal cases emphasizes quantity over quality in the disposition of criminal charges. Lawyers feel pressured to plead clients guilty rather than to go to trial in order to receive their fees and pay their own rent.

Trend 10

In nearly every judicial unit, a statutory or other ceiling exists on the fee that may be paid to an attorney who has been appointed by the court to represent an indigent criminal defendant. The ceiling is likely to be less than $500 for misdemeanor cases and less than $1,000 for felony cases, much less in many jurisdictions. Some jurisdictions have imposed a ceiling on the expenses for which an appointed lawyer may be reimbursed. The effect of these ceilings is to discourage lawyers from taking their client's cases to trial, since the time involved in preparing for a trial would escalate legal fees beyond statutory ceilings in most instances. Their effect may be also to dissuade many lawyers from making a sufficient number of pretrial motions or demanding the necessary pretrial hearings, and from commissioning a thorough investigation of the evidence that points to the client's guilt or innocence. A companion problem is the practice by the courts in many judicial units to make across the board cuts in vouchers submitted by lawyers in order to obtain their fees and expenses. Thus, in some jurisdictions, a lawyer may realize that a ceiling of $1,000 exists for fees and expenses in a given defendant's case. What he does not learn until it is too late is that the court will not authorize him to be paid for more than $800, having exercised an across the board cut to the tune of 20 percent. When the lawyer takes another appointed criminal case, if he ever does, he will be likely to devote even less effort next time compared with last time, expecting to receive a maximum of $800, instead of the statutory $1,000 ceiling.

Varieties of Bargaining

In addition to the varieties of bargains that have been noted already, at least four varieties of bargaining practices may be identified as being characteristic of the process by which criminal case dispositions are negotiated in judicial units across the United States. In recent years, a demand has been echoed throughout the criminal justice system for greater uniformity and for greater regulation in the negotiation of criminal case dispositions. This demand has met with different responses in various judicial units.

Figure 7-1 illustrates the interface of uniformity and regulation in the disposition of criminal cases without trial within selected jurisdictions that have been studied. At least four patterns of dispositional negotiations have emerged, including: (1) the laissez-faire style; (2) the open-door style; (3) the semi-regulated style; and (4) the systematically-regulated style. The interface of these styles is depicted by means of a Johari's Window in figure 7-1. For an understanding of the construction and significance of a Johari's Window, refer to figure 4-1 in chapter 4.

In figure 7-1, uniformity is plotted across the X axis while regulation is plotted along the Y axis. For this reason, as explained more thoroughly in conjunction with figure 4-1 in chapter 4 uniformity becomes higher from left to right across the X axis, and regulation becomes higher from bottom to top along the Y axis. When the cross formed by the intersection of the X and Y axes is framed, four windows emerge. A different style of negotiation in the disposition of criminal cases will be assigned to each window for descriptive and analytic purposes. As was explained in association with figure 4-1 previously, the two left windows indicate a low value of the X axis (in the case of figure 7-1, a low value in terms of uniformity), while the two bottom windows depict a low value on the Y axis (in the case of figure 7-1, a low value in terms of regulation). On the other hand, the two right windows show a high value on the X axis and consequently a high degree of uniformity, while the two top windows show a high value on the Y axis and as a result a high degree of regulation.

"SEMI-REGULATED STYLE" (L,H) Chicago New Orleans Pittsburgh San Diego	"SYSTEMATICALLY-REGULATED STYLE" (H,H) El Paso, Texas Waterloo, Iowa Alaska Others
"LAISSEZ-FAIRE STYLE" (L,L) Most Judicial Units	"OPEN-DOOR STYLE" (H,L) Detroit Los Angeles New York Washington, D.C. Others

Regulation

Uniformity

Figure 7-1. The Interface of Uniformity and Regulation in the Disposition of Criminal Cases Without Trial

These four styles of bargaining are intended to illustrate negotiation practices as these vary from one prosecutor's office to another, primarily, rather than from one assistant prosecutor to another. Of course, to the extent that uniformity of negotiation practices is lacking, these practices may well vary from one assistant prosecutor to another, particularly in offices that are characteristic of a particular bargaining style. Regulations may or may not exert a significant impact upon uniformity of bargaining practices, depending upon the type of regulation that is employed within a prosecutor's office that is characteristic of a specific bargaining style. An understanding of the differences among the four bargaining styles requires an in-depth look at each.

Laissez-Faire Style

The oldest, the most natural, and undoubtedly the most prevalent style of bargaining for the disposition of criminal cases is labeled the "laissez-faire style." Of the four styles that are identified within figure 7-1, this one ranks lowest in terms of both uniformity and regulation. As such, it exhibits a pattern that is referred to commonly as the 1,1 pattern in conjunction with a Johari's Window. It will be known as a L,L (for low, low) pattern in figure 7-1, however, since the analysis of bargaining styles involves qualitative rather than quantitative measurements and the difference between 1,1 or 1,2 or 2,1 or 2,2 would be insignificant.

Prosecutors in offices that follow a laissez-faire style of bargaining tend to be relatively unconcerned about the likelihood that similarly situated defendants in unrelated criminal transactions may not receive equal bargaining opportunities, and that as a result these defendants may not obtain bargains that are substantially the same. Moreover, in these offices bargaining choices are relegated to individual assistant prosecutors who have been assigned to handle pending criminal cases, usually at random. Very little, if any, supervision is maintained over the negotiation practices of these assistant prosecutors. Few, if any, policy controls have been announced by the chief prosecutor, and so the office does not exhibit a preference for specific dispositional alternatives.

In a laissez-faire jurisdiction, the makeup of any given dispositional agreement will depend ordinarily upon the strength of a working relationship that develops between the particular assistant prosecutor to whom a case has been assigned and the individual defense lawyer who is representing the defendant. If the interaction between these two attorneys is strained, the bargaining will be more tedious, it may take longer to consummate an agreement, and in the last analysis the bargained arrangement will be less acceptable to the defendant anyway and perhaps even to the prosecutor. Both parties will gripe that each was given short shrift. If the interaction between the two attorneys is amicable, the bargaining will be more convivial, it may take less time to consummate an agreement, and ultimately both parties may be more contented with the negotiated agreement.

This style of bargaining is not devoid of party politics, but successful negotiations are far more likely to be products of compatible personalities between the individual counsel than any other external factors. Client tradeoffs are not unknown to judicial units that have a laissez-faire bargaining style, but a defense lawyer will find it more difficult to exchange the best interests of one client for another because seldom will he have an opportunity to negotiate a large proportion of his caseload with any single assistant prosecutor. For this reason, also, court-busting is much less common within laissez-faire style judicial units than within jurisdictions where other styles exist.

Law enforcement personnel seem to prefer the laissez-faire style of bargaining to other styles, since fewer defendants who pass through the judicial process are able to dictate their own punishment in a judicial unit of this style. Naturally, even in a laissez-faire jurisdiction some assistant prosecutors can be expected to bargain more readily, more fairly, or more vigorously than others. Under the law of averages, however, the least and most aggressive balance each other out. Most assistant prosecutors seem unwilling to take personal responsibility for "giving away the courthouse," since most are beginning their legal careers and are trying to build respect in the eyes of the bar and the public. A new assistant prosecutor in a laissez-faire judicial unit may seek advice from a more experienced colleague to begin with, but as he builds experience each assistant appears to be governed by the dictates of his own conscience more than anything else.

The personal and the professional reputations of a defense counsel may carry some weight among some assistant prosecutors in a laissez-faire style jurisdiction. This seems to be truer when the assistant is considering resignation in favor of a private law practice. During the year or so prior to leaving a prosecutor's office, an assistant may be shopping around the legal community for an opportunity to become associated with a prestigious private law firm. One way in which the door to a private law firm may be opened to an assistant prosecutor is by means of his offering the clients of that firm reasonable if not favorable bargaining opportunities. In short, an assistant prosecutor working in a laissez-faire judicial unit enjoys an opportunity to bargain preferentially with some defense counsel or with some law firms over others if he chooses to do so.

Any individual defense lawyer who practices in a laissez-faire jurisdiction may buildup "credits" with individual assistant prosecutors with whom he bargains over a period of time. For instance, after bargaining properly and fairly with a particular assistant prosecutor over a period of months or years and during the course of many different case negotiations, an attorney may call in credits that he feels he has earned with this assistant by being a good fellow for a long time. He may use these credits sparingly to procure a more favorable bargain for a special client now and then, particularly if the client on whom the credit is consumed does not stand out as a serious or dangerous offender. Of course, a defense lawyer may use such credits advantageously whenever a member of his own family, a neighbor, or a close friend or employee becomes charged with a crime as long as the offense is not highly visible to the public.

The reputation of a defense lawyer as a trial advocate may exert added pressure on an assistant prosecutor to bargain both hastily and generously. In many laissez-faire judicial units, but not in all, once a case has been assigned to an assistant prosecutor he must carry that case to termination. The prospect of opposing some lawyers in the courtroom may be more ominous than the prospect of opposing other lawyers. However, since assistant prosecutors are bent on building a reputation for themselves, many relish the opportunity to appear in court against defense counsel with tough reputations. Once an assistant prosecutor has been beaten at a trial by a particular defense lawyer, however, this assistant may be reluctant to take other cases belonging to this defense counsel near the courtroom. Indeed, once an assistant prosecutor has been beaten badly by a defense lawyer at trial, he may "flinch" and offer ample bargaining perquesites to this defense counsel in the immediate future. But on the other hand, an assistant prosecutor who believes he has been cheated or deceived by a particular defense lawyer in or out of court may refuse to bargain with that counsel again for a long while, insisting upon taking as many of that lawyer's cases to trial as possible. He may lose the cases, but in the process the opposing lawyer loses time, effort, and money. In a laissez-faire jurisdiction, also, word can pass among assistant prosecutors that Lawyer X is a fair person with whom to deal, Lawyer Y is a tiger in court, and Lawyer Z is a cheat or an incompetent. After hearing that news, other assistant prosecutors may decide to play squarely with Lawyer X, stay out of court with Lawyer Y, and place as many obstacles as possible in the way of Lawyer Z.

Open-Door Style

In a few judicial units across the United States, notably the largest in terms of population density, a bargaining style is followed that can be described most pointedly as an "open-door style." This style is characterized by a high degree of uniformity coupled with a low degree of regulation. As such, it exhibits a pattern that is referred to commonly as the 9,1 pattern in conjunction with a Johari's Window. It will be known as a H,L (for high, low) pattern in figure 7-1, however, since the analysis of qualitative measurements does not yield a significant difference between 9,1 or 8,2 or 9,2 or 8,2. Most boroughs of New York City follow this bargaining style, but some (Bronx, Brooklyn, Queens) follow it more than others (Manhattan and Staten Island). Detroit, Los Angeles, and Washington, D.C. exhibit characteristics of the open-door style of bargaining, also.

Under the open-door style, the likelihood that similarly situated defendants will receive equal bargaining opportunities is not a matter of concern at all. They will inevitably. In these judicial units, prosecutors perceive themselves as being so deluged with criminal case backlogs that virtually any defendant who is willing to admit his guilt to some criminal charge will succeed in securing the immediate dismissal of most other charges pending against him without having to go through much trouble in the process. Law enforcement authorities complain rather aptly that this bargaining style involves "giving away the courthouse," since as a rule prosecutors are at the mercy of defense counsel.

It does not matter as a rule what individual prosecutor has been assigned to a defendant's case in an open-door style jurisdiction. Ordinarily, one assistant prosecutor is just like another, and the one who was assigned to handle a specific defendant's case today will not be the one who handles it tomorrow or next week. The defense attorney does not have to do much other than to sit back and wait for the right opportunity to have his client tender a guilty plea. The ripeness of the opportunity will depend upon what judge happens to be hearing guilty pleas on a given day, and of course on how much money the lawyer stands to gain from termination of the case today rather than tomorrow. Bargaining is merely a ritual in most jurisdictions exhibiting this style, and this situation gives rise to several forms of abuses.

Many of the criminal cases that are processed through open-door style judicial units will involve representation of the defendants by large and powerful public defender agencies. Court-busting and client tradeoffs are more common in open-door jurisdictions than elsewhere. Not all defendants are represented by a public defender agency, however. Some are represented by privately retained counsel who reap the benefits of a powerful public defender system. Most defendants who are not represented by the public defender are assigned to private lawyers who have been appointed by the court.

In most judicial units other than those of the open-door style, and in laissez-faire style jurisdictions, particularly, lawyers who are in private practice accept assigned indigent criminal defendant cases sparingly and on a rotation basis. They take these cases to fill-in their caseloads if they are just starting out in practice, or as a public service if they are more experienced. In open-door style jurisdictions, however, a segment of the bar tends to earn the bulk of their livelihood from accepting assigned criminal defense cases through court appointments. Some of these lawyers do more than accept these cases; they "hustle" them. These attorneys are known variously as the "Baxter Street Bar" (in New York City's Manhattan Borough), the "Fleet Street Bar" in Detroit, and the "Fifth Street Fixers" in Washington, D.C. They are known collectively in most open-door style jurisdictions as "the men in the baggy pants" who hang around the courthouse steps. Almost never do these lawyers take a case to trial, and seldom do they provide any skillful service to their clients. In substance, these lawyers hold their clients' hands while together they walk through the criminal justice process. Obviously, the defendant could do virtually the same thing by himself, and some do. Other defendants do not know the ropes in the courthouse, and may be "referred" to lawyer-hustlers by bailiffs, deputy sheriffs, and other support personnel who in turn collect an illegal "referral fee" from the lawyer to whom they have directed an unsuspecting client.

Few prosecutors prefer an open-door style of bargaining, and many who condone this style profess not to do so by choice but by necessity. An open-door style of bargaining appears to result principally from an oversaturated caseload of unterminated criminal charges that remain pending in a prosecutor's office. Without exception, prosecutors in open-door judicial units initiate more criminal charges than they have the manpower to matriculate. It goes without saying that they initiate more charges than they could ever bring to trial, but that is true in jurisdictions of other bargaining styles, also. Prosecutors in open-door jurisdictions launch more criminal charges than they can even *negotiate* feasibly, and so they begin to avoid substantive negotiations as well as trials and to routinize criminal cases along a ritualized but endless assembly line.

An open-door style of bargaining cannot endure for very long within any judicial unit unless the judges who hear the majority of criminal cases support it or at least look the other way. The value of an open-door pattern rests in the speed at which criminal cases can reach disposition without regard for the quality of most dispositions. An open-door style sacrifices substantive effectiveness to achieve procedural efficiency, although as often as not it even lacks efficiency. Judges are expected to rubber-stamp any dispositional agreement to which the prosecutor has assented, without comment usually but certainly without inquiry or scrutiny. A judge who devotes even a minimum amount of time toward examining the appropriateness or the merits of a dispositional agreement defeats the functional value of the open-door system. As has been mentioned, unless such a judge can change the system and that is unlikely, he will have to remove himself from the bench or be removed. A critical judge is an obstacle to the automation that is the essence of an open-door style of processing criminal cases.

Semiregulated Style

A third bargaining style is in the process of emerging rapidly and vigorously within a number of judicial units across the nation. This style seems to take root in the offices of prosecutors who are both energetic and fairly new in office. It does not seem to have emerged forcefully within any major jurisdiction where a prosecutor has to reckon with an aggressive or an expansive public defender agency. This style offers evidence of being partially regulated, because the chief prosecutor maintains control over latitude that is accorded to his assistants in terms of their bargaining discretion. For this reason, the style may be termed a semiregulated style.

Although a semiregulated bargaining style is accompanied by a number of policy controls which are both prescribed and enforced by top prosecution management, the regulations are directed toward the interests of the state much more than toward those of defendants. For this reason, the style is not fully regulated and does not even purport as a rule to achieve or to be concerned with achieving uniformity. Consequently, this style follows a 1,9 pattern in a Johari's Window, and in figure 7-1 it is identified as exhibiting L,H (for low, high) traits.

Prosecutors who preside over semiregulated style offices tend to be concerned primarily with the disposition of selected kinds of criminal cases that have been singled out from the lot for peculiar reasons. The disposition of other cases that have not been singled out may follow a laissez-faire style of bargaining in general. Cases that are singled out are likely to involve the commission of crimes that have outraged the community or that may enhance the political image of the prosecutor. Examples of outrageous crimes are contract murder, armed robbery, rape, and narcotics trafficking. Examples of crimes that when prosecuted may bolster a prosecutor's political image are organized rackets offenses, official corruption offenses, and crimes that involve confidence schemes or other fraudulent and deceptive practices. Thus, semiregulated jurisdictions tend to concentrate on regulating the prosecution of street crimes, organized crime, and white collar crimes.

Normally, the regulations that are imposed within a semiregulated style judicial unit do not preclude negotiated dispositions even for criminal cases that fall within categories that have been selected for regulation. It is harder for these cases to be negotiated, and much harder for a defendant (especially a repeat offender) who has been charged with one of these crimes to obtain a desirable disposition by means of negotiation. These cases are assigned to assistant prosecutors who are more experienced than average, or retained for prosecution personally by the district attorney himself or by one of his principal deputies. Greater care will be taken to investigate facts surrounding commission of these crimes, to gather sufficient admissible evidence, and to prepare witnesses for testimony in court.

A semiregulated style of bargaining has been observed by the author in Allegheny County (Pittsburgh), Pennsylvania, Cook County (Chicago), Illinois, Orleans Parish (New Orleans), Louisiana, and San Diego, California. It is estimated that up to one-fourth of the major American judicial units may have adopted a semiregulated bargaining style in one form or another to a greater or a lesser extent. In jurisdictions that have adopted a semiregulated bargaining style, defense counsel have grumbled when, as is likely, they have been unable to dispose of cases as easily or as rapidly as usual when the cases fall within the regulated classes. The decision by prosecutors to adopt a semiregulated bargaining style does not seem to have paralyzed or otherwise impeded the flow of cases that remain outside the scope of the regulations. Nor is there evidence to suggest that even those classes of cases that are regulated have become anymore backlogged than they were previously.

A semiregulated prosecutor's office tends to adopt a division of labor according to functional, compartmentalized units even for classes of crimes that are not directly regulated per se. Special screening units may be created to eliminate unprovable cases before these cases enter the courts. Assistant prosecutors may be assigned to specific departmental groups to which all cases involving specific crimes are assigned. In this way, assistant prosecutors become more familiar with the elements of the crimes which they specialize in prosecuting. They interact more intensively with the victims of these crimes. They come to know the names and faces of repeat offenders who perpetrate these crimes. Although assistant prosecutors in different departmental units may not be regulated from the front office to the same extent, they tend over time to regulate themselves by adopting and enforcing their own group norms. In this way, gradually, individual prosecutors move away from a laissez-faire style and begin to internalize the need for regulations.

Systematically Regulated Style

A fourth style of bargaining is in its formative stages within a few judicial units across the United States. This style has already come and gone in other jurisdictions, where after being tried it has been deemed an unworkable failure. Because it involves a high degree of regulation as well as a high degree of uniformity, this style may be termed a "systematically regulated style." It seems to emerge primarily on account of a reaction on the part of judges or prosecutors who have witnessed abuses in the laissez-faire bargaining style that existed in their judicial unit prior to being replaced.

In a systematically regulated jurisdiction, the regulations themselves are oriented toward generating uniformity in the disposition of criminal cases. Therefore, this style follows a 9,9 pattern in a Johari's Window, and in figure 7-1 it is identified as exhibiting H,H (for high, high) traits. In most instances when this bargaining style has been attempted, the prosecutors and the judges have joined in a regulatory coalition. More often than not, the movement toward systematic regulation has been initiated by the court or by one or more sitting judges. Opposition from defense counsel is predictable. However, most often this style of bargaining becomes doomed when the persons or groups of people who began the experiment become disillusioned with it. In other words, judges and prosecutors themselves find systematic regulations unworkable once their curiosity has worn away.

Exact attributes of a typical jurisdiction in which bargaining has become systematically regulated cannot be reported because this style does not appear to have been fully operationalized anywhere. Most judicial units that have undertaken implementation of this style have stopped before finishing the task because of difficulties inherent in constructing a workable calculus that is capable of allocating to any criminal charge, defendant, class of offense or class of offender a constant bargaining handicap. Indeed, the notion that one bargain will fit all cases that look superficially to be the same seems to be the pitfall of this bargaining style.

Except for a brief interlude when the Attorney General of Alaska attempted to prohibit plea bargaining in every form, none of the judicial units that have experimented with systematic regulation have purported to stop negotiations over the disposition of criminal cases. Instead, most of these jurisdictions have erected boundaries within which bargaining is acceptable and outside of which bargaining is unacceptable. One major example of a judicial unit that has tried to systematically regulate bargaining is El Paso, Texas. There, three Texas district judges announced to the bar of that judicial unit "an outline of (their) thinking on sentencing which involves a point system draft for (counsel) to use in judging how (to advise his client) to plead."

The El Paso judges proposed a point system under which defendants who scored nine points or less would be good candidates for probation but those who scored over nine points could expect to be sentenced to a prison term. The point system was as follows:

Crime	Points
Murder	10
Aggravated rape	10
Aggravated arson	10

Crime	Points
Aggravated robbery	7
Burglary of habilitation	6
Second degree felony	5
Third degree felony	4

Other Variables

Use of firearm	3
Use of other prohibited weapon	2
Serious injury to victim	4
Minor injury to victim	2
Little possibility of restitution (due to amount of loss)	4
Inability to supervise probation	3
Bad recidivism prediction (based on psychological test)	1

Criminal Record

Each previous felony conviction in previous five years	6
Each previous felony conviction more than five years prior to act in question	4
Each previous class A type misdemeanor conviction	3
Each previous class B type misdemeanor conviction	2
Multiple charges—"each over one"	3
Evidence indicating professionalism	4
Evidence indicating dealing in prohibited substances	6

These judges warned that in imposing probation they would be inclined to attach conditions such as curfews, prohibition against the use of alcohol, the defendant's required participation in a rehabilitation and employment training program, confinement in jail for up to thirty days, and restitution to the victim.

The El Paso district judges stated categorically that "The Court will not entertain pleas to lesser included offenses." In doing so, they reasoned that "There is no sound judicial reason why a defendant should be convicted for some crime other than the one he actually committed." They said that upon request of the district attorney they might permit prosecution of a third degree felony as a Class A misdemeanor, however.

Finally, the El Paso judges announced in the same memorandum the following "Time To Serve Chart," in which they pledged to impose similar sentences for similarly convicted offenders:

Crime	Sentence
Murder	5-50 years
Aggravated rape	5-50 years
Aggravated arson	5-50 years
Aggravated robbery (no injury)	5-15 years
Aggravated robbery (injury)	15-50 years
Enhanced third degree felony	15 years
Enhanced second degree felony	20 years
Enhanced first degree felony	50-99 years to life
Habitualized third degree felony	25 years
Habitualized second degree felony	30 years
Habitualized first degree felony	99 years, life

In other cases where the defendant has no felony record but does not qualify for probation, the judges said they would impose the following sentences:

Crime	Sentence
First degree felony	5-10 years
Second degree felony	2- 7 years
Third degree felony	2- 5 years

Finally, the judges said if the defendant has a previous felony record within the past five years, even though not indicated, enhanced or habitualized, the sentence will be in the following range:

Crime	Sentence
First degree felony	20 years
Second degree felony	15 years
Third degree felony	10 years

It is important to note that the three El Paso judges who ordained the above guidelines admonished lawyers as follows: "Do not interpret the point system to mean that we are going to judge cases arithmetically." They said that they would not be "controlled by the system but will use it as a guide." They told counsel that "Any factor not covered in the point system may be submitted to us by any lawyer at the sentence hearing and we will certainly consider the factor (as set forth in an earlier letter): Each case stands on its own merits." Thus, these judges appear to have come full-circle within the span of two memos.

National Bargaining Trends

As a result of the on-site study of more than forty judicial units throughout the United States, national trends have been observed that are descriptive of the negotiation processes through which criminal case dispositions are reached without trial. These trends include:

Trend 1

Notwithstanding the American Bar Association's Standards plus statutes, case law and judicial rules, nearly all of which admonish judges against participating in any kind of bargaining for the disposition of criminal cases, most judges across the country participate actively in bargaining. Some participate much more actively than others do, exerting enormous pressures upon defendants and defense counsel to enter guilty pleas, and doing the same to compel prosecutors into dismissing companion charges. To the extent that defendants are coerced into waiving their rights to trial, this coercion is most likely to eminate from the bench rather than from the prosecutor, defense counsel, or anyone else.

Trend 2

Superior court judges participate in dispositional bargaining more clandestinely than do judges and magistrates in courts of limited jurisdiction. Indeed, at least half of the lower court judges who were interviewed or observed during this study participate in bargaining blatantly in open court and in full public view. Most lower court judges think nothing is wrong with actively participating in bargaining, while superior court judges are likely to admit that the practice is undesirable but necessary some of the time. Judicial participation in active bargaining is certain to continue unless judges who engage in this practice are penalized.

Trend 3

In a great many judicial units across the nation, the defendant, the defense counsel, and the prosecutor recite on the court record a deliberately deceptive account of the minutes of in camera bargaining, up to even denying categorically that bargaining has occurred when in fact the guilty pleas that are about to be tendered by the defendant have been predicated upon bargained promises. In most instances of this sort, the defendant is asked by the court to state whether or not any bargaining has taken place, and if so, whether anyone has made him a promise of any kind concerning the dismissal of companion charges or the sentence that may be imposed in return for his guilty plea. Whenever this question is posed, a defendant is expected to answer in the negative. Judges routinely accept a defendant's negative reply on the record knowing that it is false, sometimes even after they have themselves participated in bargaining. Now and then, a judge will even stop the record by signaling the court stenographer, for the purpose of coaching the defendant or permitting counsel to coach a defendant into making a deceptive response when the record is resumed.

Trend 4

There is not a single prosecutor anywhere in the United States who intends to stop bargaining for the disposition of criminal cases. From time to time, prosecutors write articles or give interviews in which they contend that they have or that they will stop bargaining. Instead, the "alternative" which they propose invariably shifts the form of the bargain or the style of bargaining but eradicates neither. Prosecutors who face reelection or other community pressure may refuse to negotiate sentence concessions or guilty pleas to reduced charges, but never do they refuse to negotiate either of these inducements against a defendant's demand for trial.

Trend 5

Very few, if any, prosecutors or defense counsel believe honestly that bargaining for the disposition of criminal cases is bad practice, and nearly all subscribe to the assumption that it is inevitable. The demand for an end to plea bargaining originates in political campaigns where persons are seeking election as jurists or as prosecutors. The movement gains support from the ranks of convicted offenders who wish after the fact that they would have gone to trial. It gains credence from academics and court administration consultants who are prone to proposing new theoretical systems that have not been tested and usually cannot be tested in practice.

Note

1. 400 U.S. 25.

8 Inter- and Intrajurisdictional Policies and Practices on Pleading and Sentencing

It appears clearly that established policies relating to pleading and sentencing exist within only a small proportion of the judicial units that have been studied (see chapter 2). On the contrary, a study of the same judicial units supports the inference derived from national and statewide data (see chapter 4) that practices on pleading and sentencing are remarkably similar not only from one jurisdiction to another but within most jurisdictions among different judges, assistant prosecutors and assistant public defenders. For this reason, whatever "understandings" that may exist as to pleading and sentencing practices between judges, prosecutors, and defense counsel must be unwritten for the most part. This chapter will be concerned with the characteristics of written policies relating to pleading and sentencing practices in those judicial units where written policies have been drafted. In addition, this chapter will be concerned with the degree to which, if at all, written policies that have been established are followed. Finally, this chapter will be concerned with the degree to which, if at all, unwritten policies may contribute to pleading and sentencing practices among judges, prosecutors, and defense counsel within the same judicial unit and across jurisdictional boundaries.

Written Policies on Pleading or Sentencing

To the extent that written policies on pleading or sentencing exist, these may have been formulated at the federal, state or, county levels, although most appear to have been devised and implemented at the county level and to be applicable only within a single judicial unit. Moreover, written policies may be formulated at any level of government by either of the three branches—the legislative, executive, or judicial. For instance, a written policy may be created by a court through an appellate case decision or within special court rules. A written policy may be initiated by a legislature in the form of a statute. Or, a written policy may be the product of an executive decision reached by the attorney general of a state or by a local prosecutor. The latter seems to be the most common, although in most jurisdiction there is a paucity of written policies related to pleading or sentencing regardless of by whom they have been originated. These written policies can be grouped more easily by the level of government within which they originated than in terms of the policy's form.

Therefore, these policies will be subdivided according to federal, state, and local judicial units.

Federal Policies

Federal policies relating to pleading have been promulgated principally by the United States Supreme Court, and secondarily by several of the United States Courts of Appeals. Federal policies relating to sentencing in the *federal* courts have been set forth by the Congress, but Congress has not taken any action which would regulate either pleading or sentencing practices in the *state* courts. The United States Department of Justice has circulated internal memoranda among the various United States attorneys related to pleading and sentencing for selected federal offenses, and some United States attorneys have developed written policies related to pleading and/or sentencing practices for use among their own staff prosecutors. Some United States District Courts have announced pleading and/or sentencing "guidelines," but for the most part these have been merely to implement decisions of the Supreme Court or of the court of appeals for the circuit in which the district court is located. Of course, decisions of the United States Supreme Court are binding upon all judicial units—federal and state—throughout the United States unless specifically limited to federal jurisdictions, and court of appeals' decisions are binding upon all judicial units situated within the respective circuit, but highly persuasive in other circuits and particularly in neighboring circuits.

The Policy Impact of the Supreme Court. The United States Supreme Court began to formulate pleading policy for the nation in early 1948 when it announced Von Moltke v. Gillies.[1] In that case, the Court held that a guilty plea is invalid if the defendant does not competently, intelligently, and with full understanding of the implications waive his or her constitutional right to *counsel* as required by the Sixth Amendment.[2] Subsequently, the Court fashioned the voluntary-intelligent standard for waiver of other constitutional rights as well, including the privilege against compulsory self-incrimination, the right to a trial by jury, and the right to confront one's accusers.[3]

The Supreme Court began to formulate the nation's policy on sentencing defendants who have pleaded guilty to criminal charges in early 1962 when it announced Machibroda v. United States.[4] In *Machibroda,* the Court held that a Federal prisoner was entitled to a hearing to determine, inter alia, whether the prisoner's guilty plea had been induced involuntarily through the prosecutor's out-of-court promise that the sentence would not exceed twenty years when in fact the actual sentence imposed was forty years (a twenty-five year sentence for one crime and a fifteen year sentence for another, to run consecutively).[5]

Both *Von Moltke* and *Machibroda* involved defendants who pleaded guilty to federal charges in federal courts. However, in 1963 the Supreme Court held, in White v. Maryland, [6] that a preliminary hearing in a *state* court was a critical stage and that lack of counsel there at the time of a guilty plea vitiates a conviction even though entry of a plea was not required at the preliminary hearing. The Court in *White* began to apply federal pleading policy to the states. In two companion cases decided in 1970, the Supreme Court determined that neither a federal (Brady v. United States[7]) nor a state (Parker v. North Carolina[8]) defendant's guilty plea is per se involuntary merely because it may have been motivated by his desire to avoid the death penalty. In *Parker*, the Court held that the state defendant's guilty plea was not inherently involuntary solely because it may have been motivated by a coerced confession. Moreover, in McMann v. Richardson,[9] also decided in 1970, the Supreme Court held that a state defendant's guilty plea based on reasonably competent legal advice is an intelligent plea and not open to attack on grounds that the defense counsel may have misjudged the admissibility of the defendant's confession.

The Supreme Court began to apply federal sentencing policy to the *states* late in 1971 in Santobello v. New York.[10] The majority opinion held that a state prosecutor's recommendation of a maximum sentence for a defendant who had pleaded guilty in reliance upon a promise by this prosecutor's predecessor not to recommend any specific sentence requires either that the defendant be entitled to withdraw his plea or that the defendant be granted specific performance of the original agreement as to sentence. The majority remanded the case to state courts for election of the remedy.

In a 1978 case, United States v. Grayson,[11] the Supreme Court set its imprimatur on the long-standing practice by many trial judges of imposing much more severe sentences upon defendants convicted after trial compared with those who plead guilty. The Court reasoned that a sentencing authority such as a trial judge may consider the demeanor of an accused during trial, including the defendant's apparent truthfulness while testifying in his own defense if he chooses to do so. The Court concluded that if a sentencing judge determines that a defendant's testimony at trial contained willful and material falsehoods, this may be considered along with other presentence knowledge that bears on sentencing, because a defendant's perjury diminishes his prospects for rehabilitation. In *Grayson*, the Supreme Court stopped short of sanctioning the enhancement of a sentence solely on account of the expense and inconvenience to which a defendant puts the court and the prosecution by raising frivolous defenses while exercising his constitutional right to trial.

The Policy Impact of Congress. The United States Congress has acted to provide for minimum standards of pleading and sentencing procedures under the Federal Rules of Criminal Procedure (See appendixes A, B, and C). Rule 11 pertains to the pleas themselves, and Rule 32 imposes guidelines for imposition of sentence and judgment. Rule 410 used to provide that evidence of a plea of guilty or of *nolo contendere* and evidence of an offer by a defendant to plead guilty or *nolo contendere,* together with statements made in connection with these pleas or plea offers, is not admissible in any civil or criminal action if the plea is not made or if made is withdrawn. Rule 410 was deleted by Congress in 1975, and substantially incorporated in the text of Rule 11(e)(6) as amended, effective August 1, 1975. Congress applied these rules only to the federal courts, but in Boykin v. Alabama (1969)[12] the Supreme Court determined that it "fastens upon the States, as a matter of federal constitutional law, the rigid prophylactic requirements of Rule 11 of the Federal Rules of Criminal Procedure."[13] In his dissent, Justice Harlan termed "bizarre" the majority's opinion of Rule 11's "rigid prophylactic procedures" to the states.[14] Was Justice Harlan hostile to the procedures, to their application to the states, or to the language used by Justice Douglas in drafting the opinion of the Court? How "rigid" are the Rule 11 procedures? How "prophylactic" are they? What injuries are they designed to prevent?

In April of 1969, two months before the Supreme Court announced *Boykin,* Chief Justice Warren delivered the Court's opinion in the case of McCarthy v. United States,[15] holding that a Federal defendant whose guilty plea had been accepted in violation of Rule 11 must be afforded an opportunity to plead anew. Chief Justice Warren noted in *McCarthy* his impression of the legislative intent behind Rule 11:

> . . . the Rule (11) is intended to produce a complete record at the time the plea is entered of the factors relevant to this voluntariness determination. Thus, the more meticulously the Rule is adhered to, the more it tends to discourage, or at least to enable more expeditious disposition of, the numerous and often frivolous post-conviction attacks on the constitutional viability of guilty pleas.[16]

However, Rule 11 (and also Rule 32) was changed by Congress after *McCarthy* and *Boykin* were decided. The changes became effective in 1975. The first and the second versions of both Rules 11 and 32 are contained in appendix A.

From a policy perspective, Rule 11(e) is the most significant portion of Rule 11 that was changed by Congress in the 1975 amendments. Sections (a) and (b) pertain to types of pleas and remain unchanged. Section (c) involves the court's advice to defendants who are contemplating guilty pleas. It requires the court to summarize for the defendant: (1) the minimum and maximum penalties to which he may be exposed by pleading guilty; (2) his right to be represented by defense counsel, including an appointed lawyer if he is indigent; (3) his right to plead not guilty, demand and receive a jury trial, and with the assistance of counsel to confront and cross-examine adverse witnesses while exercising his privilege against compulsory self-incrimination; and (4) the finality of a guilty plea. The 1975 amendment added to section (d) a fifth subsection, which mandates that the court *notify* the defendant that the court may be *going to inquire* of the defendant about the details of the offense(s) to which the defendant proposes to plead guilty, and to which the defendant will have to respond under oath in the presence of his counsel and subject to subsequent prosecution for perjury if he lies. Section (d) remained unchanged after 1975, and requires the court to inquire of the defendant in open court whether the latter's willingness to plead guilty has been inspired by prior discussions between his lawyer and counsel for the prosecution.

Section (e) delineates the proper plea agreement procedures to be followed by opposing counsel in reaching a guilty plea agreement, and prohibits judicial participation in plea discussions. Subsection (1) remained unchanged after 1975, except that Congress added the stipulation that the prosecutor's recommendation or request for a particular sentence or the prosecutor's agreement not to oppose the defendant's similar request shall *not be binding upon the court.* Subsection (2) remained unchanged after 1975, except that prior to 1975 the court simply had to require the disclosure of any plea agreement in open court, whereas since 1975 the court must require the disclosure *on the record* as well as in open court unless for good cause shown the court decides to require the disclosure in camera. The court's right to accept or to reject a plea agreement remained unchanged in 1975. Section (e)(3) which provides for the court's acceptance of a guilty plea pursuant to a prior agreement between counsel became slightly more limited in 1975. Before then, the court had to inform a defendant that the sentence to be imposed would be equal to or *more* favorable than that contemplated in the agreement. Since 1975, the court is required only to inform the defendant that it will embody the judgment and sentence disposition provided for in the agreement. Section (e)(4) which provides for the court's rejection of a guilty plea agreement. Both before and since 1975, the court must inform the defendant personally that the court is not bound by the agreement, afford the defendant opportunity to withdraw his plea, and advise the defendant that if he persists in pleading guilty or *nolo contendere* he may receive a less favorable disposition than that contemplated by the plea agreement. Before 1975, the court had to so inform the defendant in open court. Since 1975, the court must do so *on the record* and in open court unless for good cause shown the court decides to do so in camera.

Subsection (5) of Rule 11(e) requires that the court be notified of the existence of a guilty plea agreement prior to trial, except for good cause shown, and remained unchanged in 1975. Subsection (6) makes evidence of plea offer or of a withdrawn plea of guilty or *nolo contendere,* together with statements made in connection thereto, inadmissible in any civil or criminal proceeding except in prosecution for perjury if the defendant falsely represented his guilt under oath, on the record, and in the presence of counsel. The perjury exception was added in 1975. Subsections (f) and (g) remained unchanged after 1975. Subsection (f) provides that the court should determine if there is a factual basis for a plea. Subsection (g) requires that a *verbatim* record be made of the defendant's plea entry, the court's advice to the defendant, plus the court's inquiry into the voluntariness and the accuracy of a plea.

One major shortcoming of Rule 11 is that in its advice to the defendant a court is *not* required specifically to inform the defendant of potential collateral consequences that may be incurred when one pleads guilty or no contest to a criminal charge. Such consequences include civil disability (loss of the right to vote or to hold public office, permanently in some states and temporarily in others); civil death (in some states, a life sentence is automatic grounds for divorce and precludes the convict from any inheritance); the possibility of deportation, loss of a passport, undesirable military discharge; the possibility that the current sentence may be imposed to run consecutively to one already being served by the defendant; or the possibility that probation or parole on prior convictions may be revoked.[17] Nor has Rule 11 been interpreted to require the judge to inquire into possible defenses (such as entrapment, insanity, justification, or privilege) or to inquire whether proper scientific tests have been conducted to establish the validity and reliability of scientific evidence allegedly possessed by the prosecution.[18]

In enacting and amending Rule 32, Congress followed basic constitutional mandates set forth by the Supreme Court, but added several other provisions which have not yet been applied by the Supreme Court to the states, such as the requirement of a presentence investigation and report. Under Rule 32(c), a presentence investigation and report must be made to the court prior to imposition of sentence unless waived by the defendant with the permission of the court, or unless the court determines that the record contains sufficient information to enable sentencing discretion and explains this finding on the record. The specific exceptions to the presentence investigation requirements were added by the 1975 amendment. Moreover, Rule 32(c) prohibits this report from being submitted to the court or its contents from being disclosed to anyone else until the defendant has been found guilty or pleaded guilty or *nolo contendere,* although a judge may inspect such a report anytime with the written consent of a defendant. Subsection (2) of Rule 32(c) recites that the presentence report shall contain any prior criminal record of the defendant and relevant information (such as his financial condition and circumstances affecting his behavior) as may help the court in imposing sentence or granting probation.

Subsection (3) of Rule 32(c) permits the defendant or his counsel, upon request, a *limited* right to read the presentence investigation report and the ensuing right to comment upon what hread and to introduce testimony or other information as to any alleged factual inaccuracy contained in the report. This rule does not permit the defendant or his counsel to read that portion of the report which makes a recommendation as to sentence, or any portion which in the court's opinion might harm the defendant's chances for rehabilitation, or breach confidentiality that was promised in order to obtain the information, or result in physical or other harm to any person. However, under subsection 3(A) if the court declines to disclose information contained in the report the court must make an oral or a written summary of that portion of the report and give to the defendant and counsel an opportunity to comment on it, to the extent that the material will be relied on in determining sentence.

Finally, Rule 32(d) of the Federal Rules of Criminal Procedure provides that a motion to withdraw a plea of guilty or of *nolo contendere* may be made only before sentence is imposed, except that such a motion may be made after sentencing to correct "manifest injustice," at the discretion of the court. This provision is in keeping with the decision of the Supreme Court in Kercheval v. United States (1927),[19] in which the Court urged lower courts to exercise their discretion and allow substitution of a plea of not guilty "if for any reason the granting of the privilege seems fair and just."[20] However, the Supreme Court has refused to reverse a lower court's refusal to permit plea withdrawal even *before* imposition of sentence in Neely v. Pennsylvania (1973),[21] notwithstanding the defendant's good faith for wanting to do so, the allegation of sufficient supporting reasons, and the absence of prejudice to the prosecution. In withdrawal motions *following* imposition of sentence, the Rule 32(d) standard of preventing "manifest injustice" has *not* been applied to the states, and while a few states[22] have adopted Rule 32(d) in toto or in a part, a majority of the states do not permit plea withdrawal for any reason except lack of jurisdiction, following imposition of the sentence; and of these most do not permit withdrawal following entry of judgment.

State Policies

State policies relating to pleading and sentencing have been established in the state courts, in state legislatures, and by executive decision of state and county prosecutors. Of course, the policies that are in effect within one state are not binding on other states, and policies that are in effect within a particular county need not be binding upon those who administer justice in another county even within the same state unless so decreed by federal or state authority. A discussion of state policy impact will be discussed separately according to the source of the policy.

The Impact of State Courts. State courts have formulated pleading policies only in very limited areas. Two of these areas stand out and merit special analysis. The first such area is the degree to which, if at all, a state judge must establish a factual basis for a plea of guilty or of *nolo contendere*. The second such area involves the conditions, if any, under which a state judge must permit a plea of guilty or of *nolo contendere* to be withdrawn, either before or after sentencing.

Since most states have not adopted Rule 11 of the Federal Rules of Criminal Procedure, and since this rule has not been applied to the states by the

Supreme Court, most states do not require their judges to inquire at all into the factual basis for pleas leading to conviction. Of those states which do require their judges to do so, this mandate is often statutory rather than judicial in origin. However, high courts in some states, especially in the Northeast,[23] have required lower court judges to question defendants personally and on the record as to the factual basis, if any, for a plea. In other states, high courts have "advised" lower court judges to do this, without requiring them to do so per se.[24] Some states, primarily those in the West,[25] have held through appellate court decisions that lower court judges may determine the factual basis for a plea leading to conviction from the record as a whole,[26] from a presentence report,[27] from a preliminary hearing transcript and a probation officer's report,[28] or even by questioning the prosecutor and the defense counsel[29] rather than by direct examination of the defendant himself. A few state appellate courts have held that lower court judges may establish the requisite factual basis for a plea through any reasonable method.[30]

The conditions, if any, under which a plea of guilty or of *nolo contendere* may be withdrawn vary widely from one state to the next to the extent that withdrawal is possible at all following acceptance of the plea by the court. Rule 32(d) of the Federal Rules of Criminal Procedure has not been applied to the states by the Supreme Court. While a few states have adopted this rule in toto or in part, mostly by legislative action,[31] a majority of the states do not permit plea withdrawal for any reason following imposition of the sentence other than due to lack of jurisdiction; and of these most do not permit withdrawal following entry of judgment. In many jurisdictions, judgment will be entered against the defendant almost immediately following the acceptance of his guilty plea by the court.

Some states do permit a defendant to withdraw a plea leading to conviction prior to imposition of sentence. Once again, most of these states do so through statutes that have parallelled Rule 32(d). A few states have done this through appellate court decisions. To the extent that state appellate courts have sanctioned presentence plea withdrawals, these courts have tended to impose standards for withdrawal. For instance, Arizona and Washington have adopted a "manifest injustice" standard similar to Rule 32(d) but through court decision rather than legislation. Montana and Florida have developed the standard of "for good cause shown" and Pennsylvania the standard of "for any fair and just reason" through appellate court decisions.[32] In most states, the standard for plea withdrawal is even stricter following imposition of the sentence.

Since a plea withdrawal motion is relegated ordinarily to the discretion of the judge before whom the original plea was directed, its denial may be reviewed only to determine if the judge abused his discretion. Abuse of discretion is difficult to show. An Oklahoma state court held that withdrawal must be permitted if a defendant alleges a defense which a jury should hear.[33] A West Virginia state court has held that a judge abuses his discretion by denying a defendant's motion for plea withdrawal when it appears that the guilty plea was entered "under some mistake, misapprehension or inducement which worked an injustice."[34] The standard of proof for a defendant's showing that a judge abused his discretion by denying a plea withdrawal motion varies among the states, also, although the burden is always on the defendant. In West Virginia a defendant must merely "create" a sufficient doubt as to the voluntariness of his plea,[35] whereas in California, Nebraska, and Wisconsin the defendant must show "clear and convincing evidence" to warrant a plea withdrawal,[36] and in Missouri, New York, and Oregon the defendant must prove that his plea was unintelligent or involuntary by a "preponderance of the evidence."[37] The New York standard is more difficult for the defendant than the California standard, which in turn is harder than the West Virginia standard.

The Impact of State Legislatures. State legislatures across the United States have exerted impact in various ways upon pleading and sentencing policies. Their most obvious impact has been upon substantive sentences, since in every state the legislature determines what specific sentences or sentence ranges are appropriate for those who are convicted of particular crimes. State legislatures may prescribe definite, indefinite, or indeterminate sentences. In the situation of indeterminate sentences, legislatures may set the boundaries for both minimum and maximum sentences, and establish criteria to be used by the sentencing judge when he decides the specific sentence or sentence range to meet-out to each defendant. Of course, a state legislature may decide the parole structure to be followed in its state, or even to eliminate parole for some or all prisoners. Moreover, a legislature may decide whether to impose capital punishment for any crime, within United States Supreme Court guidelines. Since this book is concerned with procedures much more than with substantive crimes or substantive sentences, the bulk of discussion will focus upon the legislative role in influencing pleading and sentencing procedures.

In a number of states, by statute, a prescribed number of days must elapse between the time when a defendant is arrested and the time when he pleads guilty to a criminal charge stemming from that arrest. For instance, in Alabama the minimum time allowed by statute is fifteen days, which cannot be waived by a defendant.[38] As mentioned already, various states have adopted all or portions of Rules 11 and 32 of the Federal Rules of Criminal Procedure, in toto or in part, by statute. One state, Georgia, permits presentence withdrawal of a guilty plea by a defendant as a matter of right by statute.[39]

To the extent that most states have adopted any portions of Rules 11 or 32 of the Federal Rules of Criminal Procedure, they seem to have done so to achieve very specific objectives. One such objective stands out above the others. This is an effort by at least five and probably even more states to prohibit judicial participation in plea discussions.[40] Of course, it should not be necessary for a state to adopt Rule 11(e) in order to preclude judicial participation in plea discussions, since this proscription was contained in the pre-1975 version of Rule 11(e)., Federal Rules of Criminal Procedure, which was made applicable to the states by the Supreme Court in Boykin v. Alabama (1969).[41] The fact that some states deemed it necessary to adopt some or all of Rule 11 by state statute is an indicator that state courts ignored or were reluctant to comply with the mandate of *Boykin.*

Some states have enacted legislation to adopt Rule 11(c), Federal Rules of Criminal Procedure, in toto or in part. It must be remembered that a great deal of Rule 11(c), relating to the "advice" which the court must give to the defendant before accepting a plea of guilty or *nolo contendere,* involves notification to the defendant of the latter's rights which will be forfeited upon a plea other than not guilty. However, Rule 11(c)(5) which provides for the judge to warn the defendant that the latter will be questioned under oath as to the factual basis for his plea was added by Congress in 1975, and therefore was not made applicable to the states specifically in *Boykin.* Under Rule 11(c)(5), the defendant learns of the "allocution" or "litany" of questions that may follow as the judge examines the defendant as to the factual basis for his plea. This ritual is designed to ensure "record adequacy" of a factual, intelligent and voluntary guilty plea. At least eight states have adopted the essence of Rule 11(c) by statute, while at least seven others have done so by court decision or judicial rule.[42] Another state, Montana, permits counsel to speak for the defendant at the time of the allocution, but requires one or the other to respond to the judge's satisfaction.[43] Thus, at least fifteen or nearly one-third of the states seem to be following the practice which was envisioned behind the Congressional policy that lead to passage of Rule 11(c). In the absence of applicable statute, however, some states do not require any allocution to determine the factual basis for a guilty plea, and courts in those states have sustained this void.[44]

At least three states require all guilty plea agreements to be reduced to writing by the defendant.[45] In West Virginia, a written plea agreement may be required of some but not all defendants.[46] In Minnesota, a defendant who is charged only with a misdemeanor may elect to have his attorney file a written plea agreement as an alternative to tendering the plea personally in open court.[47] Most regulations as to the form (oral or written) of a guilty plea agreement are statutory, although some are imposed by judicial rule. In some states, a guilty plea itself (as opposed to its underlying agreement) must be tendered orally by the defendant,[48] usually in open court.[49] However, a few states permit a defendant to elect whether his plea will be oral or written, while still requiring his presence in open court for the pleading.[50]

The Impact of State Executive Decisions. In most states, the authority of the state executive department over local criminal prosecutions is extremely limited. In a few states, mainly the smaller ones such as New Hampshire, the office of the state attorney general prosecutes offenders who have been charged with the most serious crimes, such as murder. In more than two-thirds of the states, however, authority of the attorney general over county prosecutors is only advisory. Most state executive decisions that have had an impact on pleading and sentencing policies have been advisory in nature and scope.

Perhaps the most prominent of the advisory opinions on these matters was the Position Paper on Plea Bargaining dated December 5, 1975 and drafted by then-California Attorney General Evelle J. Younger. This was a ten page typewritten paper which reviewed the development of judicial approval of plea bargaining as well as the rationale *against* sentence bargaining, the rationale *for* charge bargaining, and the effect of plea bargaining on number of trials. Younger's position was that, since both the United States and the California Supreme Courts "resolved" the constitutionality of plea bargaining in Brady v. United States (1970)[51] and People v. West (1970)[52] respectively, then "the exchange of benefits" between defendants and prosecutors justifies plea bargaining.[53] He warned, however, that avoiding trials or lessening punishments should be viewed only as "a means to an end, the protection of our citizens," rather than as the end itself.[54] He said these *means* toward an end should be "adjusted to achieve the maximum in citizen protection consistent with the accused's constitutional rights" but "not to achieve a benefit to individual defendants or to the officers of the state."[55] He concluded that these exchanges of benefits may provide an "excuse" but not a "sound justification" for plea bargaining.[56]

Younger questioned the rationale of the Supreme Court in *Brady,* and argued that since a defendant who receives a plea bargain is unlikely to be " contrite," plea bargaining may not result in the defendant's being rehabilitated more quickly.[57] Younger said that while greater judicial sentencing discretion is needed under California law, the solution is not to be found in judicial approval of plea bargains "which distort the truth and circumvent the law," but rather in overhaul of the state's sentencing structure.[58] Attorney General Younger noted that, in *West,* it appeared that "expediency was one of the basic concerns prompting the California Supreme Court to uphold plea bargaining,[59] pointing to the opinion of that court in *West* in which the majority reasoned, quoting from Professor Donald Newman, that "[a] steady flow of guilty pleas and the corresponding avoidance of the time, expense, and uncertainty of trials is important to the smooth functioning of most criminal courts."[60]

Attorney General Younger argued strongly against sentence bargaining. He alleged that to the extent that punishment considerations affect the determination of guilt, the "quality of criminal justice will suffer."[61] Instead, the sentencing decision should be further removed from the decision on guilt, since each decision is undermined by "bargaining one for the other."[62] Younger condemned judicial approval of bargained sentences, because this makes the judge a participant in negotiations and an "advocate of the solution agreed on."[63]

The following conclusions were offered by Attorney General Younger in his 1975 Position Paper:

> We reach the conclusion that any form of plea bargaining which involves a commitment from the court regarding probation or sentence as a condition of the entry of a plea of guilty or nolo contendere should be abandoned. The cost of sentence bargaining in terms of public confidence in the criminal justice system, the quality of the decisions on guilt and sentence and in compromising the role of the trial judge is not worth the relatively small increase in the production of guilty pleas.
>
> To implement this position we would urge legislation which would . . . prohibit the court from engaging in any discussion or consideration of probation or sentence in a criminal action prior to the determination of the guilt of the defendant. Our tradition of trial by jury has never been justified on the basis of cost efficiency. Surely at this point we are not forced to curtail the quality of justice by inducing defendants to plead guilty through the promise of a light sentence.[64]

In 1975, the Attorney General of Alaska announced a policy which directed prosecutors throughout each of Alaska's judicial divisions to cease and desist from plea bargaining. This order was enforceable against local prosecutors, because uniquely under Alaska law prosecutors throughout the judicial divisions report directly to the attorney-general. The Alaska attorney general's directive is of less significance today than the response which it prompted from the Alaska Bar Association.

In a Memorandum to the Alaska Bar Association from its Plea Bargaining Committee dated August 12, 1975, the committee urged the Board of Governors of the Alaska Bar Association to "take affirmative steps to have the attorney general's policy decision rescinded immediately.[65] The committee's supporting reasons were plentiful. The four page Memorandum noted first the "detrimental impact" which lack of plea bargaining would have on both civil and criminal trial calendars, since more criminal trials could be projected necessitating transfer of civil judges to the criminal bench.[66] The committee tendered the panicky conclusion that with plea bargaining less than five percent of the criminal cases in Alaska go to trial, but that a cessation of plea bargaining would result in rapid increase of that percentage, and that "if there is any increment in the percentage of these cases which go to trial, the trial calendar will be in havoc."[67]

The Alaska Bar Association's Plea Bargaining Committee observed, also, that the "demise of plea bargaining is certain to increase the cost of justice," due to the fact that with additional trials demanded more judges, prosecutors, public defenders, and jurors will have to be appointed at public expense, and more witnesses will have to be subpoenaed by the state.[68] Indeed, the committee warned that police witnesses would have to be paid many overtime hours just for "waiting at court."[69] The committee decried that perhaps the "harshest" result of a no plea bargaining policy would be the "social effect on the average person" who is charged with a misdemeanor or a traffic offense who would be "forced to go to trial" unless permitted to negotiate charge dismissals and sentence reductions.[70] Remarkably, this committee of the *bar* association expressed concern that the "legal fees for defending misdemeanors will necessarily rise."[71]

The committee went on to argue that the "inability of the prosecutor to make a recommendation in regard to sentence is at odds with that principle of justice."[72] It did not recite the principle. Moreover, the committee determined that without plea bargaining a full sentencing hearing would be required although one is not required under Alaska law when a plea has been negotiated; and that such a hearing alone would cause court backlogs.[73] Finally, the committee alleged that without plea bargaining defendants would suffer economic loss because "trials necessitate more time away from their jobs" and "in many cases this absence will call attention to the criminal charge and may result in the person's dismissal from his or her job."[74] In short, the committee founded its recommendations upon the premise that the attorney general's policy against plea bargaining would be tantamount to "throwing the entire court system into chaos."[75]

In a Memorandum to the Pennsylvania District Attorneys Association dated July 13, 1975 from John J. Crane, a Delaware County prosecutor,[76] the author concluded as follows:

> No matter what the rules and regulations and standards and goals, the entire system of plea bargaining is, as in most contract situations, dependent upon the integrity, common sense and forthrightness of all involved in the process. There must be complete disclosure on all sides so that the plea bargain may be open and honest and may be stated so in open court.[77]

In the same Memorandum, Crane cites with approval portions of an address once given before the National College of Distrit Attorneys by F. Emmett Fitzpatrick as District Attorney of Philadelphia: "Plea bargaining is not a new procedure, nor should it be embraced by prosecutors as the panacea for problems of the judicial system. There are abuses which are subject to proper criticism, particularly when candor is replaced by deception."[78]

Local Policies

Written policies relating to pleading and sentencing practices may be created and implemented at the local level of government as well as at federal and state levels. However, it appears evident that local authorities are much more reluctant than federal or state authorities are to announce pleading or sentencing policies in *written* form. As with federal and state policies, local policies may in theory be established by local courts, county legislative organs, or by executive decision of each local prosecutor. In practice, seldom are policy decisions of this sort made by local legislators. Once in a while, as in the case of El Paso County,

Texas, noted in chapter 7 and to be noted again below in this chapter, the local judiciary will at least attempt to implement pleading or sentencing policies. Much more often, but still not so often, local prosecutors will announce written guidelines to be followed by members of their staffs during the pleading and the sentencing processes.

The Impact of Local Courts. Most written communications on pleading or sentencing policy that are written *by* judges are written *for* brother judges sitting in the same judicial unit. Such communications may be drafted by a presiding judge or justice for the purpose of apprising other members of the judiciary as to recent changes in the law that have arisen through appellate court decisions or by new legislation. An example of such a communication is a Memorandum addressed to all the Justices of the Supreme Court assigned to Criminal Term and all Judges of the Criminal Court, Kings and Richmond Counties (New York), dated March 24, 1976 and signed by Hon. Milton Mollen as Assistant Administrative Judge for those counties. In this Memorandum, Justice Mollen noted a then-recent decision by the New York Court of Appeals[79] (that state's highest court) which noted that when problems are evident in the facts or the law surrounding a guilty plea, the court must do more than merely rely on the presence of counsel. Specifically, Justice Mollen apprised his fellow judges of circumstances "which should alert the Judge to the fact that the defendant's plea is *inappropriate,*" including evidence of (a) a dispute on the facts, (b) an incorrect charge on the face of the indictment, or (c) inadequate representation by counsel.

An example of a more detailed local judicial memorandum but one which is far more rare is a Memorandum that is undated but that was transmitted in December, 1975 to all attorneys practicing law within the 34th, 65th, and 205th Judicial Districts of Texas and signed by three judges who presided over those three respective districts: Hon. Jerry Woodard, Hon. Edward S. Marquez, and Hon. Sam W. Callan.[80] These judges, whose courts are located in El Paso, Texas, drafted this Memorandum for the purpose of terminating plea bargaining in those judicial districts on a trial basis. They notified the readers that they would "not henceforth be bound in imposing sentences by the plea bargaining recommendations of the District Attorney's Office" but would "assess such punishment in cases as we feel just and proper."[81] Attached to that Memorandum was a synopsis of the "point system" on which they proposed to predicate their sentences, which in turn has been summarized within chapter 7.

In the spring of 1976, these judges circulated among members of the local bar a second Memorandum, this time signed only by Judges Woodard and Callan, in which they reemphasized, quoting from their December, 1975 Memorandum, that they would *not* be "going to judge cases arithmetically" under their "point system."[82] In this second Memorandum, the judges insisted that they "will not be controlled by the (point) system but will use it as a guide."[83] They said the point system "is mainly for the benefit of attorneys so that they can advise their clients and not unintentionally mislead them."[84] The judges concluded that any "factor" not covered in the "point system may be submitted to us by any lawyer at the sentence hearing and we will certainly consider the factor as it is set out in the letter (of December, 1975): 'Each case stands on its own merits.' "[85]

The second Memorandum might appear to raise the inference that the judges would be conducting plea bargaining themselves. Indeed, the first Memorandum must have caused the local bar to surmise that these judges wanted counsel to negotiate with the judges' clerks, since in the *second* Memorandum the judges addressed this issue and, in denying it, contended that "it never occurred to us that anyone would think we were setting up some kind of negotiators for us. *There is not going to be any kind of negotiations of criminal cases in the 34th and 205th District Courts.*" (Emphasis in original.)[86] However, in their *second* Memorandum these judges observed that "[t]here seems to be a great deal of misunderstanding" over their *first* Memorandum[87], which of course is an inherent danger behind written judicial policy directives into areas such as pleading and sentencing.

The Impact of Local Prosecutors. To the extent that local prosecutors execute written policies relating to pleading or sentencing practices, they do so reluctantly and seldom except when they feel it is absolutely necessary to do so. What is more, many local prosecutors try not to publicize these written policies outside their office staff, although to be sure members of the defense bar who practice regularly within a single judicial unit are likely to become cognizant of these policies within a short time. Because such written policies are not made available routinely to defendants, however, the names of prosecutors and the judicial units which they serve will not be mentioned here in connection with any specific written policies by prosecutors. Instead, these policies will be summarized, and to give credence and demonstrate geographic impact, if any, specific policies will be identified only according to the state in which is located the judicial unit to which they pertain.

In a 1974 memorandum issued to his staff by a prosecutor in the state of New York, issues relating to reduction both in the number of separate charges and in the seriousness of those charges are addressed. As to defendants who are charged with multiple counts, this memorandum requires that they plead guilty to one count for each separate criminal transaction involved. However, the memorandum provides for four exceptions to this rule, as follows:

(a) Ordinarily defendants charged with street sales of drugs are not arrested unless there have been more than one street sale. A plea to one transaction on a drug indictment is in order, even though two or three street level sales are alleged.

(b) When defendants are charged with a series of frauds involving no personal injury and involving a common plan or scheme—in an indictment with a handful of counts—it will not be necessary for the defendant to plead to each separate transaction. However, if the scheme includes a very large number of transactions, and the indictment contains a multitude of counts, ordinarily pleas to multiple counts will be required to emphasize to the Court (and, ultimately, to the State Division of Parole and to future prosecutors if the defendant is again arrested) that the crime did not merely involve a single larcenous act.

(c) If the crime involves several victims at the same place and same time (e.g., the holdup of both a bar and the group of patrons in the bar at the time), a plea to a single count will be adequate. In such cases, however, . . . the aggravating factor—the number of victims, each endangered—ordinarily will result in our insistence upon a plea to the top count of the indictment and not to any reduced charge whatsoever.

(d) If the defendant has pleaded to two or more felonies before he is imprisoned on any of them, and is thereby likely to have his punishment limited by (law), then steps can be taken to cover remaining indictments. In such instances our insistence on further pleas would only result in trials in which defendants had nothing to lose as no further penalties could be imposed. In such cases, however, if there are strings of felonies, . . . the defendant should be compelled to plead to top counts of each transaction to which a guilty plea is taken.

As to the seriousness of individual charges pending against defendants, this New York prosecutor's memorandum authorizes his assistants to routinely reduce charges by one class except when the reduction will be from a felony to a misdemeanor. The memorandum stresses that the reduction is from the top "nonpuffed" count in the opinion of the assistant. Felonies will be reduced to misdemeanors only when "the gravity of the cases will not require that they be treated as felonies." Reductions of more than one class of felony will not be permitted unless the defendant consents to a *prepleading investigation,* and then only if such an outcome is justified by the investigation report. A prepleading investigation is the same as a presentence investigation except that it is conducted prior to the plea instead of between the time of pleading and sentencing.

Certain types of serious offenses will preclude any plea concessions as a rule under the terms of this New York prosecutor's seventeen page memorandum. Such offenses include kidnapping for ransom or the taking of hostages in which the victim is killed, multiple killings, murder for hire, murder when the defendant has previously been convicted of a homicide, or murder of an on-duty police officer or prison guard, any public official, or any witness. These offenses require consent of the prosecutor's homicide bureau chief before any concessions can be authorized. In addition, when a defendant who has been accused of heroin, opium or cocaine sale for profit is a *nonuser,* no lesser plea will be acceptable under the terms of this memorandum without the consent of the assistant prosecutor in charge of narcotics prosecutions. Finally, appropriate heads of bureaus within the prosecutor's office must consent to reduced pleas involving indictments for racketeering, official misconduct by public servants, unlicensed possession of a weapon, in all *multiple* robbery, rape, burglary, arson, or assault cases, and in any single robbery or rape case where the offender and the victim were strangers and the victim was injured seriously.

The New York memorandum urges assistant prosecutors not to "tempt" defendants into withdrawing arguably valid dismissal motions by offering "uniquely attractive" plea bargains that are conditioned upon the defendant's withdrawal of the motion, particularly when the defendant "acts soundly in the belief that there is no viable case against him."

In 1976, a prosecutor for a populous California judicial unit prepared a 165 page General Directive for his staff that constituted a revision of an even larger Department Operations Manual. Within this General Directive are numerous "Special Directives" to be followed by assistant prosecutors in the handling of capital charges, narcotics and obscenity-pornography offenses, felony sex crimes and "organized" crimes. Not all segments of this General Directive pertain to policies or practices of pleading or sentencing although a substantial proportion do.

The California prosecutor's General Directive is similar in many respects to the New York prosecutor's memorandum to his staff, but unlike the New York memorandum the California Directive goes into detail about selection of charges ab initio. As one example, several pages are devoted to a discussion of "felony-misdemeanor alternatives," which delineate the primary factors to be considered in determining the appropriateness of a felony sentence. Four main factors are proposed: (a) the defendant's prior record, (b) the severity of the crime, (c) the defendant's probability of continued criminal conduct, and (d) the defendant's eligibility for probation. The Directive is especially explicit in demonstrating how to evaluate the severity of a crime, in consideration of eight factors: (1) use of a deadly weapon to attempt injury; (2) causation of injuries to the victim, including even temporary injuries that are incapacitating; (3) possession of a loaded firearm during commission of the crime; (4) battery on a police officer resulting in more than minor injury; (5) property damage or loss in excess of $1,000; (6) commission or attempted commission of a residential burglary; (7) possession of controlled substances in quantities larger than ordinarily used for personal consumption; and (8) in the case of a stolen motor vehicle, its lack of recovery in the same condition as it was at time of theft, without alteration of identification features. If one or more of these factors is present in a given case, a misdemeanor plea is unauthorized by the Directive.

A large section of the California prosecutor's General Directive is entitled "Prosecutorial Alternatives," within which are discussed proper distinguished from improper bases for exercise of a prosecutor's discretion not to charge a suspect with a crime. After a review of state caselaw in point, the Directive itemizes eight proper bases for exercising discretion not to charge, including: (1) application of criminal sanctions to the suspect's conduct would be contrary to the legislative intent behind the statute; (2) the statute in question is antiquated; (3) the victim requests no prosecution and the crime did not involve violence resulting in injury; (4) leniency should *be offered* to a prospective witness in order to prosecute someone else, when the testimony is essential and the gravity of the witnesses conduct warrants leniency; (5) the violation is *de minimis;* (6) the accused is confined presently on other charges, and the new offense would not merit additional punishment; (7) the accused is facing criminal prosecution on other charges, and conviction on the new offense would not merit additional punishment; and (8) the cost of locating or transporting prosecution witnesses is highly disproportionate to the importance of prosecuting the accused.

The Directive asserts that it is improper to decline to bring a criminal charge solely because: (1) the offender has made restitution to the victim; (2) extradition would be necessary to obtain jurisdiction over the accused; (3) the victim is a relative of the offender; (4) the statute is unpopular; (5) the victim's cooperation cannot be assured throughout the prosecution; (6) prosecution would have a severe impact on the accused or his family; or (7) the complainant possesses personal motives for seeking prosecution.

The Directive outlines the conditions under which a prosecutor may accept "voluntary compliance" by the accused offender as an alternative to filing criminal charges or a civil complaint in consumer fraud, environmental law, public nuisance, and business license violation cases. For example, the Directive provides that an offense for which voluntary compliance is appropriate must not have been deliberate, part of a conspiracy, or done repeatedly; the victim(s), if any, must have received full restitution; and the prosecutor should be reasonably satisfied that the offense will not be repeated.

In addition to the New York and California policies that have been written by prosecutors, a Texas prosecutor has indicated in writing to his staff that certain crimes (murder, involuntary manslaughter while intoxicated, armed robbery, and burglary of a private residence or business) should result in imprisonment of the offender upon conviction, and that assistant prosecutors are not authorized to recommend probation in these cases without specific authorization by the first assistant district attorney. Moreover, assistant prosecutors in this Texas district are not authorized to recommend or to agree to the dismissal of any pending charge in return for the defendant's stipulation for probation revocation. Bottom-level prosecutors with less than six months experience must have all recommendations approved either by a first assistant district attorney or a trial team chief.

This Texas prosecutor has cautioned his assistants in writing that no plea or sentence recommendation is authorized until a "rap sheet" has been placed in the defendant's case file and evaluated. Moreover, any such recommendation must be written inside that case file prior to the first pretrial conference. These basic policies were drafted in a six page 1973 memorandum and then redrafted with slight modification in a seven page 1975 memorandum.

A former Florida prosecutor issued a Policy Directive to his staff in 1961 requiring that in all cases where they agree to accept a guilty plea to a lesser offense than charged in an indictment or to fewer counts than charged, they should discuss this matter in advance with the arresting officers and obtain their approval. In a 1969 Policy Directive by this same prosecutor, his staff is warned that it is "absolutely essential" for the victim of a crime to be advised prior to the disposition of a case that does not involve a trial as to the terms thereof. In 1974, this prosecutor issued another Policy Directive forbidding assistants from agreeing to probation in any homicide case or in any case that involves a serious crime without his personal approval. In a 1975 Policy Directive, this prosecutor announced to his staff that since the crime of breaking and entering into a dwelling has occurred with increasing frequency, and since a prison sentence of ten years is permitted by law to be imposed against offenders convicted of this crime in Florida, that assistant prosecutors may not negotiate a prison sentence of less than five years in the state prison for this offense without prior approval of the prosecutor, his administrative assistant, or his executive assistant.

Unwritten Policies on Pleading or Sentencing

Written pleading and sentencing policies are not easily obtained from judicial or prosecutorial officers unless they have been incorporated into the law by statute or appellate court decision. However, once obtained, the written policies are easily analyzed. Of course, this does not mean that even the written policies are followed by those who have drafted them or by those for whose benefit they have been drafted. The same is true about *unwritten* pleading and sentencing policies, but to a much greater extent. Unwritten policies, by their very nature, have not been incorporated into the statutory or case law. They exist literally from hand to mouth. The accuracy of unwritten policies diminishes as their text becomes contorted when spoken by one person to another. Unwritten pleading and sentencing policies are a living testament to the dangers posed by hearsay evidence. To the extent that unwritten policies do exist, they appear to be obeyed even less often than are written policies on pleading and sentencing. For this reason alone, an extensive commentary on the fabric of unwritten policies would be highly speculative if not altogether futile.

Many lawyers tend to confuse pleading and sentencing *practices* with policies. For instance, some judges are believed to impose more severe sentences, *ceteris paribus,* on similarly situated offenders than do other judges. Some judges more than others are believed to favor probation as a viable alternative to incarceration. Some judges are viewed as being likely to look more kindly upon certain classes of offenders, and for this reason are favored over other judges to the extent that "bench shopping" is permissible or at least possible within a given judicial unit. While it may be the *practice* of any given judge to react negatively toward certain crimes, selected offenders, or other information that is made available to the court before, during, or after pleading or sentencing, a judge remains free to alter his traditional posture from one moment to the next in the exercise of his discretion. A practice, unlike a policy and especially unlike a written policy, can be changed sporadically with little risk of the change being construed successfully as arbitrary or capricious.

In addition to judges, prosecutors and their assistants are prone to give the onlooker an impression, over time, about their individual reactions to various crimes, offender types, pleading or sentencing alternatives, and the like. Once again, as in the situation with judges, the *practice* of a prosecutor can be amended from case to case without the appearance of overt discrimination. A policy, once established by a prosecutor and particularly once published in writing even internally within the office, is more difficult to amend or to ignore on a case-by-case basis without generating at least the appearance if not the reality of selective law enforcement.

Notes

1. 332 U.S. 708 (1948).
2. Id., at 709-710.
3. These rights, secured under the Fifth and Sixth Amendments, require a voluntary-intelligent waiver as a condition-precedent to any plea (guilty or no contest) that will result in a conviction. See Boykin v. Alabama, 395 U.S. 238 (1969).
4. 368 U.S. 487 (1962).
5. Id., at 489.
6. 373 U.S. 59 (1963).
7. 397 U.S. 742 (1970).
8. 397 U.S. 790 (1970).
9. 397 U.S. 759 (1970).
10. 404 U.S. 257 (1971).
11. 404 U.S. 257, 98 S.C. 2610 (1978).
12. 395 U.S. 238.
13. Id.
14. Id., at 247.
15. 394 U.S. 459 (1969).
16. Id., at 465.
17. There is some conflict in the federal circuits on a few of these issues,

particularly on varying parole consequences of a guilty plea. The major trends are clear, however, and trial judges are generally not required to inform pleading defendants of potential consequences such as deportation [United States v. Santelises, 509 F.2d 703 (2d Cir. (1975)] or that the current sentence may be imposed to run consecutively to one already being served [Wall v. United States, 500 F2d 38 (10th Cir. 1974), cert. den. 419 U.S. 1025 (1974)] .

18. See State v. Sullivan, 482 p.2d 861 (Ariz. 1971).

19. 274 U.S. 220.

20. Id., at 224.

21. 411 U.S. 954.

22. Delaware and Alaska have adopted Rule 32(d) in toto, and Arizona, Kansas, Maryland, Missouri, Virginia and Vermont have done so in part.

23. See People v. Granello, 222 N.E.2d 393 (N.Y. 1966) and Commonwealth ex rel. West v. Rundle, 237 A.2d 196 (Pa. 1968). The Second Circuit has held that the constitution requires that the record show the existence of a factual basis for a plea leading to conviction. United States ex rel. Dunn v. Casscles, 494 F.2d 397 (1974).

24. See People v. Carlisle, 195 N.W.2d 851 (Mich. 1972). In Texas, the high court recommended that following a guilty plea the defendant confess all elements of his crime before the court. Drain v. State, 465 S.W.2d 939 (Tex. 1971).

25. Some of these western states seem to favor an indirect examination of the record rather than a direct allocution with the defendant personally and in open court. On balance, the direct allocution would seem preferable, since a record can become stale over time.

26. See State v. Durham, 498 P.2d 149 (Ariz. 1972) and Widener v. State, 499 P.2d 1123 (Kas. 1972).

27. People v. Alverez, 508 P.2d 1267 (Colo. 1973).

28. State v. Sullivan, 482 P.2d 861 (Ariz. 1971) and State v. Leger, 208 N.W.2d 276 (Neb. 1973).

29. State v. Irving, 217 N.W.2d 197 (Minn. 1974).

30. See, inter alia, People v. Rowell, 296 N.E.2d 353 (Ill. 1973). This represents the posture of the American Bar Association. ABA Standards, Pleas of Guilty 33 (1968).

31. See supra, Note 22.

32. The American Bar Association has enumerated five examples of manifest injustice: the defendant (1) did not receive effective assistance of counsel; (2) did not enter, ratify or authorize the plea; (3) pleaded involuntarily or without knowledge of the charge(s), or that the sentence actually imposed could be imposed; (4) did not receive the charge or sentence concessions contemplated by agreement; or (5) did not affirm the plea after being advised by the court that it did not concur in the agreement. ABA Standards, Pleas of Guilty 10 (1968).

33. Pierce v. State, 394 P.2d 241 (Okla. 1964).

34. State ex rel. Clancy v. Coiner, 179 S.E.2d 726, 733 (W. Va. 1971).

35. Id.

36. See, inter alia, People v. Singh, 319 P.2d 697 (Cal. 1957); State v. Krug, 192 N.W.2d 163 (Neb. 1971); and Reiff v. State, 164 N.W. 2d 249 (Wis. 1969).

37. See, inter alia, Tyler v. State, 476 S.W.2d 611 (Mo. 1972); People v. Romano, 31 N.Y.2d 980, – N.E.2d – (1973); and Kent v. Cupp, 492 P.2d 507 (Ore. 1972).

38. Code of Alabama, Title 15, section 263. The provision cannot be waived. Report of the Attorney General, October-December, 1939, p. 332. The provision is mandatory and must be complied with strictly. Patrick v. State, 43 Ala. App. 620, 197 So. 2d 782 (1967).

39. Ga. Code Ann. 27-1404. See Hamm v. State, 179 S.E.2d 272, 274 (1970) and Burkett v. State, 205 S.E.2d 496 (Ga. 1974).

40. See, inter alia, Rule 25.3(a), Arkansas R. Cr. P.; Rule 21(g)(1), New Mexico R. Cr. P.; North Carolina Cr. P. Act, sec. 15-A-1021(a); Rule 11(d)(1), North Dakota R. Cr. P.; and Rule 319(b)(1), Pennsylvania R. Cr. P. In addition, see Shavie v. State, 182 N.W.2d 505 (Wis. 1971), and Rule 402, Illinois S. Ct. R. (discretionary).

41. 395 U.S. 238.

42. See, inter alia, Rule 11A, Maine R. Cr. P.; Rule 4, Massachusetts R. Cr. P.; North Carolina Cr. P. Act, sec. 15-A-1022; Rule 21(e), New Mexico R. Cr. P.; Rule 11(B), Ohio R. Cr. P. These rules replicate Federal Rule 11(c). The following rules substantially replicate Federal Rule 11(c): Rule 15.01, Minnesota R. Cr. P.; Rule 319(a), Pennsylvania R. Cr. P.; and Rule 3A:15, Virginia Cr. P. Rule. In addition to these statutes, courts in other states have adopted Rule 11(c) in effect, as follows: Rule 11, Delaware Super. Ct. Rules; Rule 11, District of Columbia Super. Ct. Cr. Div. Rules; Rule 402(a), Illinois S. Ct. Rules; Rule 11, Rhode Island Cr. P. Rules–Super. Ct.; State v. Sisco, 169 N.W.2d 542 (Iowa, 1969) and Britain v. State, 497 P.2d 543 (Wyo. 1972).

43. Montana C. Cr. P., sec. 95-1606(b).

44. See, inter alia, James v. State, 219 A.2d 17 (Md. 1966).

45. See, inter alia, Rule 17.4(a), Arizona R. Cr. P.; Rule 21(g)(2), New Mexico R. Cr. P.; and Criminal Rule 4.2(g), Washington Super. Ct. Rules.

46. West Virginia Code, sec. 62-3-1a.

47. Rule 15, 03(2), Minnesota R. Cr. P.

48. See inter alia, Utah C. Cr. P., sec. 77-24-2.

49. See, inter alia, Arkansas R. Cr. P., Rule 24.3(a); California Penal Code, sec. 1018; Rule 11(a), Ohio R. Cr. P.

50. See, inter alia, Code of Alabama, Tit. 15, sec. 288(10).

51. 397 U.S. 742, 751-753.

52. 3 Cal.3rd 595, 604.

53. Younger, Memorandum at 3.

54. Id.
55. Id.
56. Id.
57. Id., at 3-4.
58. Id., at 4.
59. Id., at 4-5.
60. 3 Cal. 3rd 595, 604-605.
61. Younger, Memorandum at 5.
62. Id., at 7.
63. Id.
64. Id., at 10.
65. Alaska Bar Association, Memorandum at 4.
66. Id., at 1.
67. Id., at 2.
68. Id.
69. Id.
70. Id.
71. Id., at 2-3.
72. Id., at 3.
73. Id.
74. Id.
75. Id., at 4.
76. Chief Deputy District Attorney, Delaware County, Pennsylvania.
77. Crane, Memorandum at 13.
78. Id., at 14.
79. People v. Francis, 38 N.Y.2d 150 (1976).
80. Actual signatures were in alphabetical order.
81. Woodard, Marquez, Callan Memorandum at 2.
82. Callan and Woodard Memorandum at 2.
83. Id.
84. Id.
85. Id.
86. Id.
87. Id., at 1.

9 Truth in Pleading: The Need for a Written Guilty Plea Agreement

It has become fashionable over the past decade for Congress and most state legislatures to establish minimum standards for the contents of enforceable installment loan agreements, known as "truth in lending" legislation. As a result, the maker (borrower) of an installment note must be given a copy of the agreement that he signs at the time he signs the note. Normally, an installment loan agreement must contain a full disclosure of the actual interest which the borrower will be expected to pay to the lender over the life of the loan, as well as the amount of each monthly payment consisting of interest, principal reduction, and other fees, if any, such as insurance premiums. Courts have held that lenders cannot enforce "confession of judgment" clauses against individual borrowers, finding that these provisions are unconscionable and thereby void as being contrary to public policy. Indeed, courts have held that a "warrant of attorney" or a "confession of judgment" clause must be printed conspicuously on the face of an installment loan agreement in order for it to be enforceable against even a commercial (business) borrower. The Uniform Commercial Code has incorporated many of these and other requirements, varying slightly from state to state, in an effort to protect the naive consumer.

If one looks closely at the ordinary guilty plea arrangement, it should be obvious that a defendant who is about to plead guilty to a criminal offense is situated very similarly to a consumer who wants to borrow money. The defendant needs, or at least feels that he needs, an opportunity to avoid going to trial. In return, he is likely to expect that he will be compensated for saving the state the effort and the expense of a trial. However, many defendants do not seem to realize fully the rights they are waiving by pleading guilty. Most appear not to realize the advantages of their going to trial. Most appear to expect either a greater concession or a different kind of a concession for avoiding trial than they will in fact receive from the court. Many prosecutors tend to be equally unaware of the significance of some guilty pleas to the administration of justice, particularly when the offender has a history of serious criminal activity which would be likely to be aired at trial but hidden during the guilty plea process.

The defendant who contemplates pleading guilty to a criminal charge should be cognizant at the time of pleading as to what the actual cost of his plea will be to himself in terms of the direct and indirect punishments that will be imposed. A defendant should unmistakably know and understand the limits of these punishments. For instance, what is the maximum fine that may be imposed? What is the maximum length of time to which the defendant may be sentenced to serve in prison? To what prison, or to what kind of a prison, will he be committed? Will he lose his right to vote and to hold public office? If so, for how long, and what will he have to do in order to have these franchise rights restored? If he is to be sentenced to a term of imprisonment for the duration of his natural life, will his spouse acquire an absolute right to divorce him? Will a long prison sentence terminate his rights to inherit the property of close relatives, particularly through intestacy (the succession of property by operation of law when a decedent has not executed a valid will)? Can his children be adopted, or can their surnames be changed without his consent following his imprisonment and divorce from his spouse? The answers to these and other vital questions may prompt a defendant to reconsider a plea of guilty.

The major problem relating to guilty plea agreements is not that false promises are made or that specific promises once made are broken, as was the situation in the case of Santobello v. New York (1972) where the United States Supreme Court said:

> (T)he adjudicative element inherent in accepting a plea of guilty . . . must be attended by safeguards to insure the defendant what is reasonably due in the circumstances. Those circumstances will vary, but a constant factor is that when a plea rests in any significant degree on a promise or agreement of the prosecutor, so that it can be said to be part of the inducement or consideration, such promise must be fulfilled.[1]

Instead, the more common difficulty surrounds the nebulousness of guilty plea agreements. Were any promises made by the prosecutor? Even if not, did the defendant reasonably believe that any promises were made? Ultimately, the question is whether the defendant duped himself just as often as whether he was duped by the prosecution. *Santobello* protects the defendant to whom a promise was made but later broken. It is mute on the matter of what happens when a defendant possesses the mistaken belief that a promise has been made when in fact no promise was made or a promise of a different sort was made.

Most defendants who have been charged with committing a crime do not just march right into the courtroom and then plead guilty "on the nose" to the charges the next day at their first (initial) appearance before a magistrate, even if this were possible and it is not in some states.[2] As a rule, a time lapse of between six weeks and six months intervenes between time of arrest and entry of a guilty plea, and in some jurisdictions the plea will not be tendered for at least a year after arrest as a rule when charges are serious. During the time interval between arrest and plea, defense counsel and assistant prosecutors communicate before, during, and after various pretrial hearings[3] in person and, periodically, by telephone. The frequency and the intensity of these communications are likely to accelerate as time goes by following arrest and the moment for a plea draws near. As the point approaches when these negotiations begin to reach fruition, a judge may be invited to participate[4] by offering his "off-the-record" and out-of-court opinion as to the sufficiency of the consideration (trade-offs given by each side to the other) that will support an evolving agreement.

Framing the Guilty Plea Agreement

An agreement arises ordinarily out of an offer by one party, an acceptance by another, supported by sufficient consideration which constitutes the underlying value behind the exchange. A guilty plea agreement is created normally in the same fashion as any other understanding between two or more parties, and it may become a contract depending upon the nature and the extent of the legal obligation(s), if any, incurred by each party to the agreement. Sometimes, guilty plea agreements require the fulfillment of conditions, and in turn these conditions may be expressed, implied in fact (circumstantially necessary, even if unrecited) or implied in law (legally necessary, even if unrecited). As in any agreement, conditions may be *precedent* (the condition must be fulfilled first before the agreement can become binding), *subsequent* (the condition is intended to be fulfilled only after the agreement has become binding, but failure of the condition in the future may be grounds for the agreement to lose its binding effect), or *concurrent* (two or more conditions, each dependent upon the other, intended to be fulfilled before or contemporaneously with when the agreement becomes binding; also known as "mutual conditions-precedent"). Any type of condition may be breached (unfulfilled on time or at all), and if a condition is material (significant) to an agreement, its breach may nullify and void the agreement, in toto or in part.

Under any agreement, the obligations of at least one party thereto may become discharged (excused without penalty) on account of the inexcusable failure to fulfill the underlying conditions or other consideration. The purpose of a guilty plea agreement may become "frustrated" when a goal or an objective envisioned by at least one of the parties ceases to exist or to be worthwhile. A guilty plea agreement may become impossible to perform, due, for instance, to a change in the law or a change in the facts beyond the control of the parties themselves which will preclude performance under the terms of the agreement. Some agreements become dishonored intentionally by the repudiation of one of the parties. When any agreement, including one for a guilty plea, becomes breached or appears likely to be breached (anticipatory breach), at least one party is fairly certain to demand rescission of the agreement (restoration of the parties to their respective positions, the "status quo ante") prior to the time when they made the agreement. Frequently, the other party will request a court to enforce the terms of the agreement by granting specific performance.

A major difficulty with guilty plea agreements lies in defining and verifying the terms to which the parties reached an agreement. Since human beings are known to be liars in commerce, domestic relations, and in other activities of life,[5] a prudent person who enters an agreement which he feels he may want to enforce later in the courts will cause the agreement to be reduced to writing and memorialized. Indeed, to be enforceable, certain agreements must be written by law. These include contracts for the conveyance of real estate, most installment loan contracts calling for the repayment of money over a period of time, and contracts for the purchase and sale of movable goods under the Uniform Commercial Code.[6] Very few states require that guilty plea agreements be written, and therein appears to lie the major difficulty with many guilty pleas. Because guilty plea agreements involve so many contractual elements, a more detailed analysis is needed to interpolate the problems associated with each element.

Offers and Acceptances

The term *offer* is used more ambiguously during the process of guilty plea negotiations than during commercial transactions. An observer of plea discussions is likely to hear a prosecutor, a defense counsel, or both "offer" to bargain, to provide consideration for a bargain, or to indicate under what circumstances, if any, the other side's "offers" to bargain or to provide consideration might be acceptable. At what point is a formal offer made? Quite clearly, these informal proposals constitute mere preliminary inquiries, the objective of which is to enable each side (1) to ascertain the future intentions of the other; (2) to obtain from the other side a price quotation[7] indicating the quality and quantity of consideration required to construct any future agreement; and (3) to clarify the protocol for developing both the procedural and the substantive content and form for a future agreement. Until these antecedent events have transpired, it is rare for either party to suggest to the other the terms of a formal guilty plea agreement.

Either the prosecutor or the defendant may communicate to the other the terms of a guilty plea agreement, but only through defense counsel if the defendant is represented by counsel.[8] Whichever side drafts the agreement, the subject matter may be understood by the parties verbally or be reduced to writing. A verbal understanding is the most common, except in a few states where by statute guilty plea agreements must be written to be valid.

The distinction between offeror and offeree, while artificial perhaps in any context, seems less significant in relation to the guilty plea agreement than in the context of commercial transactions contemplating an exchange of real or personal property. Here, this distinction is inconsequential, more or less, because of the interface of two factors: (1) the "promise" by a defendant to plead guilty is worthless virtually and without juristic effect unless and until the defendant actually tenders the plea; and (2) in most jurisdictions a guilty plea must be tendered by the defendant personally and in open court. A defendant's out-of-court "promise," especially a verbal one, to plead guilty to a criminal charge might be an executory agreement or understanding but it cannot reach the status of an executory contract because it is not binding upon the defendant and it cannot be enforced against him. In the absence of a record to document that the defendant knowingly and intelligently waived his constitutional right to trial plus companion rights, a defendant has not assumed any legal obligation to go forward with a contemplated guilty plea, and indeed he may repudiate a "promise" to do so at will and without penalty prior to actually tendering the plea itself. The defendant's performance alone in the form of his tender of the plea constitutes the *minimum* conduct[9] necessary to transform a guilty plea agreement into a contract containing binding legal obligations on both parties. For this reason, the ordinary guilty plea agreement becomes a unilateral rather than a bilateral contract if and when it becomes a contract at all.

In those states where by statute guilty plea agreements must be executed in writing by the parties (as well as in an increasing number of judicial units within other states where this practice is encouraged by custom or rule), this agreement although memorialized in words rather than speech should not be regarded as evidence of the defendant's "promise" to plead guilty, either. The document may serve as the defendant's actual guilty plea itself when properly executed, acknowledged and delivered to the court for filing. In most states, the defendant who has executed a written plea agreement must appear in open court nevertheless to tender a personal recognizance of the written document.[10] In a few states, however, at least those individuals who are charged only with a misdemeanor may elect to execute a written petition to plead guilty or *nolo contendere* and cause this to be submitted to the court by defense counsel as an alternative to personally appearing before the court.[11] Since even under this procedure the defendant's *own* counsel transmits the petition to the court, presumably the petition may be withdrawn at the defendant's option prior to delivery of the instrument by counsel to the court simply by the defendant's communication to his attorney of an intent to repudiate. The mere fact that a guilty plea petition exists in writing should not disguise its purpose, which is to facilitate the defendant's constructive performance by means of substitute tender.[12]

An interesting but unlikely question may evolve from use of a written plea agreement or petition properly executed by a defendant out-of-court but delivered to the *prosecutor* rather than to defense counsel. If the instrument contained or were accompanied by a record of the defendant's knowing and voluntary waivers together with a factual basis for the plea, if required, could the prosecutor enforce the terms of the document notwithstanding the defendant's subsequent repudiation? To invest a prosecutor with such a privilege would seem to confer upon the prosecutor a warrant of attorney empowering him in effect to confess judgment against the defendant. In view of the many injustices associated with the confession of civil judgment, confession of criminal judgment should be unconscionable on its face, and in any event must be void unless the confession is accomplished pursuant to a written instrument which contained a conspicuous clause[13] at the time the instrument was executed to warn the defendant of this possible outcome. Even so, the prosecutor would not be enforcing a promise in this situation; he would become the defendant's agent for the substitute tender of the plea by means of constructive performance. Needless to say, a conflict of interest would emerge to create an ethical dilemma.[14]

Having reasoned that a guilty plea agreement must result in a unilateral contract if and when it becomes a contract at all, the task may remain for the order of the defendant's performance to be charted in relation to the communication of the prosecutor's correlate promises, if any, although this task approximates surplusage. In a normal unilateral contract, the offeree's performance is tendered in response to a previous communication of the offeror's promises. This order is followed in by far the majority of guilty plea agreements across the nation. Once in a while a defendant may tender a guilty plea which is conditioned upon proposed conduct by the prosecutor to which the latter has not consented previously. If at the time of tender the prosecutor does agree (or may be deemed to agree) to become bound by conditions on which the guilty plea has been tendered by a defendant, then such a sequence might be interpreted as creating a reverse unilateral contract,[15] since the performance precedes communication of the promise(s). Note, however, that if the defendant tenders an *unconditional* guilty plea in consideration of which no promises by the prosecutor are expressed or implied in fact or in law, then no contract exists at all between the defendant and the prosecutor.

One final point should be made concerning the discretion of the judge before whom a guilty plea is tendered to "accept" or "reject" the plea and/or the conditions on which a plea may be premised. This unfortunate and inaccurate use of contractual language may be confusing and misleading, especially to the layman. Only on rare occasions does the court become a principal party to a guilty plea agreement, and therefore the ordinary guilty plea agreement requires judicial *ratification* rather than acceptance or rejection. Normally, the court should be viewed as a third party upon whose satisfaction the defendant's plea, the prosecutor's promises, and ultimately the entire agreement all may be conditioned.

Consideration

The consideration or value which binds the obligations of the parties to a guilty plea agreement varies among different agreements. Separate consideration passes from each party to the other during the birth of any contract. Consideration supplied by a prosecutor to induce a defendant to plead guilty to a criminal charge may be more tangible than consideration provided by the defendant to the prosecutor. Nevertheless, consideration flows from each party to the other, and should be discussed separately in specific relation to its source.

Consideration From Prosecutor to Defendant. It is common for a prosecutor to supply one or more of at least four varieties of consideration, alone or in combination, to a defendant who is contemplating the tender of a guilty plea. These varieties include: (a) horizontal charge reduction; (b) vertical charge reduction; (c) sentence recommendation; and (d) forbearance of other action.

Horizontal Charge Reduction. In most jurisdictions, judges are unwilling (and sometimes unable) to impose consecutive sentences against a defendant except under unusual circumstances; and seldom are consecutive sentences imposed for more than two or at most three separate offenses, even if an offender has committed numerous different criminal transactions (episodes). Thus, if a defendant has been charged with a multitude of separate offenses (or separate counts of the same substantive offense), to prosecute such a defendant for more than a fraction of these charges would be meaningless in terms of sentence. For this reason, a prosecutor who is confronted with a choice between a trial or a negotiated disposition for a defendant against whom multiple charges are pending may opt for dismissing most of the charges in exchange for the defendant's plea of guilty to one or two charges. This variety of consideration flowing from prosecutor to defendant may be labelled a "horizontal charge reduction," since the quantity (number) of separate charges rather than the quality (seriousness) of any given charge constitutes the value of the concession.

Ideally, a prosecutor would prefer to dismiss the less serious charge(s) pending against a defendant in exchange for the latter's guilty plea to the more serious charge(s). In practice, however, a defendant who has been charged with numerous crimes is likely to be permitted to plead guilty to charges other than the least or the most serious. An application of the statistical principle of regression toward the mean is noticed in this context. Some prosecutors will attempt at least to require the defendant whose charges have arisen out of different criminal transactions to plead guilty to crimes resulting from at least two separate transactions. The blunt truth is that once an offender has committed a serious crime he might as well commit as many more as he encounters the opportunity to commit before being apprehended, since ultimately most of these crimes will be dismissed in consideration of his eventual guilty plea to one or two companion crimes.

Horizontal charge reduction may be preceded by horizontal overcharging as an impetus to start the guilty plea negotiation process rolling. A defendant who has been charged with five felonies may be more willing to plead guilty to at least one felony than another defendant who has been charged with only a single felony to begin with. During the course of the author's field visits, considerably less horizontal overcharging was identified than had been expected. By far the plurality of charges dismissed in most jurisdictions appeared to be legally sufficient, although to be sure the trial sufficiency of any criminal case may be in doubt until a verdict is handed down following a trial.

Vertical Charge Reduction. In addition to or instead of horizontal charge reduction, many defendants opt for an opportunity to plead guilty to an offense which is less serious than the offenses with which they have been charged. This is true particularly of defendants against whom very few charges have been filed or remain outstanding. It is true of nearly all defendants who have been charged with a criminal offense for the first time in their lives, especially if the charge is a felony. This variety of consideration flowing from prosecutor to defendant may be labelled a vertical rather than a horizontal charge reduction, since the quality (seriousness) of the individual charge(s) instead of the quantity (number) of separate charges constitutes the value of the concession.

The most significant vertical reduction is from a felony to a misdemeanor charge. Most prosecutors will not permit this to happen by negotiation unless the original felony was of a low grade or unless evidence supporting a higher grade of felony was or has become weak. The ABA standards[16] recommend that in a situation where the seriousness of a charge is reduced the lesser offense should bear some relationship to the greater offense. The most common reduction is to a lesser included offense (LIO), where the relationship is obvious. It is common for a defendant to plead guilty to a lesser but nonincluded offense or even to a nonincluded offense of virtually equal magnitude, however, for a special purpose such as to avoid the social stigma associated with a sex offense conviction.

Vertical charge reduction may be preceded by vertical overcharging, also, since a defendant who has been charged with an offense for which a sentence of life imprisonment may be imposed tends to be more eager to plead guilty to some grade of felony compared with another who has been charged with an offense for which a maximum sentence of two years in prison is possible. Jurisdictions which do abuse the charging process are likely to utilize both forms of overcharging, but the predominant form used seems to be a function of the method by which crimes are classified in the state.

Sentence Recommendation. In addition to either a horizontal or a vertical charge reduction, or both, most defendants opt for an agreement pursuant to which the prosecutor promises to make or to abstain from making a specific recommendation to the court on the matter of the defendant's sentence following a guilty plea. The failure of the prosecutor to fulfill such an agreement was the issue in *Santobello.*[17] If under the law or local custom in a jurisdiction a charge reduction fixes the sentence to the defendant's satisfaction, then a prosecutor's recommendation or lack thereof becomes immaterial. Usually, on the contrary, the sentencing judge retains discretion whether to impose an unconditional discharge, probation, or a sentence involving commitment, and whether to suspend execution thereof. Even when commitment is a certainty, the judge retains discretion to narrow or widen the potential time interval between the minimum and maximum lengths of an indeterminate sentence. In addition, the judge may exercise influence if not authority over the specific location of confinement, such as a county jail or a reformatory as opposed to the state prison.

In nearly every jurisdiction, the prosecutor is afforded an opportunity by the court to tender a sentence recommendation. Most judges across the nation admit that they will be persuaded by a prosecutor's recommendation much of the time, especially if the recommendation is favorable to the defendant. If a favorable recommendation cannot be obtained, a prosecutor's silence at the time of sentencing is preferable to a negative recommendation from a defendant's point of view, since unless aggravating circumstances surrounding commission of the crimes are communicated to a judge he is likely to impose a sentence of average severity in relation to the charges, notwithstanding that the offender's conduct may have been peculiarly reprehensible. Seldom does information contained in a presentence investigation report provide a judge with sufficient insight into an offender's character to facilitate substantive justice.

Forbearance of Other Action. In addition or instead of agreeing to a charge reduction or a sentence recommendation, a prosecutor may decide to refrain from filing additional criminal charges against a defendant in exchange for the latter's guilty plea to one or more charges already filed. Similarly, a prosecutor may agree that special allegations will not be filed against a defendant in conjunction with the charges to which the defendant pleads guilty. Special allegations, if filed, might aver that the defendant is a predicate (recidivist or habitual) felony offender for whom enhanced punishment is warranted; or that the defendant possessed or used a weapon during commission of the offenses charged. Also, a prosecutor may refrain from initiating probation or parole revocation proceedings related to previous convictions for which the defendant was on conditional release at the time when the offenses in question occurred. Less frequently, a prosecutor might agree not to file criminal charges against the defendant's friends or relatives, particularly if the other persons might otherwise be named as the defendant's accomplices or co-conspirators.

Consideration from Defendant to Prosecutor. In the ordinary course of events a prosecutor receives some value in return for a defendant's guilty plea, even if the defendant has received a substantial benefit, also. The offices of most state prosecutors throughout America operate at full or almost full trial capacity throughout the year. Regardless of what may be the level of capacity in a given jurisdiction (whether the jurisdiction is able to try one or twenty cases per week), prosecutors in most judicial units across the country at least perceive that the peak of their trial capacity has long since been reached. Accurately or not, they feel precluded from bringing to trial more than a fixed number of cases at a time. Based on this assumption, for them to bring one case to trial means that at least one other case which otherwise would have been tried must be disposed of in some other way.

In most state judicial units, prosecutors are elected to office. A prosecutor's political reputation and public image may be marred or scarred when he loses at trial, especially in high visibility cases. Evidence against some defendants is stronger than against others, and trial assistants are able to prepare some cases more completely than others. For these reasons, a common phrase recited by prosecutors is: "half a loaf is better than none." A conviction is a conviction whether obtained by a guilty plea or by a verdict after trial.

A prosecutor benefits from the caseload reduction achieved whenever a defendant pleads guilty and eliminates the need for a trial. When a conviction can be obtained against a defendant without trial, the victims of the crimes will be spared the trauma of public testimony and embarrassing cross-examination; the resources of the prosecutor's investigative staff can be concentrated on other and possibly more important cases; and the state may be spared the almost prohibitive expense of transporting witnesses to trial from distant localities. Most important, undoubtedly, is the greater certainty that conviction will be final after a guilty plea compared with after a trial. During a trial the defense counsel enjoys an unlimited opportunity to maneuver both the prosecution and the trial judge into procedural errors which, if deemed prejudicial rather than harmless on appeal, may compel a reversal of the conviction and in turn a new *trial* for the defendant.

Some authorities, primarily penologists, have theorized that an offender's progress toward rehabilitation will be inspired by his admission of guilt.[18] Whether this is true or not, a guilty plea does result in easing the conscience of the prosecutor and the general public. A defendant who is convicted of a crime following a trial has been proven guilty beyond a reasonable doubt, but the question of innocence may survive the lingering doubt, however unreasonable this may be. A defendant who pleads guilty to a crime knowingly and voluntarily cannot be totally blameless, since even if innocent of the crime(s) charged he must bear factual guilt at least for the perjured plea. In short, the guilty-pleading defendant quiets the controversy surrounding his wrongdoing.

Conditions

Most guilty plea agreements are predicated upon the fulfillment of one or more conditions. These may be conditions-precedent or conditions-subsequent, and each may be expressed in the agreement, or implied in fact or in law (constructive conditions). Different agreements contain different conditions, but a number of similarities are discernible within most guilty plea agreements from state to state, and these are worthy of individual notation.

Conditions-Precedent. Most conditions that are applicable to guilty plea agreements are conditions-precedent and as such must be fulfilled before the parties to the agreement incur binding legal obligations under an emerging contract. It may be helpful to discuss varieties of conditions-precedent separately in relation to the conduct of the parties.

Defendant's Conduct. Before any guilty plea agreement can achieve juristic effect, the defendant must waive his constitutional rights to a jury trial, to confront his accusers, to present witnesses in his own defense, to remain silent, and to be convicted by proof beyond a reasonable doubt. Although these underlying rights are procedural, the waivers thereof should be regarded as being substantive waivers, since by his forbearance a defendant relinquishes the fundamental protection afforded by our judicial process.

In addition to substantive conditions-precedent, a defendant must fulfill several procedural conditions-precedent before a guilty plea plea is tendered that his waiver of each constitutional right enumerated is done voluntarily, knowingly and intelligently, and that he understands the elements of the charges to which he is pleading as well as at least the direct consequences of the conviction which will result from a judgment based on a plea of guilty. When required by the court, a defendant is expected to supply for the record his personal account of the factual basis for the plea, and to recite for the record his age, educational level, and a synopsis of the discussions, if any, he has enjoyed in consultation with his defense attorney. Some courts will request a defendant to capitulate for the record in his own words the material terms of the agreement on which tender of the guilty plea is based. If a written instrument is required by law or custom to memorialize the guilty plea event, the defendant must execute portions of the document in his own handwriting, or at the very least subscribe his signature and acknowledge the same under oath.

Prosecutor's Conduct. In any given jurisdiction, conditions-precedent which are required of the prosecutor may be fewer in number than those required of a defendant in order to give juristic effect to a guilty plea agreement. In some states, for instance, the prosecutor must make a sentence recommendation, if one is to be made at all, before the defendant tenders the plea.[19] When a condition such as this is required by statute or rule, it is implied in law and therefore serves as a constructive condition-precedent to the emergence of any guilty plea contract providing for a sentence recommendation by the prosecutor. In states where the prosecutor's sentence recommendation does not have to be made prior to the defendant's tender of a plea, the agreement itself may require this sequence of events by its expressed terms or by implication in fact.

In most jurisdictions, the court will require the prosecutor to summarize for the record the factual basis for the guilty plea, together with the material terms of an underlying plea agreement if one exists. A number of courts demand that a prosecutor recite on the record his reasons for agreeing to either charge or sentence concessions. This sort of conduct when mandated of a prosecutor by law or custom may be viewed as a condition-precedent to the materialization of an agreement into a guilty plea contract.

An agreement is likely to contain expressed provisions detailing the specific charge concessions which a prosecutor may have agreed to permit in consideration of the defendant's guilty plea. Specifically, an agreement may call for the prosecutor to make a motion (either verbally in open court, or in a written petition to be filed with the court, depending upon local practice) to dismiss or to *nolle prosequi* one or more companion charges pending against the defendant. The order of events entails ordinarily the dismissal or *nolle* being made immediately following either the defendant's tender of a plea or the court's ratification thereof. If there is no bar to reinstatement of the charges upon failure of the defendant's plea, whether companion charges are dropped before or after tender of the plea is immaterial. A condition requiring a prosecutor to dismiss or *nolle* companion charges should not be viewed as a condition-subsequent even if the prosecutor's motion is made following defendant's tender of a plea, since no valid judgment could be entered on the plea until after fulfillment of this condition. Normally, the parties anticipate this condition to be fulfilled as coterminously with the defendant's plea tender as possible, and indeed this condition might be regarded as being concurrent with the defendant's plea tender. A concurrent condition is a condition-precedent.

Judicial Conduct. Most guilty plea agreements are conditioned upon the satisfaction of one very important third party—the judge before whom the guilty plea is tendered, who must ratify the guilty plea and the agreement before either acquires juristic effect. The condition-precedent of third party satisfaction will become the subject-matter for a more elaborate analysis in conjunction with judicial ratification.

Under the laws of many states, primarily those which have adopted Rule 11 of the Federal Rules of Criminal Procedure, the judge before whom a guilty plea is tendered must cause an allocution or "litany" of questions and answers to appear on record as a condition-precedent to announcing his satisfaction or dissatisfaction with the plea. Failure of a judge to make proper inquiry of a defendant on record in a Rule 11 jurisdiction will invalidate the guilty plea and void any judgment based thereon. In contrast, some states have held that such a ritual is not a necessary condition-precedent to judicial ratification of a guilty plea agreement.[20]

Conditions-Subsequent. In the guilty plea context, most conditions-precedent seem to relate to conduct by the defendant, while nearly all conditions-subsequent relate to conduct by the prosecutor. Now and then, a defendant may agree to cooperate with the prosecution by turning state's evidence as part of a plea agreement. However, if the defendant fails to testify as expected following the disposition of pending charges, the prosecutor retains very few, if any, weapons to enforce this aspect of the agreement. In effect, once a defendant tenders a guilty plea little more can be demanded of him notwithstanding the provisions in a guilty plea agreement. Little enough can be compelled from the prosecutor at this juncture.

The most common condition-subsequent associated with a guilty plea agreement involves a condition requiring the prosecutor to make a sentence recommendation to the court at a point in time which will occur following tender and ratification of the plea. In most jurisdictions, a sentence recommendation is made on the day when sentence is scheduled to be imposed, which in turn may be several weeks after judgment has been entered pursuant to an earlier tendered and ratified plea, to allow time for preparation of a presentence investigation report. This type of a condition-subsequent is likely to consist of a duty without a promise by the prosecutor. The duty is for the prosecutor to make the sentence recommendation as contemplated by the defendant when the agreement was struck. Without language of promise within the agreement to show that the prosecutor guaranteed a specific sentence, the prosecutor will not be held responsible for failure of the court to follow the recommendation.

A prosecutor must discharge a duty imposed by a condition-subsequent to a plea agreement, however, notwithstanding the likelihood that to do so may be futile. *Santobello* makes this clear, since there the Supreme Court vacated the sentence solely because of the prosecutor's failure to make a sentence recommendation on which the defendant had earlier relied to his detriment by tendering a guilty plea, even though the trial judge indicated that he intended to impose the maximum sentence despite any recommendation to the contrary.[21]

Judicial Ratification of the Guilty Plea

A defendant who has been charged with a criminal offense does not possess a right to have judgment entered pursuant to his tender of a guilty plea. By statute in most states, a judge before whom a guilty plea is tendered is invested with discretion to "accept" or to "reject" the plea. If the judge does "accept" the plea, he retains authority to concur or not to concur in the underlying plea agreement, if one exists. The better view is to regard the judge as a third party upon whose satisfaction the guilty plea agreement is conditioned, rather than as a principal party to the making of the agreement itself. In this way, the role of the judge becomes to ratify or not to ratify the plea as tendered together with other conditions upon which the plea may have been premised in the agreement.

The condition-precedent of third party (judicial) satisfaction is present expressly or implicitly in every guilty plea agreement. Even if not expressed, it is a constructive condition in every agreement for a guilty plea, being implied in law in every state. If the judge were simply to ratify a plea agreement as drafted at the moment the plea is tendered, the condition of judicial satisfaction would be easy to understand. While some judges do this, many do not, and judicial satisfaction which is itself a condition of a guilty plea agreement becomes imposed conditionally in turn. Once this happens as it does frequently, the resulting contractual implications become difficult to interpret and it is not hard to envision that in the ensuing confusion the misapprehension of the defendant may become phenomenal.

The judicial ratification process entails necessarily *two* phases: (1) ratification of the charges to which the plea is tendered; and (2) ratification of the sentence recommendation contemplated in the plea agreement. In most states, therefore, the judge before whom a guilty plea is tendered pursuant to an underlying agreement is empowered to choose among the following five alternatives: (a) ratify the plea to the charges as tendered and ratify the sentence recommendation as drafted in the agreement; (b) ratify the plea to the charges as tendered but ratify the sentence recommendation contemplated in the agreement conditionally or provisionally; (c) ratify the plea to the charges as tendered but refuse to ratify the sentence recommendation contemplated in the agreement; (d) ratify the plea to the charges conditionally or provisionally and delay consideration of the sentence recommendation; and (e) refuse to ratify the plea to the charges as tendered, in which instance the issue of ratifying the sentence recommendation abates. There may be other combinations or permutations of this ratification process, but these five should serve to outline the complexity and the variety of choices. Each merits separate analysis.

The Ratification Process

Ratification of the Plea as Tendered and of the Sentence Recommendation as Drafted

The easiest choice which a judge may make is to ratify the plea as tendered and thereupon to ratify also the sentence recommended in the agreement. Since this is the easiest choice, it seems to be followed by the average judge in most judicial units throughout America. A judge who exercises this choice repeatedly may be considered to have abdicated his judicial function and conferred upon the prosecutor the de facto authority to act as a surrogate jurist. In less creditable but equally accurate terminology, such a judge acts as a "rubber-stamp" and simply imprimaturs the charge and sentencing decisions made by the prosecutor. This course of action requires the least judicial time and effort and offers the most certainty to a defendant that his negotiated agreement will be ratified without alteration or even hesitation.

When both the plea to the charges as tendered and the agreement on sentence as drafted are ratified judicially, the condition of third party (judicial) satisfaction is fulfilled at the time the plea is tendered by the defendant. As long as justice was accomplished by both the negotiation of the charges and the negotiation of the sentence, there is little about which to complain. However, as a rule this ratification pattern ignores the need for a sentencing judge to review and be guided by the presentence investigation report of the defendant. While justice delayed may be justice denied, the same result may occur when justice is administered too swiftly and on a pro forma basis. For this reason, thoughtful judges who bear in mind the need to protect the community from the predatory conduct of the offender who avoids prolonged incapacitation through his capability (or that of his lawyer) for plea bargaining tend to be reluctant to follow this ratification pattern. Contractual complexity may be the result.

*Ratification of the Plea as Tendered but of the
Sentence Recommendation Conditionally or Provisionally*

As an alternative to ratifying both the plea as tendered and the sentence recommendation as drafted in the plea agreement, some judges will ratify the plea as tendered but the sentence recommendation only conditionally or provisionally. A common example is the judge who will accept a guilty plea to one count of theft (larceny) when the offender was charged originally with two counts of robbery (hence, the defendant has received both horizontal and vertical charge concessions) but who prefers to delay ratification of the prosecutor's sentence recommendation pending receipt and scrutiny of a presentence investigation report.

Ordinarily, if the judge ratifies the sentence recommendation conditionally he reserves the right to modify (increase) the sentence if the presentence investigation report reveals the defendant's criminal history to be substantially different from that represented by counsel to the court. As long as the report buttresses the representations of counsel, the defendant can expect that the sentence recommendation will be ratified eventually. On the other hand, a judge may ratify a sentence recommendation provisionally, reserving the right to alter the ratification and modify (increase) the sentence if specific events should take place between the time of the plea tender and imposition of sentence. These events may include the ability of the defendant to retain his present employment, or to be accepted into a diversion or probation program, or to make restitution to the victims of his offenses.

This ratification pattern should not impose undue hardship onto a defendant, since the conditions or the provisions are identified clearly by the court and the defendant and/or his counsel are admonished as to what action, if any, must be taken by them to ensure eventual ratification of the recommended sentence. Judges who follow this pattern of ratification tend to be concerned with rehabilitation and reintegration of the offender back into the community. This type of judge is less concerned about the charges than about the sanctions to be imposed, and solicit the cooperation of the defendant in determining the proper sanctions in an effort to achieve some measure at least of substantive justice.

Ratification of the Plea as Tendered But Refusal to Ratify the Sentence Recommendation as Drafted

Another alternative which is available to a judge before whom a guilty plea is tendered is to ratify the plea to the charges as tendered but to refuse to ratify the sentence recommendation as drafted in the plea agreement. Only a minority of judges follow this course of action routinely. However, from time to time nearly every judge may be called upon to deny the sentence recommendation which he feels has been negotiated without due regard for the protection of the community. The derivative question which emerges immediately is whether as a result of this judicial nonratification of the sentence recommendation the defendant should be permitted to withdraw tender of his plea to the charges. A second derivative question is whether the judge must or should make a revelation of the sentence which he prefers to impose prior to the moment when the defendant is called upon to withdraw or to reaffirm his plea.

Whenever the judge refuses to ratify the sentence recommendation made by the prosecutor pursuant to a guilty plea agreement, the actual sentence which will be imposed eventually becomes an aleatory matter. As a result, the defendant is put into an unenviable position of mistrust, uncertainty, and worry. For some judges, this practice is followed routinely as a part of the punishment process intended to unnerve defendants. For other judges, this ratification pattern is followed in an effort to prolong the sentencing decision and to procrastinate one of the most important judicial functions. In either event, it does not seem necessary or prudent to delay announcement of the sentencing decision for any longer than is absolutely necessary following tender and ratification of the guilty plea itself.

Ratification of the Plea Conditionally or Provisionally and Delay of Sentence

Until the plea is ratified as tendered or retendered as suggested by the court to ensure ratification, the issue of a sentence must be delayed. On occasion, judges refuse to ratify a guilty plea as tendered, but prefer (or the defendant may request them) to ratify the plea to the charges conditionally or provisionally, if at all. Normally, a guilty plea must be ratified or the ratification must be refused at the time the plea is tendered. However, under the laws of a number of states, final disposition of charges may be made conditionally, provisionally, or delayed altogether pending the completion of some event to take place in the future. Such an event may be the defendant's good conduct for a period such as a year's time, or the defendant's successful completion of a diversion or a probation program, or the defendant's restitution to his victims in installments. This type of a disposition may be known locally as an adjournment in contemplation of dismissal, or as accelerated rehabilitation. Usually the array of conditions or provisions are recited by statute and little doubt lingers in the defendant's mind concerning the conduct required of him to achieve a final disposition of the charges in question.

Refusal to Ratify the Plea as Tendered and
Abatement of the Issue of Sentence

A judge before whom a guilty plea is tendered may exercise the option to refuse to ratify the plea at all, in which case the matter of the sentence will not be reached unless the defendant submits a revised plea or proceeds to trial and is convicted. It is rare in most judicial units for a judge to refuse to ratify a tendered guilty plea altogether, perhaps because of the necessity for disposing of criminal cases expeditiously in most courts. In most jurisdictions, when a judge does refuse to ratify a guilty plea tendered by a defendant, the plea is deemed automatically to have been withdrawn, and the defendant is permitted at his own option either to plead anew or to proceed to trial on the question of his guilt.

Memorializing the Guilty Plea Agreement

Guilty pleas seem to be products of negotiation and agreement within nearly every American judicial unit most of the time. On the other hand, very few of these agreements are memorialized in written form within most judicial units, and even when they are, the writing seldom recites the complete text of the agreement. Moreover, except in a few jurisdictions, it is never apparent on the face of the writing that the defendant has read, understood, and agreed to its context. Usually, a written guilty plea agreement is nothing more than a one page, mimeographed form containing a form list of the constitutional rights which a defendant supposedly waives by entering a plea of guilty or of *nolo contendere,* together with a few handwritten or typewritten notations (such as the defendant's name, the charges, the date) to personalize it, plus the defendant's signature at the bottom of the paper.

In many instances, what purports to be a written guilty plea agreement may actually be of less value than an oral guilty plea agreement. At least with an oral understanding, when one party begins to fabricate its context the other can follow suit also, which in turn serves as a deterrent to each party's potential for deceit. On the other hand, once a writing is created there will be a strong tendency for at least one of the parties to argue that the written form recites the entire agreement even if it does not do so. There is ample precedent that our society countenances intricately written instruments that are used to preclude consideration of parole (oral) evidence. Witness the "battle of the forms" in commercial transactions between merchants, as well as the long battle for consumer protection against misleading clauses on notes and order forms.[23] Even if a written plea agreement is an accurate and complete expression of the understanding as it existed between the parties at the time of its inception, many defendants will not forsake the opportunity to disavow portions of its contents (especially those aspects unfavorable to the defense) at time of pleading while arguing that the balance of the instrument must be accorded full force and effect.

Care must be taken not to confuse a written *plea* form and a written *plea agreement* form. At least two states, Washington and Minnesota, have enacted prescribed guilty plea forms into their statutes.[24] The form required by the State of Washington contains fourteen separate paragraphs of printed matter plus a *jurat* (oath of truthfulness) clause that must be read by or to the defendant in open court and signed by the defendant there in the presence of his counsel, the prosecutor, and the judge. The judge must also sign the instrument. The Minnesota form is very similar, but a little longer. Both of these required state forms contain printed clauses in which the defendant represents that the guilty plea is not based upon any agreement other than what may be attached to the form, and that in no event is the guilty plea based on any agreement or apprehension as to selection of sentence. Of course, this is where the plea forms call for the defendant, opposing counsel and even the presiding judge to lie or at least to stretch the truth visibly, since this study and other studies have determined that most defendants plead guilty only in anticipation of a particular sentence reduction for having done so.

The first four clauses of the Washington plea form recite the defendant's name, age, lawyer's name, and the charge together with the maximum sentence that may be imposed on that charge. Apparently, a separate form is used for each charge if the defendant is pleading to multiple charges. Clause five recites the defendant's understanding of the rights he will waive by pleading guilty, while clause six contains space for his actual plea and the charge label. The seventh clause states that the defendant makes the plea "freely and voluntarily." In clauses eight and nine, the defendant represents respectively that no threats or promises have been made. In clause ten, the defendant recites on slightly more than one line that he has "been told the Prosecuting Attorney will take the following action and make the following recommendation to the court," while in clause eleven the defendant acknowledges that he has been told and fully understands that the court does not have to follow the prosecutor's sentence recommendation and may impose "any sentence it sees fit." Clause twelve summarizes the state's parole structure. In clause thirteen, the defendant must state briefly (within 1.75 lines) what he did that resulted in his being charged with the crime in question. In clause fourteen, as in most installment loan agreements, the defendant acknowledges that he has received a copy of the instrument, and in addition that he has "no further questions to ask of the court."

The Minnesota plea form is similar to the Washington plea form, but it conatins several notable additions. In clause five, the defendant must represent the following:

a. I feel that I have had sufficient time to discuss my case with my attorney.
b. I am satisfied that my attorney is fully informed as to facts of this case.
c. My attorney has discussed possible defenses to the crime that I might have.
d. I am satisfied that my attorney has represented my interests and has fully advised me.

There is not much doubt as to the presence of input from the Minnesota Bar Association on this form, since the practical purpose of clause five seems to be for the defendant alone to assume the risk of pleading.

In clauses six and seven respectively, the defendant represents *whether* or not he has ever been a patient in a mental hospital or "talked with or been treated by a psychiatrist or other person for a nervous or mental condition," while the defendant must state in clause eight *whether* or not he has been ill recently and in clause nine *whether* or not he has been taking pills or other medicines recently. One wonders indeed whether the defendant who responds affirmatively to any of these questions will be permitted to plead guilty, or whether involuntary commitment for diagnostic purposes may be ordered by the court prior to acceptance of the plea. In clauses ten through twelve respectively, the defendant is asked *whether* or not he waives the defenses of intoxication, self-defense or defense of others, and *whether* or not his pretrial confinement was necessitated because he could not post bail. In clause thirteen, the defendant must "waive all right to successfully object to" either the absence of or errors in his probable cause hearing if he had one. Clause thirteen sounds extremely akin to a prior restraint, the validity of which may be questionable.

Neither the Minnesota nor the Washington forms are reprinted in this book, because in the author's opinion neither is acceptable and each may be found in the respective state's statutes. Two written *plea* forms (as opposed to plea agreement forms) are reprinted in appendix D because they are representative of similar plea forms used across the country. However, neither of these (Bergen County, New Jersey, and Hamilton County, Tennessee) is adequate, either, in the opinion of the author. Finally, one exemplary guilty plea form is reprinted within this chapter itself. The San Bernadino, California form (form 9-1) will be used as a model and is highly recommended for use elsewhere when modified, if necessary, to conform with state or local rules and customs.

The Bergen County, New Jersey form is very simple, perhaps over-simplified, and most typical of similar guilty plea forms presently in use within medium-sized counties throughout the nation. Primarily, this form asks the defendant simply to write "yes" or "no" in answer to questions such as the meaning of the charge, the existence of promises or threats, whether the defendant pleads guilty and whether the defendant has been assisted in the preparation of his answers to this form. One good feature of the Bergan County form is that the defendant is asked to write down on the form the specific sentence he alleges he has been promised, while just above that space the maximum sentence that may be imposed by law is recited. The form demands the basic answers that are essential preconditions to a guilty plea, but unfortunately it makes no attempt to verify these answers other than to compare the actual sentence with the defendant's stated version thereof. The form must be signed by the defendant, and "certified" by his counsel to the best of counsel's "knowledge and belief."

The Bergen County form does contain one conspicuous warning: "The judge is not bound by those promises. If he decides not to follow the recommendations, you will be allowed to take back your guilty plea and plead not guilty."

This warning is atypically beneficial to defendants. It informs them that the court is not bound by the promises, if any, made by the prosecutor but concedes that the defendant will not be bound by his plea unless those promises, if any, are fulfilled by the court. This warning is required under New Jersey law, but it may not be required under *Santobello*.[25] If the prosecutor himself fulfills his promises, such as to make a recommendation as to sentence, must the court follow the recommendation or permit the defendant to withdraw his plea? In many states, courts do not believe *Santobello* stands for that premise. Indeed, in many states a nearly opposite warning appears on guilty plea forms, admonishing defendants that since the court has not been a party to promises, if any, made by the prosecutor, the court will not consider itself bound to fulfill those promises nor will the court consider itself bound to permit the defendant to withdraw his guilty plea if the promises are not fulfilled. Whether or not *Santobello* holds that prosecutorial promises inure to the detriment of the court, a defendant who has defied a written warning and purported to agree that the court will not be bound by promises is less able than Rudolph Santobello was to challenge the unrealization of the promises later.

A longer and more rambling form is used routinely for written guilty pleas in Hamilton County, Tennessee (see appendix D). For one thing, this form requires the defendant to represent that he has candidly informed his attorney of the "facts and surrounding circumstances" which led to the charges in question. It contains a warning that the court may impose consecutive sentences upon the defendant's guilty plea to more than one criminal charge. It requires the defendant to declare that no promises as to kind or length of sentence have been made by any officer or agent of any branch or level of government. Finally, it informs defendants that the court will not accept a guilty plea from a defendant who maintains his innocence. This provision is constitutional, since in North Carolina v. Alford (1970)[26] the Supreme Court left to the discretion of trial judges whether to accept guilty pleas accompanied by protests of innocence by defendants.

The Hamilton County form requires the defendant to sign each page, which is prescient, since defendants may be expected to argue that unsigned pages are forgeries, following the example of dissatisfied beneficiaries and heirs who challenge the authenticity of provisions made by a testator in a will. Even more significantly, however, the Hamilton County plea form requires counsel for a defendant to sign a certificate in open court, not only attesting to the contents of his advice to his client, but "recommending" to the court that the guilty plea be accepted.

In San Bernadino County, California, two guilty plea forms, are used routinely, a shorter one in Municipal Court (see appendix D) and a longer one in Superior Court (form 9-1). The most significant difference between these forms and guilty plea forms used elsewhere in most judicial units lies in the requirement that the defendant *initial* each clause of the form after reading it. In this way, obviously, a defendant who contends subsequently that he was not advised of his rights will inculpate himself to a perjury prosecution, unless he can show that the instrument is a forgery. Such a showing would be difficult to substantiate, to say the least, since the instrument must be notarized.

Even the misdemeanor plea form used in San Bernadino County must recite whether the plea is the product of plea bargaining. If the defendant is represented by counsel, the lawyer must *stipulate* that the document may be received by the court as evidence of the defendant's intelligent waiver of his constitutional rights enumerated therein, and be retained by the court as a permanent waiver of those rights.

The Superior Court plea form (form 9-1) used routinely in San Bernadino County, California has been drafted even more carefully. In addition to the provisions contained in the misdemeanor plea form already noted, this form, used almost exclusively for felony pleas, contains space for the defendant to plead guilty to multiple charges at the same time, and for the maximum punishments for each charge to be recited separately. Since in California a court may not sentence a defendant on a felony charge without first having ordered

Form 9-1

A Model Written Plea Entry Form Used in San Bernadino County, California

SUPERIOR COURT OF THE STATE OF CALIFORNIA
FOR THE COUNTY OF SAN BERNARDINO

PEOPLE OF THE STATE OF CALIFORNIA,
                              Plaintiff,

vs.   NO. CR_____

_____
                              Defendant.   CHANGE OF PLEA
                                                           (GUILTY)

DECLARATION BY DEFENDANT

1. My true name is_____, born_____/____/_____

2. The_____filed herein accuses me of the offense(s) of:
              (Information/Indictment)

    _____

    _____   _____

3. I desire to change my plea(s) and plead guilty to:

    _____

    (Set forth count and code section(s) including lesser offense(s) to which plea to be made.)

    _____

    _____

4. I understand that the maximum punishments I could receive for each crime are

    COUNT NUMBER   NAME OF CRIME   MAXIMUM PUNISHMENTS

    _____   _____   _____

    _____   _____   _____

    _____   _____   _____

5. I understand that, as to the charge(s) against me, my Constitutional rights include: *Initial*
                                                                                                After Reading
    a.   The right to a speedy and public trial by jury.   [   ]
    b.   The right to see, hear and question all witnesses against me.   [   ]
    c.   The right to have the Judge order into Court all the evidence and to order my witnesses to attend the trial
          without cost to me.   [   ]
    d.   The right at the trial to present evidence in my favor.   [   ]
    e.   The right to remain silent or, if I wish, to testify for myself.   [   ]

6. As to each crime I now intend to plead guilty to:
    a.   I waive and give up each of the above Constitutional rights.   [   ]
    b.   I understand that I will continue to have the right to the aid of an attorney at all further proceedings before
          the Court and that if I cannot afford an attorney the Court will appoint an attorney to represent me.   [   ]

7. I understand that the Court will not decide whether to impose sentence or extend probation until a probation
    officer makes an investigation and reports on my background, prior record (if any) and the circumstances of the
    case.   [   ]

8. Except as otherwise stated herein, no one has promised or suggested to me that I will receive a lighter sentence,
    probation, reward, immunity or anything else to get me to plead guilty as indicated.   [   ]

9. No one has used any force or violence or threats or menace or duress or undue influence of any kind on me or
    anyone dear to me to get me to plead guilty as indicated.   [   ]

10. I am freely and voluntarily entering the plea(s) of guilty as indicated:

    a.   Because I am guilty and for no other reason, or

    b.   As a result of plea bargaining after discussing with my attorney the possibility of my being convicted on other or more serious charges and risking the possibility of a longer sentence, or

    c.   Because the District Attorney has agreed to

_____

_____

_____

11. I understand that even though the Court may approve the agreement for sentence set forth, the Court is not bound by the agreement, and that the Court may withdraw its approval at any time before pronouncement of judgment, in which case I shall be able to withdraw my plea should I desire to do so.

I understand that any agreement as to sentence applies only in the original sentence and that a violation of probation may cause the Court to send me to the state penitentiary (county jail) for the maximum term provided by law.

12. My lawyer's name is _____.

I have personally initialed each of the above boxes and I fully understand all that I have stated and all consequences. I am satisfied that I have had all the time that I have needed to discuss this plea with my attorney.

I declare under penalty of perjury that the above is true and correct.

        SIGNED on _____ at _____, California.
                 (Date)   *(Place)*

                                              _____
                                              Signature of Defendant

_____ states that he is the above-named defendant's attorney in the above-entitled criminal action; that he personally read and explained the contents of the above declaration to the defendant; that he personally observed the defendant sign said declaration; that he concurs in the defendant's withdrawal of his plea(s) of not guilty; and that he concurs in the defendant's plea(s) of guilty to the charge(s) as set forth by the defendant in the above declaration.

Dated this _____ day of _____, 19____.

                                              _____
                                              Attorney's Signature

The People of the State of California, plaintiff in the above-entitled criminal action, by and through its attorney, James M. Cramer, District Attorney, concur in the defendant's withdrawal of his plea(s) of not guilty and in the defendant's plea of guilty to the charge(s) as set forth by the defendant in the above declaration.

Dated this _____ day of _____, 19____.

                                       District Attorney

                                   By: _____
                                           Deputy District Attorney

ORDER

Having ascertained in open Court that: (1) the defendant fully understands his Constitutional rights, the nature of the crime(s) charged in the Information/Indictment, and the consequences of his guilty plea(s), (2) the defendant understandingly and voluntarily pleads guilty and waives his Constitutional rights, and (3) the defendant is factually guilty of the crime(s) to which he pleaded "guilty," or that the plea is made on the basis of a plea agreement.

IT IS ORDERED that the defendant's plea(s) of guilty be accepted and entered in the minutes of the Court.
DATED: _____   _____
                                             Judge of the Superior Court

and received a presentence investigation report, clause seven of the San Bernadino County Superior Court form contains this notation. Moreover, the felony form advises the defendant that the court will not be bound by the sentence recommendation, if any, offered by the prosecution, but that if after the presentence investigation the court imposes a more severe sentence than promised by the prosecutor and disclosed to the court on the plea form, the defendant will be given an opportunity to withdraw his guilty plea and plead not guilty. Finally, the judge before whom the plea has been offered must sign the form, acknowledging that he has performed the allocution required under California law.

It does not appear that any state requires a specific guilty plea *agreement* form (as opposed to a guilty *plea* form, as required in Minnesota and Washington). Some judicial units do, however, by order of the court or by discretion of the prosecutor, use guilty plea agreement forms. Most judicial units do not require that any specified plea agreement form be used, and of these, most appear not to use any form at all except under special circumstances such as when the crime is very serious or when the prosecution and/or the court mistrusts the integrity of either the defendant or his counsel or both. In California, most prosecutors use written plea agreements, whether on preprinted forms or by drafting the agreement separately for each case. Plea agreement forms tend to vary widely from one judicial unit to another, and even within units these may vary from one court to the next, from one assistant prosecutor or even one judge to the next.

The most simple "plea bargain" agreement form, which is typical of similar forms used across the nation in nearly all of the limited number of judicial units where plea agreements are written, is the one that is reprinted from Bergen County, New Jersey, (see appendix E). It contains only the defendant's name and the names of opposing counsel, the date, the docket and indictment numbers, plus five lines on which may be recited the "proposed plea bargain." There is space for the signature, initials or other reflection of the person by whom it is to be "approved." This form may memorialize a verbal agreement, but on its face clearly it does not reach contractual dimensions, since it does not even pretend to contain evidence of approval from more than one of the parties.

Plea agreement forms used in Bernalillo County, New Mexico, Chester County, Pennsylvania and Pima County, Arizona are reprinted within appendix E, also. Of these, the Bernalillo form is printed and the other two are mimeographed from a typewritten stencil. The Bernalillo County plea agreement form is contained on a single page, and calls for the defendant's signature along with those of opposing counsel and the approving judge or magistrate. The language in this agreement recites that the defendant "agrees to plead" either guilty or no contest to the charges in question, which will be inserted onto the form. The plea is premised on "understandings, terms and conditions" as enumerated by the parties in rather ample space provided on the form. The form contains space for a clear recitation of the specific charges, if any, which may be dismissed or which, if not yet filed, will not be brought pursuant to the agreement. Other clauses provide, inter alia, that the agreement may be withdrawn prior to acceptance by the court, and that it may be rejected by the court. If withdrawn or rejected, the agreement by expressed terms included within the form provides that the original charges against the defendant will be reinstated automatically. However, the Bernalillo County form contains a very unusual clause which provides that "no more severe than the following disposition will be made" on the charges to which the defendant proposes to plead guilty or no contest. Another form clause provides that the agreement will be "null and void" and the plea may be withdrawn by the defendant if a more severe disposition is imposed by the court following the presentence report.

The Chester County, Pennsylvania plea agreement form is more vague, for the most part, than the Bernalillo County form. As is the case with most guilty *plea* forms such as those already noted, the defendant is advised only as to the "maximum permissible sentences" that he may receive, rather than of the actual sentence which will be recommended or considered pursuant to the agreement. The Chester County form contains a clause which provides expressly that the defendant will be left "in the same position as though no negotiations or bargain had taken place" in the event the court refuses to approve the bargain. Unlike most plea and plea agreement forms used elsewhere, the Chester County and the Bergen County, New Jersey forms utilize the words "plea bargain" rather than plea agreement on their faces.

The most exemplary plea agreement form known to the author, once again as was the case with guilty plea forms, is the one being used in San Bernadino County, California (form 9-2). It provides that a "plea bargain" has been reached between the defendant and a specified deputy district attorney whose name is to be recited within the appropriate space. This assures personal responsibility within the prosecutor's office, and of course also exhibits apparent authority on the part of this official to enter into the agreement. Terms of the bargain are to be recited, but in synopsis form. Indeed, the agreement form should be much shorter than the plea form, since if the defendant refuses to plead in open court, in most states, his agreement to do so is inoperable. The prosecutor does not have to waive any constitutional rights, but needs only to provide the defendant with a capsulized summary of their understanding.

The flaws in the San Bernadino plea bargain form, if there be any, would be in two areas. First, there is space for the form to be "approved" by a judge. This may be unwise, since prior to accepting the plea itself (presumably, on the *plea* form rather than on the agreement form) the court should refrain from participation in the negotiations. His approval of the agreement, especially in advance of receiving the plea and therefore probably in advance of reading a presentence report, may be unwise and may bind the court into the agreement. Secondly, the defendant is asked to approve the form, on which is contained the

Form 9-2
A Model Written Plea Agreement (as opposed to plea entry) Form Used in San Bernadino County, California

COUNTY OF SAN BERNARDINO, STATE OF CALIFORNIA

_____COURT

THE PEOPLE OF THE STATE OF CALIFORNIA,)
                          Plaintiff,)
)   **PLEA BARGAIN AGREEMENT**
              vs.   )
)   **Case No.**_____
                    Defendant   )
_____)

    A plea bargain has been reached in this case between Deputy District Attorney_____ and Defendant.

    PLEA: The Defendant pleads guilty to _____

    TERMS:
I.   A.   _____withheld/suspended and probation for a period of_____

                       _____

       B.   FINE_____ P.A./P.O.T. _____ TOTAL_____

                 Payment Terms:_____

       C.   TRAFFIC SCHOOL: Notice of completion to be filed by_____

       D.   ALCOHOL PROGRAM: Defendant to attend _____

                 _____

       E.   JAIL TERM:_____. Defendant to appear at San Bernardino County

                 Central Jail, 630 Cardiff, San Bernardino at _____ m. on _____

II.   OTHER: _____

    _____

    _____

    _____

I consent and agree to the terms of the PLEA BARGAIN and to the entry of same in the minutes of said Court, and acknowledge receipt of a copy of this document.

I realize that willful violation of the terms of this agreement may be a misdemeanor and therefore subject to Bench Warrant and further penalties.

Dated_____   District Attorney

                                                By _____
_____
      Attorney for Defendant   _Deputy District Attorney_
                                  APPROVED:

_____   _____
             Defendant   _Judge_

                                                             91-11834-000 Rev. 11/74

Constitutional Rights

A defendant's rights include a speedy and public trial by jury. In addition, the defendant has a right to see, hear, and question all witnesses against him, and the right to have the Judge order into Court all the evidence, and to order witnesses for his defense to attend the trial without any cost to the defendant. At the trial, the defendant has the right to present evidence in his favor and the right to remain silent or to testify in his own defense.

Provisions of Plea Bargain

A defendant who agrees to a plea bargain has waived and given up each of the above constitutional rights. However, he will continue to have the right to the aid of an attorney at all further proceedings before the Court and, if the defendant cannot afford an attorney, the Court will appoint an attorney to represent him.

Another provision of this plea bargain is that the Court will not decide whether to impose sentence or extend probation until a probation officer makes an investigation and reports on the defendant's background, prior record (if any), and the circumstances of the case.

For this plea bargain to be valid, the defendant must not have pleaded guilty as indicated because he was promised or it was suggested to him that he would receive a lighter sentence, probation, reward or immunity, or because of some other persuasion. In addition, for this plea bargain to be valid, no force or violence or threats or menace or duress or undue influence of any kind was used on the defendant or anyone dear to him to get him to plead guilty as indicated.

For persons currently on probation, this plea bargain in no way limits the authority of the Court to revoke, modify or terminate the probation previously granted.

Finally, in the event the defendant fails to abide by all of the terms of any probation granted as a provision of this plea bargain, the Court retains full authority to modify, terminate or revoke that probation and sentence the defendant as provided by law.

following warning: "I realize that willful violation of the terms of this agreement may be a misdemeanor and therefore subject to Bench Warrant and further penalties." It is extremely doubtful that any penalties may constitutionally ensue from a defendant's refusal at time of plea to honor his antecedent promise to plead guilty. Indeed, to enforce such an agreement would seem to constitute a prior restraint. Moreover, the presence of such a clause could become grounds afterwards for rescission of the agreement and withdrawal of the plea on grounds of coercion. With those exceptions, however, the form is useful. If the "willful violation" clause were modified so as it would be limited to post-plea breaches, then it would appear to be acceptable. Similarly, the judge's approval should not take place before the plea acceptance, and to avoid confusion afterwards and minimize exposure to challenge the instrument should note that the judicial approval is made at the time of pleading and not before.

Notes

1. 404 U.S. 257, 262 (1971).
2. At least fifteen days must elapse between time of arrest and time of pleading guilty under Alabama law. Code of Alabama, Tit. 15, sec. 263. This provision cannot be waived by a defendant. Report of the Attorney General, October-December 1939, 332.
3. Opposing counsel are likely to begin tete-a-tete discussions once they have met face-to-face at a pretrial hearing. Before that time, they may talk on the telephone (as they may continue to do, also, afterwards) but discussions seldom lead to a serious resolution prior to completion of pretrial proceedings.
4. Although participation itself contravenes the A.B.A. Standards, many state judges do not seem to mind giving a "hypothetical" indication of what sentence a defendant may receive upon pleading guilty to proposed charges.
5. Why do people divorce after promising a lifetime union? Why does one party often break an executory contract, such as an "agreement" to purchase real estate, by refusing to tender or accept a deed? Why do deeds and mortgages need to be recorded? Why are certificates of title issued for motor vehicles?
6. See section 2-201 thereof providing that a contract for the sale of goods for the price of $500 or more is not enforceable by way of action or defense unless there is some writing sufficient to indicate that a contract for sale has been made between the parties and signed by the party against whom enforcement is sought or by his authorized agent or broker. See also exceptions under sections 2-201, 2-206, and 8-318 of the Code; and Note, The Doctrine of Part Performance Under UCC Sections 2-201 and 8-319, 9 B.C. Ind. & Com. L. Rev. 355 (1968). See also Note, The Doctrine of Equitable Estoppel and the Statute of Frauds, 66 Mich. L. Rev. 170 (1967).
7. In the context of the guilty plea negotiation, a price quotation would

not involve dollars but instead it would consist of an estimate of the number of charges or counts to which the defendant would be expected to plead guilty or *nolo contendere,* the seriousness of these charges or counts, the minimum and the maximum sentences that would be recommended by the prosecutor and the likelihood of a disposition not involving commitment (for example, probation).

8. Argersinger v. Hamlin, 407 U.S. 25 (1972).

9. In some states, permission of the prosecutor is required at the time when the plea is tendered. See South Carolina Code, Ch. 9, sec. 17-511.

10. At least three states require all guilty plea agreements to be reduced to writing. See Rule 17.4(a), Arizona R. Cr. P.; Rule 21(g)(2), New Mexico R. Cr. P.; and Criminal Rule 4.2(g), Washington Super. Ct. R. Elsewhere, defendants may be required to execute a guilty plea agreement. See West Virginia Code, sec. 62-3-la. In Utah, all guilty pleas must be oral. Utah Code Cr. P., sec. 77-24-2. In most states, a guilty plea itself (as opposed to an underlying agreement, if any, on which it is based) must be tendered by the defendant orally in open court. See, inter alia, Rule 24.3(a), Arkansas R. Cr. P.; California Penal Code, sec. 1018; Rule 11(a), Ohio R. Cr. P.

11. In Minnesota, a defendant charged only with a misdemeanor may elect to have a guilty plea petition filed by his counsel as an alternative to tendering the plea personally in open court. Rule 15,03(2), Minnesota R. Cr. P.

12. If delivered by someone other than the defendant, then the one who does deliver the petition (presumably, defense counsel) and causes that to be filed acts as the agent of the defendant to *constructively* perform the plea tender. As with a deed for the conveyance of real property, a written plea petition should not be viewed as a promise to tender a plea but as the plea itself which is *not* tendered until delivered to the court under the defendant's authority and actually filed as required by law.

13. To be "conspicuous," a clause must be printed on the face (rather than on the obverse side) of the instrument and be in type that is at least as large (preferably larger) than the average type of the instrument. Often, to ensure conspicuousness and to minimize the success of subsequent challenge, a clause that is intended to be conspicuous will be printed in red ink.

14. See, inter alia, A.B.A. Code of Professional Responsibility, EC (ethical consideration) 5-1 et seq.; DR (disciplinary rules) 5-101 through 5-107; California Rules of Professional Conduct, Rules 4-101, 5-101 through 5-103.

15. The traditional unilateral contract envisions the offeror as the promisor, while in a "reverse" unilateral contract the promisor would become the offeree since performance would precede the promise. See Restatement of Contracts 2d, sec. 57 (illustration 1); 1 Corbin on Contracts, sec. 71.

16. For instance, assault bears some relationship to rape since rape is a particular kind of assault. However, "disorderly conduct" bears little relationship, if any, to check forgery.

17. 404 U.S. 257 (1971).

18. In *Santobello,* Chief Justice Burger noted that the guilty plea "enhances whatever may be the rehabilitative prospects of the guilty when they are ultimately imprisoned." 404 U.S. 257, 261 (1971).

19. See, inter alia, Indiana Stats., Tit. 35, sec, 35-5-6-2(a).

20. See inter alia, James v. State, 242 Md. 424, 219 A.2d 17 (1966).

21. A series of delays due primarily to tardiness in the preparation of a presentence investigation report caused an elapse of more than six months between tender of Rudolph Santobello's plea on June 16, 1969 and imposition of sentence on January 9, 1970. 404 U.S. 257, 258 (1971). Another prosecutor appeared at time of sentencing, replacing the one who had negotiated the plea. Id., at 259. The sentencing judge declared: "I am not at all influenced by what the District Attorney says, so that there is no need to adjourn the sentence, and there is no need to have any testimony. It doesn't make a particle of difference what the District Attorney says he will do, or what he doesn't do." Id., at 259-260.

22. The condition (-precedent) of third party satisfaction is well-known to the law of contracts. It is often a constructive condition, being implied in law. See 3A Corbin on Contracts, sec. 645. Such a condition has been used typically in construction contracts requiring that a certificate of approval (evidencing satisfaction) be issued by a prenamed architect or engineer as a condition-precedent to payment of the contractor's final installment for services rendered. Third party satisfaction by the judge before whom a guilty plea is tendered is required by law in every jurisdiction, since there is no absolute right for a defendant to have a judgment pursuant to a guilty plea. Lynch v. Overholser, 369 U.S. 705, 719 (1962).

23. This culminated in congressional legislation known as the Federal Truth in Lending Act.

24. Criminal Rule 4.2(g), Washington Ct. R.—Super. Ct. and Appendix A to Rule 15, Minnesota R. Cr. P.

25. 404 U.S. 257 (1971).

26. 400 U.S. 25.

10 Findings and Implications of the Research

The process through which criminal cases reach a disposition has been described in connection with a number of specific judicial units across the United States which were visited by the author or for which statistical data happens to be available. It is time now to explain the aggregate significance of traits that reflect the manner in which criminal cases are processed throughout the nation, based upon a study of sample jurisdictions that are thought to be representative of most other jurisdictions across the country. Altogether, there are twelve findings.

Finding One

Prosecutors and defense counsel have reached a "gentlemen's agreement" to which many judges have joined, also, under the terms of which an artificial quota has been placed upon the proportion of pending criminal cases that will be taken to trial at any given time in virtually any American judicial unit. In the mid-1970s, in most jurisdictions, this quota is less than 10 percent of pending criminal cases. In some instances, it is much less than 10 percent, and seldom is it much greater.

Table 10-1 shows that among twenty-four states plus the District of Columbia for which comparable information is available for the mid-1970s, only six states took *10* percent or more of their pending criminal cases to trial in courts of general criminal jurisdiction, while three states and the District of Columbia tried less than *1* percent of their major criminal cases. In about three-fourths of these jurisdictions, therefore, fewer than 10 percent of the criminal caseload went through a completed trial. Table 10-2 shows that in the years since 1960, moreover, the United States District Courts have tried about *15* percent of their pending criminal cases, on the average. The percentages of criminal cases that go to trial are very similar from one state to the next most of the time in Table 10-1, and even more strikingly similar from one year to the next since 1960 among federal courts as seen in table 10-2.

Finding Two

Some of the most densely populated states seem to have the lowest quotas on the number of criminal cases that will be taken to a trial at any given time. In

Table 10-1
Percentage of Criminal Cases[a] Taken to Trial in Twenty-Four States and the District of Columbia: Most Recent Year Available

Rank of State in Percentage of Cases Tried	State	Percentage of Cases Tried	Number of Criminal Trials
1	Pennsylvania	29.0	22,044
2	Kansas	19.4	1,289
3	Iowa	13.7	1,933
4	Utah	13.2	349
5	Missouri	12.4	2,018
6	Minnesota	10.9	651
7	Vermont	9.8	154
8	Ohio	8.3	164
	South Dakota	8.3	139
10	North Carolina	7.9	3,524
11	North Dakota	7.1	38
12	Michigan	7.0	505
	Wyoming	7.0	85
14	Illinois	6.7	2,480
15	Colorado	6.3	481
16	South Carolina	5.7	1,141
17	Alaska	3.7	485
18	Delaware	2.5	155
19	Texas	2.0	139
20	Connecticut	1.9	109
21	Louisiana	1.1	84
22	District of Columbia	0.6	102
23	New Jersey	0.4	98
	New York	0.4	98
	Upstate	0.5	67
	New York City	0.3	63
25	California	0.3	129

Sources: See table 4-1, adding: **Iowa:** 1974 Rep. Re. to the Courts of the State of Iowa 56 (Table 3) and 57 (table 4) (1975); **Michigan:** 1974-1975 Rep. of the State Court Administrator 49 (1976); **Missouri:** Judicial Dept. of Missouri, Ann. Jud. Conf. Statis. Rep., 1975, 58 (1976).

[a]Data pertains to courts of general criminal jurisdiction, excluding in most instances companion data for courts of inferior (limited) jurisdiction such as those without full felony jurisdiction. Cases may be offender- or charge-based.

the mid-1970s, this quota has been less than 1 percent for California, New York, New Jersey, and the District of Columbia.

It does not seem credulous that 99 percent of all criminal charges that are brought against defendants in four or more jurisdictions can be settled fairly without benefit of trial, when in most other jurisdictions at least up to 10 percent of the criminal charges have to be resolved by means of a trial. At least in the absence of evidence to the contrary, of which there is none available at the moment, the implication that emerges is that defendants in these and other jurisdictions where trials are a total rarity are either being coerced into pleading guilty under circumstances where their factual or legal guilt is in doubt, or that defendants against whom evidence is overpowering are not being convicted of crimes for which they should be punished.

Finding Three

Based upon data that is available today, there appears to have been a quota on the proportion of pending criminal cases that were taken to trial at any given time in state courts during the 1930s, also, although forty years ago the population of the United States was smaller and less concentrated in urban centers.

Table 10-3 shows that in 1937 among twenty-eight states and the District of Columbia for which comparable information was collected and remains available, nine states took *10* percent or less of their pending criminal cases to trial, and only five tried *20* percent or more of their criminal cases. Forty years ago, about one-half of the states for which information remains available took fewer than *15* percent of their criminal cases to trial. In the 1930s, excluding 1935, about *12* percent of criminal cases pending in federal courts went to trial, as table 10-2 indicates.

On the average, fewer criminal cases are being terminated as a result of trial now compared with forty years ago in state courts. What is more, in 1937 states with large and densely concentrated populations such as California, New Jersey, New York, and the District of Columbia terminated criminal cases by trial at about the same rate as did the average state at the time, trying 15 percent of their cases or more, while states that tried less than 10 percent of their criminal cases included less populous ones such as New Hampshire, Vermont, Rhode Island, North Dakota and South Dakota. In the mid-1970s, the most densely populated states take the smallest percentage of their criminal cases to trial, while the less populous ones take cases to trial at an average rate.

Information is available for sixteen states plus the District of Columbia that reflects the proportion of criminal cases terminated by trial in the mid-1970s compared with 1937, as shown in table 10-4. The proportion of criminal cases terminated by trial has decreased significantly in about half of these jurisdictions, and this proportion has increased in only four of them. Decreases range from 1 percentage point in South Dakota to 18 percentage points in California and New Jersey. This proportion decreased substantially in other jurisdictions which have become very populous over the past forty years, including the District of Columbia, Michigan, New York, and Pennsylvania. Even though Pennsylvania had the highest proportion of criminal cases terminated by trial in both the 1930s and the 1970s, its trial rate dropped from 43.6 percent in 1937 to 29 percent almost forty years later, although the number of trials more than doubled.

Table 10-2
Percentage of Criminal Cases[a] Taken to Trial in the United States
District Courts, 1908-1975

Fiscal Year	Percentage of Cases Tried	Number of Criminal Trials
1908	20.3	2,631
1909	15.6	2,181
1910	14.4	2,210
1911	14.2	2,085
1912	14.5	2,347
1913	15.2	2,546
1914	12.6	2,288
1915	14.0	2,684
1916	28.1	5,735
1917	24.6	4,377
1918	20.0	6,189
1919	16.5	5,881
1920	17.3	5,936
1921	13.8	6,523
1923	14.5	9,906
1924	13.1	9,597
1925	9.6	8,884
1926	10.9	8,308
1927	14.7	9,157
1928	11.3	9,955
1929	8.4	7,159
1930	11.3	9,352
1931	9.5	8,742
1932	9.0	8,757
1934	11.1	5,054
1935	21.1	4,341
1936	12.2	6,493
1937	12.5	6,509
1938	12.0	6,200
1939	12.4	6,577
1940	13.0	6,331
1945	13.0	6,331
1946	9.8	3,578
1947	8.3	3,045
1948	7.2	2,461
1949	7.0	2,537
1950	7.2	2,699
1951	6.4	2,615
1952	7.8	2,997
1953	8.6	3,259
1954	9.0	3,858
1955	10.4	4,050
1956	11.7	3,714
1957	11.7	3,492
1958	12.0	3,642
1959	10.7	3,298
1960	12.0	3,671
1961	15.2	4,954
1962	15.4	5,097
1963	14.9	5,186

Table 10-2 continued

Fiscal Year	Percentage of Cases Tried	Number of Criminal Trials
1964	12.5	4,172
1966	13.4	4,278
1967	13.3	4,200
1968	15.1	4,807
1969	14.6	4,791
1970	15.5	5,637
1971	14.4	6,416
1972	15.3	7,583
1973	15.7	7,358
1974	15.3	7,335
1975		

Source: See table 5-4.

aCases may be offender- or charge-based.

The meaning of this change is unclear, but ominous implications are possible. What it may mean is that at least part, and perhaps a significant or a substantial part, of the *decrease* in the percentage of criminal cases that are tried in some states is attributable to the fact that criminal cases which need to be tried and which would have been tried forty years ago are not tried today. Thus especially in states where the decrease involves 15 percentage points more or less, some of these points may account for cases in which either the defendant is coerced or beguiled into pleading guilty or in which charges against guilty defendants are dismissed for no valid reason. The occurrence of either situation is unconscionable, and ludicrous if inspired simply to achieve a uniformly low trial rate.

Finding Four

Quotas on the number of criminal cases that can be brought to a trial in the mid-1970s appear to vary a little from one judicial unit to another in association with the density of the unit's population, but they do not seem to vary substantially on this basis.

Conversion of data that has been presented in table 4-3 indicates that the proportions of criminal cases are terminated by trial vary in association with the population density of the judicial unit (county) in which the cases have been brought, as table 10-5 shows. Based on this information, which pertains only to eight states, it would appear that the judicial units that serve the largest populations try the largest proportions of their criminal cases. Clearly, however, the observation of a quota applies across judicial units serving populations of

Table 10-3

Percentage of Criminal Cases[a] Taken to Trial in Twenty-Eight States and the District of Columbia, 1937

Rank of State in Percentage of Cases Tried	State	Percentage of Cases Tried	Number of Criminal Trials
1	Pennsylvania	43.6	9,852
2	Utah	28.4	107
3	Indiana	21.2	1,073
4	Michigan	23.4	1,106
5	Massachusetts	20.1	611
6	New Mexico	19.8	166
7	New Jersey	19.2	1,011
8	California	19.2	825
9	District of Columbia	17.8	306
10	Colorado	17.2	270
	Montana	17.2	101
12	Idaho	17.0	73
	New York	17.0	1,753
14	Ohio	16.5	992
15	Arizona	14.3	119
16	Washington	13.6	215
17	Kansas	13.1	234
18	Nebraska	12.9	133
19	Wisconsin	11.6	353
20	Wyoming	10.7	35
21	Oregon	10.1	84
22	South Dakota	9.3	49
23	North Dakota	8.6	46
24	Connecticut	8.4	98
25	Minnesota	8.1	154
26	New Hampshire	7.6	32
27	Iowa	7.0	110
28	Vermont	4.2	27
29	Rhode Island	1.2	7

Source: See table 5-1.

[a]Cases may be offender- or charge-based.

different size. In jurisdictions other than the very largest, 10 percent of the criminal cases or fewer are terminated by trial.

Finding Five

As in state jurisdictions, there appears to be a quota on the number of criminal cases that can be taken to a trial in the United States District Courts at any given time. This quota has not varied significantly from one year to the next for most years since 1908, averaging at about 15 percent of cases filed, or at least 5 percentage points higher than similar quotas appear to be for many states. For

Table 10-4
Comparison of Percentages of Criminal Cases[a] Taken to Trial in
1937 and in a Selected Year of the Mid-1970s, Sixteen States and
the District of Columbia

State	Percentage of Cases Tried, 1937	Number of Criminal Trials, 1937	Percentage of Cases Tried, Mid-1970s	Number of Criminal Trials, Mid-1970s	Change in Percentage Points Up or Down
California	19.1	825	0.3	129	−18.8
Colorado	17.2	270	6.3	481	−10.9
Connecticut	8.4	98	1.9	109	−6.5
District of Columbia	17.8	306	0.6	102	−17.2
Iowa	7.0	110	13.7	1,933	+6.7
Kansas	13.1	234	19.4	1,289	+6.3
Michigan	23.4	1,106	7.0	505	−16.4
Minnesota	8.1	154	10.9	651	+2.9
New Jersey	19.2	1,011	0.4	98	−18.8
New York	17.0	1,753	0.4	130	−16.6
North Dakota	8.6	46	7.1	38	−1.5
Ohio	16.5	992	8.3	164	−8.2
Pennsylvania	43.6	9,852	29.0	22,044	−14.6
South Dakota	9.3	49	8.3	139	−1.0
Utah	28.4	107	13.2	349	−15.2
Vermont	4.2	27	9.8	154	+5.6
Wyoming	10.7	35	7.0	85	−3.7

Source: See table 5-1 for 1937 data; see table 4-1 for mid-1970s data.
[a]Cases may be offender- or charge-based.

several years during World War I, federal trial quotas were higher than they have been since by between 5 and 10 percentage points, reaching an all-time high of 28.1 percent in 1916. For ten years following the end of World War II, federal trial quotas were lower than they have been at any other time since 1908 by between 5 and 10 percentage points, reaching an all-time low of 7 percent in 1949.

The implication of this finding is that available time and space dictate whether many, if not most, criminal cases that need to be tried will reach a trial. Of course, this does not mean in any sense that every criminal charge must be or should be resolved by trial. Undoubtedly, some charges can be resolved fairly only through trial, since even the defendant himself may not be fully cognizant of his guilt or of the degree to which he is guilty, if at all. No one could argue responsibly that just because a courtroom is empty someone should be accused of a crime in order that a trial may be held. It is equally silly to suppose that just because all available courtrooms are filled no other pending cases require trial. Yet, it appears as if in state courts, and particularly in the federal courts, a concerted effort by prosecutors and defense counsel is directed at regulating the flow of trials at an even pace.

Table 10-5
Trial Terminations of Criminal Cases in Association with County Population Density, Eight Reporting States[a]

Population of County	Percentage of Cases Tried	Number of Criminal Trials
Over 1,000,000	12.1	11,491
500,000-1,000,000	11.0	3,680
250,000-500,000	10.3	2,547
100,000-250,000	9.0	2,323
50,000-100,000	7.5	1,767
25,000-50,000	5.4	950
10,000-25,000	7.2	777
Under 10,000	7.5	231

[a]These states are recited in table 4-3.

Finding Six

Certain kinds of criminal cases appear to be taken to trial more often than do other kinds. The "gentlemen's agreement" on the proportion of criminal cases that can be tried seems to bend or be broken more often for violent compared with nonviolent offenses.

Data relating to the disposition of criminal cases in the United States District Courts has been presented earlier from sources cited in connection with tables 4-5 and 5-2. Based upon the same data, table 10-6 illustrates the differential rates at which selected types of criminal cases have been taken to trial in the federal courts between 1946-1970 (between 1961-1970 for homicides and sex offenses). Without any doubt, trials in the federal court are most likely to be held when the crime involves actual violence and least likely to take place when the crime does not involve actual or threatened violence. In the middle are crimes such as robbery where violence must be threatened but does not have to be used, followed by narcotics offenses and burglary which do not have to involve even the threat of violence but which may precipitate use or threat of violence.

Data relating to the disposition of criminal cases by type of offense charged has been presented earlier based upon sources cited in table 4-4 and pertaining to three states (California, Pennsylvania, and Texas) for which compatible information is available. Based upon the same data, table 10-7 illustrates the differential rates at which selected types of criminal cases have been taken to trial during the mid-1970s in state courts. Notice that in these state courts, as in the federal courts, trials are more likely to take place when the crime involves actual violence and least likely to be held when the crime does not involve actual or threatened violence. In the middle are crimes such as driving a motor vehicle while intoxicated (D.W.I.), robbery, and arson where violence may be threatened

Table 10-6
Differential Trial Rates of Criminal Cases in Federal Courts,
by Type of Crime[a]

Type of Crime	Percentage of Cases Tried	Number of Criminal Trials
Sex offenses	35.9	906
Homicides	33.7	345
Assaults	31.2	2,015
Robberies	23.1	4,436
Narcotics violations	18.6	17,645
Burglaries	14.3	894
Larceny-thefts	12.2	10,160
Fraud offenses	10.2	18,079
Auto Thefts	9.8	11,129
Forgery-counterfeiting	9.1	8,640
Embezzlements	6.9	2,626

[a]Data for type of crime obtained from table 4-5.

but physical harm need not necessarily occur to any victim, followed once again by narcotics offenses and burglary which do not have to involve even the threat of violence but which may precipitate use or threat of violence. Although the trial rates are conclusive for the federal courts, information relating to only three states cannot support a generalization insofar as the same rates would apply to other states. The evidence is strong enough to support the general finding, however, that type of crime charged influences the likelihood of trial quite often in state as well as federal courts, to the limited extent that a particular state judicial unit conducts any significant number of trials at all.

Finding Seven

Neither an offender's prior criminal record nor the viciousness of his conduct during commission of any particular type of crime appears to exert much influence on the number of different crimes or on the seriousness (degrees) of the culpability of which he will be accused; and neither seems to exert any significant influence in most judicial units over prosecutorial discretion to accept a negotiated guilty plea in lieu of trial.

Although type of crime charged seems to have some impact on the likelihood that an offender will be put on trial, among defendants who stand charged with the same or similar crimes, the chance that any individual defendant will be compelled to proceed to trial does not depend, as perhaps it should, on either his criminal history or his demeanor during the course of the criminal conduct. Qualitative research within prosecutors' offices indicates that many do not even bother to inquire about a defendant's criminal history before

Table 10-7
**Differential Trial Rates of Criminal Cases in State Courts,
by Type of Crime[a]**

Type of Crime	Percentage of Cases Tried	Number of Criminal Trials
Homicides	38.5	1,405
Rapes	27.4	528
Assaults	26.4	1,746
Driving-while-intoxicated offenses	21.5	3,633
Robberies	18.9	2,070
Auto thefts	15.8	747
Arsons	14.6	59
Narcotics offenses	13.3	4,505
Burglaries	10.9	3,118
Larceny-Thefts	8.6	1,707
Forgeries	4.0	303

[a]Data for type of crime obtained from table 4-5.

reaching a plea agreement as a rule (see chapter 7), and that even among prosecutors who are knowledgeable of a defendant's criminal record that information is rarely used in determining either the charges that will be brought or the manner in which these charges will reach a disposition. Thus, the career criminal who is charged with any given crime is offered an opportunity to have the charge reduced just as if he were a first or a second offender. The same qualitative research indicates that prosecutors in most American jurisdictions do not seem interested in learning from victims or witnesses the details surrounding commission of most crimes. Hence, among similarly situated offenders, the one who has terrorized his victim and the one who has not are likely in many judicial units to receive equally generous charge and sentence concessions in consideration of their agreements to plead guilty and avoid trial. Because of this, there is considerably little impetus for an offender to desist from terrorizing his victims.

Even within judicial units where PROMIS (Prosecution Management Information System) is used to rank defendants during the pretrial stage in terms of priority for prosecution, those offenders who are singled out as being unusually dangerous generally become comingled with ordinary offenders well in advance of the moment when their cases are terminated. Therefore, while PROMIS identifies and isolates offenders who should not receive charge or sentence concessions, and who should be compelled to plead guilty as charged or go to trial, this information is not used subsequently in most jurisdictions when multiple charges pending against a given defendant are dismissed or reduced and the defendant is encouraged to plead guilty to the one or two remaining charges (see trend 1 in chapter 7).

Finding Eight

Despite their rhetoric, very few prosecutors in the United States seem to be concerned at all for obtaining a conviction on at least one charge relating to each separate criminal episode (transaction) in which a defendant is known to have participated. For this reason, it is to the advantage of the sophisticated and persistent offender (and he knows it) for him to perpetrate as many separate criminal transactions as possible between the moment he commits the first and the time he is imprisoned, as well as during virtually all periods of pretrial or postconviction release.

Most prosecutors are concerned far more with processing defendants than with processing charges. As long as they can manage to obtain at least one conviction against each defendant who stands charged with any number of offenses, prosecutors appear satisfied much of the time (see trend 2, chapter 7). For this reason, more than for other potential reasons, crime seems to pay directly in proportion to the number of crimes committed and the frequency at which those crimes are committed by an offender before being placed in confinement (see chapter 3). A few prosecutors are beginning to become concerned about the type of offender who is suspected or accused of perpetrating many different criminal transactions. One reason all prosecutors should be concerned about this group of offenders is that they terrorize a large number of victims and generally appear to take pleasure in doing so. The politically oriented prosecutor has finally recognized this group of offenders as being extremely newsworthy if caught and convicted for numerous crimes involving multiple transactions (see chapter 5). However, some of these prosecutors tend to limit their pursuit to the multiple-transaction offender who has committed frauds and other white-collar crimes. There are many more multiple-transaction offenders who commit terrorizing and usually violent offenses.

Finding Nine

Most prosecutorial decisions from initial charging to finalization of a guilty-plea agreement are made by underqualified, inexperienced, and career-motivated assistants who believe it is to their personal advantage to process criminal cases as expeditiously as possible without much regard for the public safety and with paramount concern that prominent members of the defense bar not become annoyed at them.

Very few lawyers spend more than three years working in the office of a prosecutor, and many spend only between one and two years there. Usually, assistant prosecutors are recent law school graduates who are using the prosecutor's office for initial clinical experience and as a means toward employment in a private law firm. Many have never actually tried a criminal case, and of these, most shudder at the prospect of doing so. Assistant prosecutors know that members of the private bar (including but not limited to the private criminal defense bar) are observing their activities while scouting for future associates. Since defense counsel tend to prefer winning to losing cases and consider a plea bargain to be a partial success, the wise assistant prosecutor will opt for this type of a disposition. By going to trial, he runs the risk of losing, and demonstrating what he believes to be his own incompetence, or winning, and obviating what he feels opposing defense counsel will interpret to be the latter's incompetence. In either situation, most prosecution assistants do not view criminal trials as being compatible with their personal career goals. Whether these perceptions by assistant prosecutors are accurate (and they may not be) is really immaterial since the prosecutor's impression of what is good for him will be his motivating force rather than the accuracy of that impression.

Finding Ten

The person who is the key figure in guilty-plea negotiations in many judicial units throughout the United States is the judge before whom a defendant's pending charges will reach a disposition. Most American judges seem to ignore ethical and even statutory proscriptions against active participation in plea discussions, although the frequency and the intensity of judicial participation appears to vary rather widely from one jurist to the next. To the extent that judges do become involved in plea discussions, these invariably hover around sentence rather than charge concessions.

Judges tend to play various roles in the process by which criminal cases reach disposition. Quite often, judges function as plea brokers (see chapter 6). Jurists continue to participate actively in plea discussions even within those states that have forbidden this practice by law, yet seldom is a judge ever disciplined for this breach of ethics or prosecuted for such a violation of the law. In many American judicial units, only one or two judges participate actively in plea negotiations on a routine basis, but their colleagues on the bench are not averse to this participation upon occasion, as a rule with some limited exceptions.

Judges rarely become interested in the caption of a criminal charge. Instead, they focus attention upon the severity of the sentence that *may* be imposed against a particular defendant in consideration of the total number of crimes of which he stands accused. With this in mind, ordinarily, a judge will impose a single sentence that he considers appropriate in view of how serious he perceives the offender's average offense to be, rather than in view of how rampant an offender's criminal activities have been.

Finding Eleven

American judges as a group have failed abysmally in their responsibility to impose sentences upon convicted criminal offenders with consistency and fairness both to the offender and to the public. Similarly situated offenders can expect to receive significantly different sentences from one judge to the next for reasons that appear to correlate with each judge's perception of the extent to which the offender cooperates with the court and the prosecution, and the public can expect that repeat offenders will avoid severe punishment for most severe crimes because they manipulate prosecutors and judges. Consecutive sentences are imposed by judges as a rule only because of an offender's hostility toward the court rather than because of the offender's criminal conduct on the street.

Only a handful of American judges make it their practice to impose consecutive sentences against offenders regardless of the number of separate criminal transactions with which a particular offender has been charged. Judges are more inclined toward imposing consecutive sentences upon offenders who have been convicted after trial than upon those pleading guilty to crimes. The implication is clear that judges impose consecutive sentences against offenders to whom they as judges have taken a personal dislike. When this happens, the source of the hostility between judge and offender seems to invariably originate in the courtroom rather than in the conduct of the offender on the street at the time he committed the crimes for which he must be sentenced. Since different judges possess different notions about which crimes and which offenders most deserve imprisonment as opposed to probation, the actual sentence imposed upon any given offender is most likely to be a function of the correctional philosophy of the particular judge who sentences him rather than a function of his criminal record, the number or the circumstances of the crimes charged.

Finding Twelve

Throughout most of the twentieth century, criminal cases have reached disposition by negotiation much more often than by trial in nearly every American judicial unit, regardless of population density. The "experts" such as lawyers and judges who administer the criminal justice system have replaced the citizen-jurors as triers of fact in ordinary criminal cases. As a consequence, the notion of trial by a jury of the defendant's peers as envisioned by the framers of the Constitution has been denigrated. This seems to be one vital reason that as the rate of serious crimes committed during any time period continues to rise, both the proportion of offenders who are punished, and the severity of the punishment imposed for any given criminal offense at least remain constant, and generally decline. When the incidence of crime increases but rates of detection, apprehension, prosecution, conviction, and actual punishment for any single crime remain constant or decline, the net result is the emergence and continuous escalation of crime without punishment.

The disposition of criminal cases without trial is not new to the American criminal justice system. This practice has been followed continuously throughout this century in both state and federal courts serving both urban and rural judicial units (see chapter 5). This practice operates to defeat the spirit of the Sixth Amendment, since the practice is incompatible with the notion of a speedy trial before a jury of ordinary citizens who are peers of the defendant. Negotiated justice is not speedy, and the decision makers are not ordinary citizens. Instead, justice is delayed as it is being administered by a select class of judges and lawyers who have usurped the Sixth Amendment's mandate that laymen should decide issues of fact such as a defendant's guilt and degree of culpability. Since there are fewer judges and lawyers than citizens generally, the number of fact finders has diminished since ratification of the Constitution in 1789. More than any other single factor, this reduction in the size of the array of fact finders has contributed to the inordinate delays in the administration of criminal justice which, in turn, have precipitated an escalation of crime without punishment.

11 Recommendations for Change

After devoting a number of chapters to the analysis and the criticism of the American judicial process, it is incumbent upon the author to propose a set of recommendations which, if implemented, would be likely to exert a beneficial impact upon the quest for justice in the courts. Some of these recommendations can be implemented cheaply in most jurisdictions while others would require considerable expense. Some can be implemented unilaterally by a prosecutor or a court, while others would require a concerted effort by the executive or the legislative branches of government, or both. Undoubtedly, some of these recommendations are obvious and simple while others are so sweeping that if implemented they would alter at least the appearance if not the fabric of the scales of justice. These recommendations are not presented in any particular order of importance. Each is considered vital. Some will be grouped together so that their interface or aggregate as well as individual significance will become more apparent.

Recommendations Pertaining to Guilty Plea Negotiations

The first fifteen recommendations pertain to the disposition of criminal charges by guilty plea negotiations. These include:

Recommendation One. *A defendant or his counsel should be permitted to bargain with a prosecutor only on charges resulting from one criminal transaction at a time; and bargaining on any other charges resulting from any other transactions should be delayed until the defendant has been sentenced for all charges on which bargaining has been commenced.*

The greatest evil inherent in the negotiation of criminal charge dispositions is not the plea bargain but an expanded form of dismissal bargaining which may be identified as transaction bargaining. The professional criminal is able to wipe out several months' or even several years' worth of known crimes in a single stroke in many jurisdictions, simply by pleading guilty to all or some of the charges resulting from one or two transactions out of the many criminal transactions of which he stands accused. One victim of crime is no less important than another, but this is the result when an offender avoids conviction and thereby escapes punishment for offenses against many victims merely by pleading guilty to an offense against a single victim. By confining the bargaining to charges related to one criminal transaction at a time, a prosecutor can focus in upon actual harm perpetrated against the victims of this one transaction exclusively, as can the sentencing judge. Moreover, the multiple offender is more likely to be dealt with as a recidivist when he is compelled to bargain, *ad seriatim,* the charges resulting from his many criminal episodes.

Recommendation Two. *A defendant or his counsel should be permitted to bargain with a prosecutor only on charges resulting from the earliest transaction pending against him.*

A defendant's impetus to bargain for a suitable disposition of criminal charges pending against him diminishes once he succeeds in avoiding trial on the most serious of these charges. So also does this impetus diminish as the time between arrest and disposition increases, since he knows the testimonial evidence pending against him will decline in strength over time. For these reasons, a prosecutor should at least make an effort to avoid bargaining away recent charges pending against a defendant who still has older charges not yet terminated. Judges should support this restraint on prosecutorial discretion. It is important for a variety of reasons to dispose of criminal charges in the order they arose. First among these reasons is the necessity of determining at the time a defendant proposes to bargain on any charge whether at the time he committed the underlying offense he was a predicate felony offender, in order to provide for a penalty enhancement if prescribed by law. This task becomes difficult and may be ignored unless charges are disposed of swiftly and in consecutive order. Another reason for disposing of charges in sequence is to permit the presentence investigation report for subsequent charges to reflect the prior convictions, not merely prior arrests, in order to keep sentencing judges informed of the outcome of prior bargaining efforts.

Recommendation Three. *Under no circumstances should a prosecutor consent to or should a judge accept a defendant's guilty plea to one criminal charge in exchange for the dismissal or the reduction of any other criminal charges that resulted from any separate criminal transactions.*

Transaction bargaining has become a way of life in some jurisdictions. It is a danger to defendants, but a greater danger to society. Transaction bargaining poses a danger to defendants who gamble that they will receive the desired sentence or sentence ceiling for all pending offenses. When they lose this gamble by receiving a substantially more severe penalty, they seek to void their guilty plea. If this plea pertained only to one criminal transaction, they would be free to commence new negotiations on subsequent transactional charges or to proceed to trial on these. Less would be at stake in any given bargaining process. Transaction bargain poses a threat to society by creating the risk, and often the reality, that a sentencing judge will determine how long a defendant should spend in prison for the total offenses of which he stands accused, rather than for each sequence of offenses separately. Although perhaps this statement is crass, it should be none of a judge's business how many years of confinement a defendant becomes culpable for as a result of multiple criminal transactions. A judge should impose a penalty based upon the character of each separate transaction.

Recommendation Four. *At the time of formal charging, the prosecutor, the victims if known, all witnesses and the arresting police officers if any should be compelled by law to execute an affidavit under oath and on penalty of perjury averring* whether or not *the criminal transaction from which said charges resulted involved (1) possession, (2) use not resulting in injury, or (3) use resulting in injury (a) by the defendant or (b) by an accomplice of any lethal or dangerous weapons; this allegation should accompany all charges pertaining to that transaction throughout the criminal justice process; this allegation should never become the object of bargaining; and a charge which reflects the possession or use of a lethal or a dangerous weapon during a criminal transaction should never be dismissed or reduced to a charge which does not reflect said possession or use.*

Possession or use of a weapon during commission of a crime is as serious a violation of the law as can be committed. The law looks too often at the presence or absence of actual harm and too seldom at the risk of harm. By making each person who has a role in the prosecution of criminal offenders swear that the offender either did or did not possess or use a weapon at the time of a crime, a step is taken to establish as part of the defendant's criminal history the specific danger which he posed to his victims and to society during his criminal behavior.

Recommendation Five. *At the time of formal charging, the prosecutor should be compelled by law to execute an affidavit under oath and on penalty of perjury averring that a complete investigation of the defendant's criminal history has been made and, pursuant to said investigation,* whether or not *the defendant is known to have been previously convicted of a felony and if so on how many occasions; this allegation should accompany all charges pertaining to this defendant throughout the criminal justice process; this allegation should never become the object of bargaining; and enhanced punishment based upon the defendant's conviction for a second or subsequent felony, if prescribed by law, should be imposed without regard for the defendant's guilty plea or for any accompanying bargain.*

Recidivism is rampant in the United States, especially among serious violent criminal offenders. If our society desires to mete out leniency to first offenders, these offenders must be distinguished from repeat offenders and the latter must receive enhanced punishment. By making a prosecutor swear that an offender either does or does not have a previous criminal record, a step is taken to establish as part of the defendant's criminal history at time of charging rather than at a latter point whether he deserves leniency or enhanced punishment. A seasoned offender should not be permitted to masquerade up to and even beyond sentencing as a naive first offender, or to unjustly reap benefits not due him.

Recommendation Six. *Whether an individual jurist should participate in the dispositional bargaining of criminal cases should be a choice left open to the judge himself; but a true and complete record capable of transcription should be made of all conversations relating to the disposition of a criminal case which take place between a judge and a prosecutor or a defense counsel, a judge and a defendant, or a prosecutor and a defense counsel or a defendant in the presence of a judge; and disciplinary action should be initiated against a judge or a member of the bar who represents for the record a false or a deceptive summary of in camera bargaining or who knowingly permits such a false or deceptive summary to be made.*

It is extremely difficult to regulate judicial discretion, as it should be if judges are to continue exercising discretion. Some jurists are indiscreet, however, and display at least the appearance of impropriety in the course of their participation in bargaining. Rather than to remove all judges from bargaining, the more sensible alternative is to compel all judges to maintain a record of conversations engaged in during bargaining, so that in the event the defendant alleges impropriety following sentencing or in the event any other dispute develops, a review of the record rather than a hearing de novo may resolve the questions. Those who purport to administer criminal justice should not condone falsification of the records of a proceeding in order to conceal from scrutiny improprieties which have occurred in camera.

Recommendation Seven. *Not even a tentative commitment as to sentence should be made by a judge prior to considering the contents of a complete presentence investigation report; and prior to imposition of sentence for a criminal charge of which a defendant was convicted without trial a presentence hearing should be conducted for the purpose of determining mitigating as well as aggravating factors, if any, surrounding commission of the transaction from which conviction resulted; and victims if known, all witnesses and the arresting police officers if any should be notified of and afforded this opportunity to participate in the sentencing decision.*

In countless jurisdictions which have been visited the judge who is called upon to impose sentence on a defendant who has pled guilty to a criminal charge seems unaware of either the aggravating or the mitigating circumstances surrounding commission of the crime to the extent a judge who presided at the trial of such a defendant would be. To combat this ignorance at sentencing, a presentence hearing should be mandatory in all jurisdictions at which hearing each person who has participated in any way in the prosecution of the defendant should have an opportunity and be encouraged to provide input into the sentencing process. Many judges choose to avoid asking questions about a defendant's conduct during commission of his crimes which never arise because bargaining is less revealing of a defendant's conduct than is a trial. These judges would find greater difficulty avoiding the impact of these questions upon sentencing if the answers were a matter of public record.

Recommendation Eight. *Legislation should be enacted, or alternatively, courts should intervene to prohibit by law any negotiations over the disposition of charges surrounding a criminal transaction consisting of any charges for which a sentence of capital punishment may be imposed, regardless of the likelihood that such a sentence will be imposed against the particular defendant or that, if imposed, such a sentence will be carried out.*

Too much opportunity for coercion exists under circumstances where a defendant faces the alternative of pleading guilty and remaining alive or being found guilty and being executed. The magnitude of capital punishment is so great that when capital charges are pending against a defendant he cannot be expected to make a voluntary choice on the issue of whether to plead guilty or to demand a trial. If the evidence against him is strong and persuasive, and especially if he is guilty and knows it, he cannot intelligently do anything but plead guilty if he is given that option. Justice at least appears to be perverted, if it is not perverted in fact, when the sole reason why one defendant lives and another dies for committing the same crime is due to the fact that the latter has exercised his constitutional right to a trial before a jury of his peers.

Recommendation Nine. *The value and the wisdom of funding a public defender agency to represent the bulk of the indigent criminal defendant caseload in any judicial unit should be questioned.*

While a public defender agency may represent its clients well at early stages in the criminal justice process (such as at initial appearance and preliminary hearing), a voluminous caseload may impede the total effectiveness of such an agency in reaching an effective disposition particularly for the felony defendant. A more viable alternative to a public defender agency may be the assignment of indigent criminal defendants to members of the local bar who are engaged in private practice, on a properly managed rotational basis. A defendant who is assigned to an individual lawyer may enjoy a more direct and intensive attorney-client relationship which in turn should culminate in the greater likelihood of substantive justice.

Recommendation Ten. *If members of the local bar who are in private practice are assigned to represent indigent criminal defendants on a rotational basis, these attorneys should be paid for their legal services,* ad seriatim, *in installments upon completion of the client's case at each stage of the criminal justice process.*

When an appointed counsel is paid in toto at the disposition of a case, some lawyers tend to plead their clients guilty as soon as practicable for no reason other than to turn over their caseload often and get paid sooner. Similarly, each jurisdiction should evaluate the necessity for imposing a ceiling on the fee which may be paid to counsel per defendant per charge, together with the reasonableness of such a ceiling, if one is needed. At the very least, a lawyer should be granted an opportunity to argue before the court (or other agency which supervises the appointment of counsel to represent indigent defendants) for the payment of fees exceeding the normal ceiling in extraordinary cases.

Recommendation Eleven. *Classification of crimes should be altered so that offenses that involve the intent to inflict substantial terror upon a victim would be the only crimes known and punished as felonies. Examples of these crimes are murder and voluntary manslaughter, armed robbery, forcible rape or forcible sodomy between strangers, mayhem, kidnapping for hostage or ransom purposes, arson of a building not in the exclusive possession of the offender, plus the relatively new offenses commonly associated with terror such as air piracy ("skyjacking") and terroristic bombings.[1] No one should be permitted to plead guilty to any of these offenses as a result of either a charge or a sentence concession.*

Over the last two hundred years in the United States, the word "felony" has eroded to the extent that in some subcultures it has actually become a badge of honor. The nefarious meaning of this word should be restored, so that a convicted felon is recognized officially by the police and socially by his peers as a physically dangerous person who contrives to harm others. These are the chief crimes for which lengthy imprisonment and even death should be considered as punishments. In addition to the crimes that involve intent to inflict actual terror, some crimes may be presumed on their face to include the offender's intent to inflict constructive (indirect) terror on the victim. An example might be the sale of an addictive drug to a nonaddict, since by becoming addicted the victim's health will be terrorized at least at the point of withdrawal. All of these crimes either do or should expose an offender to punishment so severe that as a matter of law no offender should be permitted to accept the same voluntarily by pleading guilt. Thus, conviction by trial rather than by guilty plea should be mandated.

Recommendation Twelve. *Classification of crimes should be altered so that offenses that do not involve the intent to inflict substantial terror upon a victim would not be labeled or punished as felonies. Current felonies in this category should be identified and reclassified as misdemeanors or as gross misdemeanors. Examples of such crimes are involuntary manslaughter; unarmed robbery, battery or assault; use of nonfatal force including sexual force between members of legal or constructive family units (people who are living together); arson of* *property that is in the exclusive possession of the offender; sale of addictive drugs to addicts or sale of nonaddictive controlled drugs to anyone; and property offenses such as burglary, criminal mischief, criminal trespass and grand theft when committed without a physical confrontation between the offender and victim.*[2] *Unlike true felonies that do involve the intent to inflict terror in a victim, these terrorless offenses do not require punishment in every instance,*[3] *and the offender should enjoy an opportunity to negotiate the type and amount of punishment, if any, that is appropriate.*

The distinction between what is and what should be a felony rather than a misdemeanor has become confused in the statutes of most American jursidictions. Surely one reason so many serious felony offenders who have terrorized their victims avoid punishment commensurate with the harm they have caused is that they are grouped together in the eyes of the law with less serious offenders whose crimes, inaccurately, have been termed felonious. To the extent that persons who are charged with a criminal offense are permitted an opportunity to reach a negotiated disposition, every effort should be made to secure such an opportunity for the offender who has not terrorized his victim rather than for the one who has.

Recommendation Thirteen. *Every offender who is or should be charged with a crime that involves the intent to inflict substantial terror upon a victim, based on the factual allegations of a victim or a witness should be compelled to stand trial without enjoying any opportunity for charge or sentence negotiation. Whether or not guilt is determined by a judge or a jury, the maximum sentence allowable by law for the specific crime in this category should be reducible only by concurrence of the trial judge and a jury of lay citizens, or by order of an appellate court of competent jurisdiction. A jury should be convened to decide the issue of sentence in cases where the defendant has been convicted of a crime in this category after a bench trial.*

True felony offenders who stand charged with committing a crime involving the infliction of terror upon a victim should not be permitted to negotiate either the charge or the punishment, since indeed this negotiation process itself may become the source of additional terror to the victim who cannot help but believe that the offender is conspiring with the prosecution and the court to be set free only to terrorize him again. Moreover, a person who stands accused of having terrorized one or more members of a community should be compelled to face citizen representatives of that community as *both* the issue of his guilt and the issue of his punishment are determined. One major reason offenders continue to terrorize their victims is that they themselves continue to avoid being terrorized by juries in the courtroom.

Recommendation Fourteen. *Offenders who are charged with crimes that do not involve the intent to inflict substantial terror upon a victim should be permitted* *and encouraged to participate in the original charging process and in sentencing. No offender should be committed to a state prison solely because of being convicted of one or any number of crimes in this category. At most, economic sanctions such as fines and public service should be imposed along with supervised probation whenever necessary to ensure compliance. Conviction of a crime in this category should not be followed by any punishment at all[4] other than the stigma of the conviction itself unless the offender has previously been convicted of a crime that is equally or more serious than the current conviction. Even then, prosecutors and judges should seriously consider the propriety of imposing a formal sanction against an occasional or situational offender when most serious career criminals avoid punishment on the majority of their systematic offenses. If there has to be crime without punishment, the trivial rather than the serious offender should go unpunished.*

Offenders who have not terrorized their victims constitute the overwhelming majority of persons who stand charged with criminal behavior at any given moment in virtually every jurisdiction. Yet, in order to matriculate these persons as defendants through the criminal justice processes, cases involving more serious criminal conduct become backlogged. We propose that offenders who are convicted of crimes not involving the intent to inflict substantial terror upon a victim need not and therefore should not be imprisoned. Indeed, first, second, situational and even other occasional offenders who engage in criminal behavior only sporadically and then only in relatively nonserious criminal behavior may not require any formal punishment other than the record of conviction itself. Since our system of administering criminal justice is far short of being perfect, and many criminal offenders avoid punishment altogether even for serious and terrorizing crimes, if a choice must be made as to whom to punish, the selection process should favor the offender who causes the least harm.

Rather than dismiss serious charges against career criminals in order to reduce case backlog, prosecutors and judges should at least consider as an alternative dropping all charges pending against less serious defendants. One method of doing so would be for prosecutors to accept consent decrees from individual defendants (as they do routinely from corporate defendants accused of unfair trade or discriminatory practices) whereby the defendants would accept conviction on the record but without being subjected to any other sanction at all. Another alternative would be for defendants to accept a notation rather than a conviction, realizing that subsequent accusation within a prescribed time period would result at least in conviction and possibly in economic sanctions as well. In an age of costly and sophisticated machinery for the administration of criminal justice, we must finally realize that not all crimes *can* be punished, but that those crimes which are punished should be the ones that cause the most terror to the community. Presently, we live with an informal system of crime without punishment. Perhaps we should formalize this system as it pertains to the least serious offenders and offenses.

Recommendation Fifteen. *A significant proportion (at least 10 percent) of the defendants who stand charged at any given time with repeat offenses involving the intent to inflict terror upon a victim should be selected by lot to stand trial as charged without enjoying any opportunity for charge or sentence concessions. Selection should be by scientific random sampling whereby every similarly situated defendant would have an equal statistical probability of being put on trial for each terrorizing crime of which he is accused. As an alternative, sampling frames may be stratified according to the number and/or the seriousness of each defendant's prior convictions. In most jurisdictions where defendants with short criminal records outnumber those with long ones, stratification would subject career criminals to an increasingly greater likelihood of being selected for trial with every additional crime charged.*

Random sampling of defendants for trial should serve as a deterrent to both serious crime and prosecutorial overcharging. If those criminal offenders who perpetrate serious crimes systematically knew that now and then they would be compelled to face trial at which time the enormity of their brutality would be publicized, undoubtedly some would be more hesitant to commit further crimes. If prosecutors faced the prospect of having to go to trial with a significant percentage of the charges filed, they would be less inclined to launch unwarranted charges, on peril of having defendants acquitted in court. Random sampling of offenders for trial should not violate the Fourteenth Amendment, since indeed offenders would enjoy *statistical* equal protection under the law.

Recommendations Pertaining to Judicial Administration

The next set of recommendations pertain to the efficient and orderly administration of criminal justice in the courts, and refer to the scheduling of proceedings, the use of space when it is available, and the need to balance convenience against the mandate that criminal charges be resolved as soon as possible after being initiated. These recommendations include:

Recommendation Sixteen. *Courtroom space should be allocated according to priority usage. The highest priority use of most courtrooms should be for the trial of criminal cases, followed by preliminary and evidentiary hearings in criminal matters. Piggy-backed trials and hearings should be encouraged with as few recesses as possible, even if this necessitates the ongoing rotation of judges from one courtroom to another. Judicial matters that do not require use of a courtroom can better be conducted elsewhere, such as in chambers.*

One factor above all others that contributes to delay and case backlog in American courts is that formal proceedings are scheduled to begin in a courtroom but their commencement is delayed, proceedings become informal, or activity in the courtroom is recessed. The courtroom is a vital arena to the administration of justice, and it cannot remain vacant during times of the day or week when it should be in use. A courtroom should not be misused as an office or a lounge. It should not serve as a waiting room except for persons whose cases are about to involve proceedings that must take place in open court.

Recommendation Seventeen. *Formal criminal proceedings should be scheduled during most if not all days of the week and during most if not all hours of the day and night, around the clock if possible, to maximize the use of valuable courtroom space. Proceedings requiring testimony from witnesses should be scheduled during the day or the evening whenever possible to avoid inconvenience. Misdemeanor proceedings should be scheduled for the evening rather than the day, as a rule, to avoid loss of work time for defendants and witnesses and to minimize conflict with the scheduling of more serious felony proceedings during the day. Once begun, formal proceedings should not be interrupted except for necessary meals and emergency recesses until at least eight hours have passed or the issues at bar have been resolved.*

The common syndrome in *most* American courts where proceedings take place between ten and twelve o'clock in the morning and two to four o'clock in the afternoon must be stopped. There is no legitimate reason why judges and prosecutors cannot be assigned to evening or night shifts instead of to the day shift, perhaps on a seniority basis, just as police are. Defense counsel can be on call around the clock just as are members of the health professions, especially physicians. Felony proceedings can be scheduled from eight o'clock in the morning until four o'clock in the afternoon; misdemeanor proceedings from four until midnight. The period between midnight and eight o'clock the next morning can be used for proceedings that do not involve testimony by unofficial witnesses, such as initial appearances, guilty pleas, sentence impositions, and so on. Indeed, negotiations can be conducted better at times other than peak business hours.

Recommendation Eighteen. *More judges, more magistrates, and more assistant prosecutors should be appointed or elected to cope with the size of criminal caseloads in nearly every American judicial unit.*

These public officials should collectively represent a cross-section of the American public, in terms of age, sex, and race. Therefore, younger judges and older assistant prosecutors should be appointed, as should qualified female and minority candidates for each type of position. Magistrates who are attorneys can preside over misdemeanor trials as effectively as judges can, and they can do the same at pretrial proceedings for both felony and misdemeanor cases. Judges should spend their time presiding over adversarial proceedings in the courtroom. When negotiations between counsel require a moderator, this role can be fulfilled by the appointment of a master or the selection of an arbitrator.

Recommendation Nineteen. *Many, if not most, misdemeanor charges can be resolved through binding arbitration rather than by trial or negotiation.*

Unlike the California "slow plea" practice whereby written stipulations are submitted to a judge on a transcript, an arbitrator should take the opportunity to see and listen to all parties and witnesses before reaching a decision in a criminal case. This recommendation does not conflict with the constitution and it should not conflict with most statutes, case law or court rules, since a defendant should retain his right to trial before a judge and a jury unless he waives that right.

Recommendation Twenty. *Sentences that have been imposed by state courts against defendants who have been convicted on felony charges should be reviewed separately from other questions on appeal, and sentence reviews should be appealed to or* considered sua sponte *by a single court in every state, preferably by one that has been created exclusively for this purpose. Sentences that have been imposed by federal and state courts against defendants who have been convicted on felony charges should be reviewable by appeal to or* sua sponte *by a United States Court of Sentence Appeals which Congress should create. The appropriate state or federal court of competent jurisdiction should be charged with overseeing that similarly situated offenders are punished as uniformly as possible, and judges thereof should possess the authority to reduce or to increase sentences in their own unfettered discretion with or without announcing their reasons for doing so in any given case.*

One major reason why so many criminal cases are appealed to existing appellate courts at both the state and federal levels is that defendants contest the fairness of their sentences. If fundamental sentence fairness could be ensured, presumably many of these appellants would desist from arguing procedural errors and other legal technicalities, some of which drag on from one appeals court to the next throughout the duration of the appellant's confinement. To ensure that state courts supervise the uniformity of sentences, a new specialized federal court needs to be created, and it would exercise a supervisory role over federal sentences, also. This court would reduce significantly the caseload of the United States Supreme Court, which could defer *certiorari* of criminal convictions until sentence review has been completed.

Notes

1. See Jones, *Crime and Criminal Responsibility* (1978).
2. Id.
3. Punishment, and particularly imprisonment, is a dangerous practice when imposed without regard to the seriousness of the crime, the circumstances

surrounding the conduct, and the characteristics of the offender. For trivial crimes and unsophisticated (situational) offenders, no punishment may be preferable to confinement, if only because of the health risks which an offender is likely to experience during confinement. See Jones, *The Health Risks of Imprisonment* (Lexington Books, D.C. Heath, 1976).

    4. Id.

Appendix A
Rule 11. Pleas (Federal Rules of Criminal Procedure)

Rule 11. Pleas (Federal Rules of Criminal Procedure)
(Prior to 1975 Amendments)

(a) Alternatives. A defendant may plead not guilty, guilty, or nolo contendere. If a defendant refuses to plead or if a defendant corporation fails to appear, the court shall enter a plea of not guilty.

(b) Nolo contendere. A defendant may plead nolo contendere only with the consent of the court. Such a plea shall be accepted by the court only after due consideration of the views of the parties and the interest of the public in the effective administration of justice.

(c) Advice to defendant. The court shall not accept a plea of guilty or nolo contendere without first, by addressing the defendant personally in open court, informing him of and determining that he understands the following:

(1) the nature of the charge to which the plea is offered; and

(2) the mandatory minimum penalty provided by law, if any, and the maximum possible penalty provided by law for the offense to which the plea is offered; and

(3) that the defendant has the right to plead not guilty, or to persist in that plea if it has already been made; and

(4) that if he pleads guilty or nolo contendere there will not be a further trial of any kind, so that by pleading guilty or nolo contendere he waives the right to a trial.

(d) Insuring that the plea is voluntary. The court shall not accept a plea of guilty or nolo contendere without first, by addressing the defendant personally in open court, determining that the plea is voluntary and not the result of force or threats or of promises apart from a plea agreement. The court shall also inquire as to whether the defendant's willingness to plead guilty or nolo contendere results from prior discussions between the attorney for the government and the defendant or his attorney.

(e) Plea agreement procedure.

(1) In General. The attorney for the government and the attorney for the defendant or the defendant when acting pro se may engage in discussions with a

view toward reaching an agreement that, upon the entering of a plea of guilty or nolo contendere to a charged offense or to a lesser or related offense, the attorney for the government will move for dismissal of other charges, or will recommend or not oppose the imposition of a particular sentence, or will do both. The court shall not participate in any such discussions.

(2) Notice of such agreement. If a plea agreement has been reached by the parties which contemplates entry of a plea of guilty or nolo contendere in the expectation that a specific sentence will be imposed or that other charges before the court will be dismissed, the court shall require the disclosure of the agreement in open court at the time the plea is offered. Thereupon the court may accept or reject the agreement, or may defer its decision as to acceptance or rejection until there has been an opportunity to consider the presentence report.

(3) Acceptance of plea. If the court accepts the plea agreement, the court shall inform the defendant that it will embody in the judgment and sentence the disposition provided for in the plea agreement or another disposition more favorable to the defendant than that provided for in the plea agreement.

(4) Rejection of plea. If the court rejects the plea agreement, the court shall inform the parties of this fact, advise the defendant personally in open court that the court is not bound by the plea agreement, afford the defendant the opportunity to then withdraw his plea, and advise the defendant that if he persists in his guilty plea or plea of nolo contendere the disposition of the case may be less favorable to the defendant than that contemplated by the plea agreement.

(5) Time of plea agreement procedure. Except for good cause shown, notification to the court of the existence of a plea agreement shall be given at the arraignment or at such other time, prior to trial, as may be fixed by the court.

(6) Inadmissibility of plea discussions. Evidence of a plea of guilty, later withdrawn, or a plea of nolo contendere, or of an offer to plead guilty or nolo contendere to the crime charged or any other crime, or of statements made in connection with any of the foregoing pleas or offers, is not admissible in any civil or criminal proceeding against the person who made the plea or offer.

(f) Determining accuracy of plea. Notwithstanding the acceptance of a plea of guilty, the court should not enter a judgment upon such plea without making such inquiry as shall satisfy it that there is a factual basis for the plea.

(g) Record of proceedings. A verbatim record of the proceedings at which the defendant enters a plea shall be made and, if there is a plea of guilty or nolo

contendere, the record shall include, without limitation, the court's advice to the defendant, the inquiry into the voluntariness of the plea including any plea agreement, and the inquiry into the accuracy of a guilty plea.

Rule 11. Pleas (Federal Rules of Criminal Procedure)
(Paragraph 11(e)(6) is effective August 1, 1975
while the balance of Rule 11 is effective
December 1, 1975.)

(a) Alternatives. A defendant may plead not guilty, guilty, or nolo contendere. If a defendant refuses to plead or if a defendant corporation fails to appear, the court shall enter a plea of not guilty.

(b) Nolo contendere. A defendant may plead nolo contendere only with the consent of the court. Such a plea shall be accepted by the court only after due consideration of the views of the parties and the interest of the public in the effective administration of justice.

(c) Advice to defendant. Before accepting a plea of guilty or nolo contendere, the court must address the defendant personally in open court and inform him of, and determine that he understands, the following:

(1) the nature of the charge to which the plea is offered, the mandatory minimum penalty provided by law, if any, and the maximum possible penalty provided by law; and

(2) if the defendant is not represented by an attorney, that he has the right to be represented by an attorney at every stage of the proceeding against him and, if necessary, one will be appointed to represent him; and

(3) that he has the right to plead not guilty or to persist in that plea if it has already been made, and that he has the right to be tried by a jury and at that trial has the right to the assistance of counsel, the right to confront and cross-examine witnesses against him, and the right not to be compelled to incriminate himself; and

(4) that if he pleads guilty or nolo contendere there will not be a further trial of any kind, so that by pleading guilty or nolo contendere he waives the right to a trial; and

(5) that if he pleads guilty or nolo contendere, the court may ask him questions about the offense to which he has pleaded, and if he answers these questions under oath, on the record, and in the presence of counsel, his answers may later be used against him in a prosecution for perjury or false statement.

(d) Insuring that the plea is voluntary. The court shall not accept a plea of guilty or nolo contendere without first, by addressing the defendant personally

in open court, determining that the plea is voluntary and not the result of force or threats or of promises apart from a plea agreement. The court shall also inquire as to whether the defendant's willingness to plead guilty or nolo contendere results from prior discussions between the attorney for the government and the defendant or his attorney.

(e) Plea agreement procedure.

(1) In general. The attorney for the government and the attorney for the defendant or the defendant when acting *pro se* may engage in discussions with a view toward reaching an agreement that, upon the entering of a plea of guilty or nolo contendere to a charged offense or to a lesser or related offense, the attorney for the government will do any of the following:

(A) move for dismissal of other charges; or

(B) make a recommendation, or agree not to oppose the defendant's request, for a particular sentence, with the understanding that such recommendation or request shall not be binding upon the court; or

(C) agree that a specific sentence is the appropriate disposition of the case. The court shall not participate in any such discussions.

(2) Notice of such agreement. If a plea agreement has been reached by the parties, the court shall, on the record, require the disclosure of the agreement in open court or, on a showing of good cause, in camera, at the time the plea is offered. Thereupon the court may accept or reject the agreement, or may defer its decision as to the acceptance or rejection until there has been an opportunity to consider the presentence report.

(3) Acceptance of a plea agreement. If the court accepts the plea agreement, the court shall inform the defendant that it will embody in the judgment and sentence the disposition provided for in the plea agreement.

(4) Rejection of a plea agreement. If the court rejects the plea agreement, the court shall, on the record, inform the parties of this fact, advise the defendant personally in open court or, on a showing of good cause, in camera, that the court is not bound by the plea agreement, afford the defendant the opportunity to then withdraw his plea, and advise the defendant that if he persists in his guilty plea or plea of nolo contendere the disposition of the case may be less favorable to the defendant than that contemplated by the plea agreement.

(5) Time of plea agreement procedure. Except for good cause shown, notification to the court of the existence of a plea agreement shall be given at the arraignment or at such other time, prior to trial, as may be fixed by the court.

(6) Inadmissibility of pleas, offers of pleas, and related statements. Except as otherwise provided in this paragraph, evidence of a plea of guilty, later

withdrawn, or a plea of nolo contendere, or of an offer to plead guilty or nolo contendere to the crime charged or any other crime, or of statements made in connection with, and relevant to, any of the foregoing pleas or offers, is not admissible in any civil or criminal proceeding against the person who made the plea or offer. However, evidence of a statement made in connection with, and relevant to, a plea of guilty, later withdrawn, a plea of nolo contendere, or an offer to plead guilty or nolo contendere to the crime charged or any other crime, is admissible in a criminal proceeding for perjury or false statement if the statement was made by the defendant under oath, on the record, and in the presence of counsel.

(f) Determining accuracy of plea. Notwithstanding the acceptance of a plea of guilty, the court should not enter a judgment upon such plea without making such inquiry as shall satisfy it that there is a factual basis for the plea.

(g) Record of proceedings. A verbatim record of the proceedings at which the defendant enters a plea shall be made and, if there is a plea of guilty or nolo contendere, the record shall include, without limitation, the court's advice to the defendant, the inquiry into the voluntariness of the plea including any plea agreement, and the inquiry into the accuracy of a guilty plea.

Appendix B
Rule 32. Sentence and Judgment (Federal Rules of Criminal Procedure)

Rule 32. Sentence and Judgment (Federal Rules of Criminal Procedure) (Prior to 1975 Amendments)

(a) Sentence.

(1) Imposition of sentence. Sentence shall be imposed without unreasonable delay. Before imposing sentence the court shall afford counsel an opportunity to speak on behalf of the defendant and shall address the defendant personally and ask him if he wishes to make a statement in his own behalf and to present any information in mitigation of punishment.

(2) Notification of right to appeal. After imposing sentence in a case which has gone to trial on a plea of not guilty, the court shall advise the defendant of his right to appeal and of the right of a person who is unable to pay the cost of an appeal to apply for leave to appeal in forma pauperis. There shall be no duty on the court to advise the defendant of any right of appeal after sentence is imposed following a plea of guilty or nolo contendere. If the defendant so requests, the clerk of the court shall prepare and file forthwith a notice of appeal on behalf of the defendant.
(c) Presentence investigation.

(1) When made. The probation service of the court shall make a presentence investigation and report to the court before the imposition of sentence or the granting of probation unless the court otherwise directs for reasons stated on the record.

The report shall not be submitted to the court or its contents disclosed to anyone unless the defendant has pleaded guilty or nolo contendere or has been found guilty, except that a judge may, with the written consent of the defendant, inspect a presentence report at any time.

(2) Report. The report of the presentence investigation shall contain any prior criminal record of the defendant and such information about his characteristics, his financial condition and the circumstances affecting his behavior as may be helpful in imposing sentence or in granting probation or in the correctional treatment of the defendant, and such other information as may be required by the court.

223

(3) Disclosure.

(A) Before imposing sentence the court shall upon request permit the defendant, or his counsel if he is so represented, to read the report of the presentence investigation exclusive of any recommendation as to sentence, unless in the opinion of the court the report contains diagnostic opinion which might seriously disrupt a program of rehabilitation, sources of information obtained upon a promise of confidentiality, or any other information which, if disclosed, might result in harm, physical or otherwise, to the defendant or other persons; and the court shall afford the defendant or his counsel an opportunity to comment thereon.

(B) If the court is of the view that there is information in the presentence report which should not be disclosed under subdivision (c)(3)(A) of this rule, the court in lieu of making the report or part thereof available shall state orally or in writing a summary of the factual information contained therein to be relied on in determining sentence, and shall give the defendant or his counsel an opportunity to comment thereon. The statement may be made to the parties in camera.

(C) Any material disclosed to the defendant or his counsel shall also be disclosed to the attorney for the government.

(D) Any copies of the presentence investigation report made available to the defendant or his counsel and the attorney for the government shall be returned to the probation officer immediately following the imposition of sentence or the granting of probation. Copies of the presentence investigation report shall not be made by the defendant, his counsel, or the attorney for the government.

(E) The reports of studies and recommendations contained therein made by the Director of the Bureau of Prisons or the Youth Correction Division of the Board of Parole pursuant to 18 U.S.C. 4208 (b), 4252, 5010 (e), or 5034 shall be considered a presentence investigation within the meaning of subdivision (c)(3) of this rule.

(d) Withdrawal of plea of guilty. A motion to withdraw a plea of guilty or nolo contendere may be made only before sentence is imposed or imposition of sentence is suspended; but to correct manifest injustice the court after sentence may set aside the judgment of conviction and permit the defendant to withdraw his plea.

(e) Probation. After conviction of an offense not punishable by death or by life imprisonment, the defendant may be placed on probation if permitted by law.

(f) Revocation of probation. The court shall not revoke probation except after a hearing at which the defendant shall be present and apprised of the grounds on which such action is proposed. The defendant may be admitted to bail pending such hearing.

Rule 32. Sentence and Judgment (Federal Rules of Criminal Procedure) (Effective December 1, 1975)

(a) Sentence.

(1) Imposition of sentence. Sentence shall be imposed without unreasonable delay. Before imposing sentence the court shall afford counsel an opportunity to speak on behalf of the defendant and shall address the defendant personally and ask him if he wishes to make a statement in his own behalf and to present any information in mitigation of punishment. The attorney for the government shall have an equivalent opportunity to speak to the court.

(2) Notification of right to appeal. After imposing sentence in a case which has gone to trial on a plea of not guilty, the court shall advise the defendant of his right to appeal and of the right of a person who is unable to pay the cost of an appeal to apply for leave to appeal in forma pauperis. There shall be no duty on the court to advise the defendant of any right of appeal after sentence is imposed following a plea of guilty or nolo contendere. If the defendant so requests, the clerk of the court shall prepare and file forthwith a notice of appeal on behalf of the defendant.
(b) Judgment.

(1) In general. A judgment of conviction shall set forth the plea, the verdict or findings, and the adjudication and sentence. If the defendant is found not guilty or for any other reason is entitled to be discharged, judgment shall be entered accordingly. The judgment shall be signed by the judge and entered by the clerk.

(2) Criminal forfeiture. When a verdict contains a finding of property subject to a criminal forfeiture, the judgment of criminal forfeiture shall authorize the Attorney General to seize the interest or property subject to forfeiture, fixing such terms and conditions as the court shall deem proper.
(c) Presentence investigation.

(1) When made. The probation service of the court shall make a presentence investigation and report to the court before the imposition of sentence or the granting of probation unless, with the permission of the court, the defendant waives a presentence investigation and report, or the court finds that there is in the record information sufficient to enable the meaningful exercise of sentencing discretion, and the court explains this finding on the record.

The report shall not be submitted to the court or its contents disclosed to anyone unless the defendant has pleaded guilty or nolo contendere or has been found guilty, except that a judge may, with the written consent of the defendant, inspect a presentence report at any time.

(2) Report. The report of the presentence investigation shall contain any prior criminal record of the defendant and such information about his characteristics, his financial condition and the circumstances affecting his behavior as may be helpful in imposing sentence or in granting probation or in the correctional treatment of the defendant, and such other information as may be required by the court.

(3) Disclosure.

(A) Before imposing sentence the court shall upon request permit the defendant, or his counsel if he is so represented, to read the report of the presentence investigation exclusive of any recommendation as to sentence, but not to the extent that in the opinion of the court the report contains diagnostic opinion which might seriously disrupt a program of rehabilitation, sources of information obtained upon a promise of confidentiality, or any other information which, if disclosed, might result in harm, physical or otherwise, to the defendant or other persons; and the court shall afford the defendant or his counsel an opportunity to comment thereon and, at the discretion of the court, to introduce testimony or other information relating to any alleged factual inaccuracy contained in the presentence report.

(B) If the court is of the view that there is information in the presentence report which should not be disclosed under subdivision (c)(3)(A) of this rule, the court in lieu of making the report or part thereof available shall state orally or in writing a summary of the factual information contained therein to be relied on in determining sentence, and shall give the defendant or his counsel an opportunity to comment thereon. The statement may be made to the parties in camera.

(C) Any material disclosed to the defendant or his counsel shall also be disclosed to the attorney for the government.

(D) Any copies of the presentence investigation report made available to the defendant or his counsel and the attorney for the government shall be returned to the probation officer immediately following the imposition of sentence or the granting of probation, unless the court, in its discretion, otherwise directs.

(E) The reports of studies and recommendations contained therein made by the Director of the Bureau of Prisons or the Youth Correction Division of the Board of Parole pursuant to 18 U.S.C. §§ 4208(b), 4252, 5010(e), or 5034 shall be considered a presentence investigation within the meaning of subdivision (c)(3) of this rule.

(d) Withdrawal of plea of guilty. A motion to withdraw a plea of guilty or nolo contendere may be made only before sentence is imposed or imposition of sentence is suspended; but to correct manifest injustice the court after sentence may set aside the judgment of conviction and permit the defendant to withdraw the plea.

(e) Probation. After conviction of an offense not punishable by death or by life imprisonment, the defendant may be placed on probation if permitted by law.

(f) Revocation of probation. The court shall not revoke probation except after a hearing at which the defendant shall be present and appraised of the grounds on which such action is proposed. The defendant may be admitted to bail pending such hearing.

Appendix C
Rule 410. Offer to Plead Guilty; Nolo Contendere: Withdrawn Plea of Guilty (Federal Rules of Evidence)

Rule 410. Offer to Plead Guilty; Nolo Contendere; Withdrawn Plea of Guilty (Federal Rules of Evidence) (Prior to 1975 Amendments)

Except as otherwise provided by Act of Congress, evidence of a plea of guilty, later withdrawn, or a plea of nolo contendere, or of an offer to plead guilty or nolo contendere to the crime charged or any other crime, or of statements made in connection with any of the foregoing pleas or offers, is not admissible in any civil or criminal action, case, or proceeding against the person who made the plea or offer. This rule shall not apply to the introduction of voluntary and reliable statements made in court on the record in connection with any of the foregoing pleas or offers where offered for impeachment purposes or in a subsequent prosecution of the declarant for perjury or false statement.

This rule shall not take effect until August 1, 1975, and shall be superseded by any amendment to the Federal Rules of Criminal Procedure which is inconsistent with this rule, and which takes effect after the date of the enactment of the Act establishing these Federal Rules of Evidence.

Rule 410. Offer to Plead Guilty; Nolo Contendere; Withdrawn Plea of Guilty (Federal Rules of Evidence) (Rule has been superseded by Federal Rule of Criminal Procedure 11(e)(6) (as amended))

Appendix D
Plea Entry Forms

IN THE _____ COURT OF _____ JUDICIAL DISTRICT
COUNTY OF SAN BERNARDINO, STATE OF CALIFORNIA
Address: _____

People of the State of California,
 	
                             Plaintiff,
 	
    vs.
 	
_____
   (Print name of defendant)
	DEFENDANT'S WAIVER OF CONSTITUTIONAL RIGHTS FOR ENTRY OF GUILTY PLEA
	Case No. _____
	
	_____
	 (Print name and address of defendant's attorney)

Defendant Initial
after reading

1.   DEFENDANT: I understand that I am charged with the offense of _____

_____
(number and name of charge)

2.   DEFENDANT: I understand that I have the **right to be represented by an attorney** at all stages of the proceedings until the case is terminated. Further, that if I cannot afford an attorney, one will be appointed for me for whom I **may** have to pay no more than the court finds I can afford.

3a.   DEFENDANT: I understand that I have a right to a speedy and public **trial by jury.**

3b.   DEFENDANT: I understand that by entering a guilty plea I am waiving or giving up the right to a **jury trial** and that is my desire.

4a.   DEFENDANT: I understand that I have the right to be **confronted by witness(es)** against me and to cross examine them myself or through an attorney, and that I have the right to the free process of the court to subpoena witnesses in my behalf.

4b.   DEFENDANT: I understand that by entering a plea of guilty, that I will be waiving or giving up the right to be **confronted by witness(es)** against me and to subpoena witnesses in my behalf and that is my desire.

5a.   DEFENDANT: I understand that I have the right to testify on my own behalf but that **I cannot be compelled to be a witness against myself.**

5b.   DEFENDANT: I understand that by pleading guilty I am waiving or giving up **the right to testify on my own behalf** and **to not be compelled** to testify against myself if I choose not to testify and that is my desire.

6.   DEFENDANT: I understand that I am pleading to the offense(s) of_____

_____ and that
the maximum penalty provided by law for said offense(s) is/are _____

_____

6a.   The penalties provided by law for violations of Sections 23102(a) V.C. and 23105 V.C. are as follows:
First offense: Up to six (6) months in County Jail and/or $500 fine and possible suspension of driver's license.
Second offense within five (5) years of the first offense: Up to one (1) year in County Jail and/or $1,000 fine; mandatory loss of driver's license for one (1) year; mandatory minimum of two (2) days in County Jail; and a mandatory minimum fine of $250 plus $65.50 penalty.
Third offense within seven (7) years of first: Same penalty as for second offense except that loss of driver's license is for three (3) years.
With respect to all offenses, possible assignment to a drivers / alcoholic school at the discretion of the judge.

Accepted _____
Rejected _____
Ref. to P. O. _____

_____ confirmed

_____
Judge

_____
Dep. Dist. Atty.

02-11486-000 Rev. 12/74
Page 1

6b. I understand the penalties provided by law for violation of section 23103 V.C. are as follows:
Not less than five nor more than ninety days in County Jail or by a fine of not less than $25 nor more than $250 plus $65.50 penalty or by both such fine and imprisonment. The court may suspend all or any portion of the above and may impose an assignment to a driver's improvement school.

7. DEFENDANT: (If applicable) My lawyer has told me that if I ask to plead guilty, the District Attorney will recommend to the Court that the following penalty be imposed: _____
_____

8. DEFENDANT: I have personally initialed each of the foregoing boxes and I understand each and every one of the rights outlined, and I hereby waive or give up each of them in order to enter my guilty plea to the above charges. **I am entering a plea of guilty or authorizing my attorney to enter a guilty plea in my behalf because:** (Initial appropriate reason)

   a. I am guilty and for no other reason.

   b. Because the plea is a result of plea bargaining.

   c. Other: _____

       _____
       (If addtional space is needed, use reverse side of sheet)

Dated: _____ Signed: _____
                                                                      (Defendant)

9. DEFENDANT'S ATTORNEY ONLY: I am attorney of record and I have explained each of the above rights to the defendant and I concur in his/her decision to waive them and enter a plea of guilty. I further stipulate that this document may be received by the court as evidence of defendant's intelligent waiver of these rights and that it shall be filed by the clerk as a permanent record to that waiver.

Date: _____ Signed: _____
                                                                      (Attorney)

10. IF DEFENDANT HAS NO ATTORNEY: I freely and voluntarily give up the right to be represented by an attorney having been completely advised as to the nature and extent of this right.

Date: _____ Signed: _____
                                                                      (Defendant)

State of California   )
) ss
County of San Bernardino)

On this _____ day of _____ , 19 _____ , before me, a notary public in and for the said county and state, residing therein, duly commissioned and sworn, personally appeared _____ ,
known to me (or proved to me on the oath of _____)
to be the person whose name is subscribed to the within instrument, and acknowledged to me that ____he executed the same.

In witness whereof I have hereunto set my hand and affixed my official seal the day and year in this certificate first above written.

_____
Notary Public in and for said County and State

NOTE: If defendant is appearing through an attorney only under 1429 P. C. and will not be present to acknowledge this document in court, his/her signature must be acknowledged before a Notary Public.

After reading, initialing, and signing, give to courtroom clerk.

                                    SUPERIOR COURT OF NEW JERSEY
                                            CRIMINAL DIVISION
                                    COUNTY _____

STATE OF NEW JERSEY. :   INDICTMENT # _____
                                ACCUSATION # _____
            v.   :

Deft: :

Address: :

                      :   Statement by Defendant

                      :

1. You are charged with _____

    a. Do you know what that means? _____

    b. Do you understand that for the offense to which you are

        about to plead guilty the court could impose a sentence

        of not more than _____ or a fine of not more than

        $_____ or both? _____

2. Has the prosecutor promised either to recommend the dismissal

    of any charge against you or recommend that a particular sentence

    be given to you, or both? _____ Put the number of any

    indictment, count of any indictment, accusation or complaint to

    be dismissed here _____.

    Write out the specific sentence you were promised _____

    _____

    The judge is not bound by those promises. If he decides not to
    follow the recommendations, you will be allowed to take back your
    guilty plea and plead not guilty.

3. Have any other promises, recommendations or inducements been made

    to you by the prosecutor or anyone else concerning this plea of guilty? _____ If your answer was yes, explain what

was told to you: _____

4. Did anyone threaten or force you in any way to cause you to

offer this plea of guilty? _____ If you answered yes,

explain the nature of the force or threats and who made them:

_____

5. In view of your answers to the above, do you now enter a plea

of guilty to _____?

6. Did anyone help or assist you to write the answers to these

questions? ___ _____ If your answer is yes, who helped

you? _____

Date: _____   Signed by: _____
                                            Defendant

I certify that the answers to the foregoing questions were made
by the defendant, that they are true to the best of my knowledge
and belief, and that this statement was signed by the defendant
in my presence.

Date: _____   Signed by: _____
                                        Attorney for Defendant
                                      _____
                                            Address

IN THE CRIMINAL COURT

HAMILTON COUNTY

STATE OF TENNESSEE

STATE OF TENNESSEE   #   DIVISION NO._____
                            #
     VS   #
                            #   Criminal Case No._____
                            #
_____
Defendant

PETITION TO ENTER PLEA OF GUILTY

    I, the above named defendant, respectfully represent to the
Court as follows:

(1)   My true full name is _____,
and I declare that all proceedings against me be had in the name
which I here declare to be my true name.

(2)   I am represented by counsel, and the name of my attorney is
_____.

(3)   I have received a copy of the indictment before being
called upon to plead, and have read and discussed it with my attorney,
and believe and feel that I understand every accusation made against
me in this case.

(4)   I have told my attorney the facts and surrounding circumstances as known to me concerning the matters mentioned in the
indictment, and believe and feel that my attorney is fully informed
as to all such matters. My attorney has since informed me, and has
counselled and advised with me as to the nature and cause of every
accusation against me, and as to any and all possible defenses I
might have in this case.

(5)   My attorney has advised me that the punishment which the
law provides is as follows:

also, that probation may or may not be granted; and that if I plead
"GUILTY" to more than one offense, each indictment being considered a
separate offense, the Court may order the sentences to be served consecutively, one after another.

(6)   I understand that I may, if I so choose, plead "Not Guilty"
to any offense charged against me, and that if I choose to plead "Not
Guilty" the Constitution guarantees me (a) the right to a speedy and
public trial by jury; (b) the right to see and hear all witnesses
against me; (c) the right to use the power and process of the Court
to compel the production of any evidence, including the attendance of
any witnesses, in my favor; and (d) the right to have the assistance
of counsel in my defense at all stages of the proceedings.

                                     _____
                                        Defendant

Page One of Petition to Enter Plea of Guilty

Petition to Enter Plea of Guilty

(7)   I also, understand that if I plead "GUILTY" the Court is
authorized to impose immediately the same punishment as if I had
pleaded "Not Guilty", stood trial, and been convicted by a jury.

(8)   I declare that no officer or agent of any branch of government (Federal, State or local), nor any other person, has made any
promise or suggestion of any kind to me, or within my knowledge to
anyone else, that I would receive a lighter sentence, or probation, or
any other form of leniency, if I would plead "GUILTY". I hope to
receive probation, but I am prepared to accept any punishment permitted by law which the Court may see fit to impose. However, I
respectfully request that the Court consider in mitigation of punishment at the time of sentence the fact that by voluntarily pleading
"GUILTY" I have saved the Court the expense and inconvenience of a
trial.

(9)   I believe and feel that my attorney has done all that anyone
could do to assist me, and that I now understand the proceeding in
this case against me.

(10)   I know the Court will not accept a plea of "GUILTY" from
anyone who claims to be innocent and, with that in mind and because
I make no claim of innocence, I wish to plead "GUILTY", and respectfully request the Court to accept my plea, as follows:

(11)   I declare that I offer my plea of "GUILTY" freely and voluntarily and of my own accord; also that my attorney has explained to
me, and I feel and believe I understand, the statements set forth in
the indictment, and in this petition, and in the "Certificate of
Counsel" which is attached to this petition.

(12)   I further state that I wish the Court to omit and consider
as waived by me all reading of the indictment in open court, and all
further proceedings upon my arraignment, and I pray the Court to
enter now my plea of "GUILTY" as set forth in paragraph (10) of this
petition, in reliance upon my statments made in this petition.

            Signed by me in open court in the presence of my attorney,
this the _____ day of_____, 19_____.

                              _____
                                       Defendant

Page Two of Petition to Enter Plea of Guilty

CERTIFICATE OF COUNSEL

The undersigned, as attorney and counsellor for the foregoing named defendant,
in Criminal Case No. _____, hereby certifies as follows:

(1)   I have read and fully explained to the defendant all the accusations against the defendant which are set forth in the indictment in this case;

(2)   To the best of my knowledge and belief each statement set forth in the foregoing petition is in all respects accurate and true;

(3)   The plea of "GUILTY", as offered by the defendant in paragraph (10) of the foregoing petition, accords with my understanding of the facts as related to me by the defendant, and is consistent with my advice to the defendant;

(4)   In my opinion the defendant's waiver of all reading of the indictment in open court, and of all further proceedings upon arraignment is voluntarily and understandingly made; and I recommend to the Court that the plea of "Guilty" be now accepted and entered on behalf of the defendant as requested in paragraph (10) of the foregoing petition.

Signed by me in open court in the presence of the foregoing named defendant, this _____ day of_____,19____.

_____
Attorney for the Defendant

*

O R D E R

Good cause appearing therefor from the foregoing petition of the foregoing named defendant and the certificate of his counsel and from all proceedings heretofore had in this case, IT IS ORDERED that the petition be granted and that the defendant's plea of "GUILTY" be accepted and entered as prayed in the petition and as recommended in the certificate of counsel.

Done in open court this _____ day of_____,19___.

_____
Criminal Court Judge

THIS DOCUMENT
ENTERED ON MINUTES OF COURT
  DIVISION NO._____
DATE_____BY_____
  ENTERED ON RULE DOCKET
DATE_____BY_____
MICROFILM
REF. NO._____

STATE OF TENNESSEE   )
)
)   No._____
)
          VS   )   CHARGE:_____
)
_____   )   In the_____Division of Criminal
)   Court of Hamilton County, Tennessee
_____   )

MOTION TO ALLOW WAIVER OF TRIAL BY JURY

Comes the above named defendant_____,
personally and by his attorney Mr._____,
and moves the Court to allow said defendant to waive his right to a
trial by jury and to submit this case to the trial judge for decision
both as to guilt and punishment, pursuant to the provisions of Section
40-2504, Tennessee Code Annotated.

                              _____
                                         Defendant

                              _____
                                    Attorney for Defendant

Attested to before me,

this_____day of

_____,19____.

_____
Deputy Criminal Court Clerk

                              Approved and concurred in by:

                              _____
                                 Asst. District Attorney General

      Defendant's motion to waive his right to a trial by jury is
hereby sustained and defendant's plea of_____guilty is hereby
accepted.

_____   _____
          Date   Judge

        THIS DOCUMENT
ENTERED ON MINUTES OF COURT
   DIVISION NO._____
DATE_____BY_____
     ENTERED ON RULE DOCKET
DATE_____BY_____
MICROFILM
REF. NO._____

Appendix E
Plea Agreement Forms

A Simple Plea Bargain (agreement as opposed to plea entry) Form Used in
Bergen County, New Jersey

<u>PLEA BARGAIN</u>

Defendant's Name: Docket #:

_____   _____

Indictment Number(s):   Asst. Pros. Assigned:

_____   _____

_____   Defense Counsel:

_____   _____

Proposed Plea Bargain:

_____

_____

_____

_____

_____

APPROVED: DATE:

_____   _____

1st ASST. PROSECUTOR'S COPY

IN THE SUPERIOR COURT OF THE STATE OF ARIZONA

IN AND FOR THE COUNTY OF PIMA

THE STATE OF ARIZONA,   )

            Plaintiff,   )   No. _____

            vs.   )   PLEA AGREEMENT

)

_____ Defendant(s).)

     It is hereby agreed by the State of Arizona and the defendant, _____, that this case shall be disposed of as provided herein.

     1. The defendant, _____, hereby agrees to plead _____ to the charge(s) of:

     2. The statutory range of sentence is:

     3. The parties agree that the defendant shall receive the following sentence:

     4. The parties agree that the following charges pending against defendant shall be dismissed upon pronouncement of judgment and sentence on the plea above:

     5. In addition, the following charge(s) not yet filed shall not be filed against the defendant:

     6. The parties further agree:

     a. That this agreement serves to amend the complaint, indictment, or information previously filed in this case so as to charge the offense(s) to which the defendant pleads without the filing of any additional pleading. If the plea is rejected or withdrawn, the original charges shall be reinstated. If, after accepting the plea, the Court concludes that any of the terms or provisions of this agreement are unacceptable, both parties shall be given the opportunity to withdraw from this agreement, or the Court can reject the agreement. In the event of such withdrawal or rejection, the plea and this agreement shall be declared null and void by the Court and the original charges shall be reinstated.

CA-53 (3/75)
1 of 2

   b. That if the charge to which the defendant pleads is a felony offense not charged in the original pleading, the defendant hereby waives any and all preliminary proceedings including a probable cause determination thereon.

   c. That unless the plea is rejected or withdrawn, the defendant hereby gives up any and all motions, defenses, objections, appeals, or requests he has made or raised, or could assert hereafter, to or against the Court's entry of judgment and imposition of sentence upon him consistent with this agreement.

   d. That the defendant understands the following rights and understands that he gives up such rights by pleading _____:

        1. His right to a jury trial;

        2. His right to confront the witnesses against him and cross-examine them;

        3. His right to present evidence and call witnesses in his defense, knowing that the State will compel such witnesses to appear and testify;

        4. His right to be represented by counsel (appointed free of charge, if he cannot afford to hire his own) at trial of the proceedings, and

        5. His right to remain silent, to refuse to be a witness against himself, and to be presumed innocent until proven guilty beyond a reasonable doubt.

   e. In the event that defendant appeals the judgment and/or sentence in this matter, the State is relieved of the obligations previously enumerated under subdivisions 4 and 5 of this agreement dealing with the dismissal of pending charges and other charges not yet filed. Such pending charges dismissed as a result of this agreement shall be reinstated at the request of the State and the State shall be free to file any charges not yet filed as of the date of this agreement.

   f.

   I, _____ , have read this agreement with the assistance of counsel, understand its terms, understand the rights I give up by pleading _____ in this matter, and agree to be bound according to the provisions herein.

_____   _____
Date   Defendant

   I have discussed this case and the plea agreement with the defendant. I have advised him of his rights and the consequences of his plea, and I concur in his entry of this plea.

_____   _____
Date   Defense Counsel

   I have reviewed this agreement and agree on behalf of the State of Arizona that the terms and conditions set forth herein are appropriate and are in the interests of justice.

_____   _____
Date   Deputy Pima County Attorney

COMMONWEALTH OF PENNSYLVANIA   :   IN THE COURT OF COMMON PLEAS

                                    :   CHESTER COUNTY, PENNSYLVANIA

        -vs-   :   CRIMINAL ACTION

                                    :   NO.

PLEA BARGAIN

The following agreement is entered between the above-named defendant and his attorney and the District Attorney of Chester County through his subscribing representative. By agreeing hereto the defendant acknowledges:

1. That he understands the nature of the charges to which he is pleading guilty.

2. That by pleading guilty he admits committing certain acts which constitute the crime charged.

3. That he has the right to a trial by jury, or to a trial by a judge without a jury, at which he is presumed innocent until he is found guilty and that the Commonwealth must prove that guilt beyond a reasonable doubt.

4. That by pleading guilty he is severely limiting any appeal rights he may have and generally may appeal only the legality of the sentence or whether his plea was voluntarily and intelligently entered.

5. That he has been advised of the maximum permissible sentences for the crimes with which he is charged.

6. That he has consulted with his counsel before entering this plea and has authorized his counsel to conduct plea bargaining on his behalf.

7. That the Court has not participated in negotiations leading to this agreement and it is not binding until approved

by the Court.

    8. That the Court may refuse to approve the bargain, leaving the defendant in the same position as though no negotiations or bargain had taken place.

Acknowledgment:

_____
Defendant

    The parties hereby agree to the following, which is to be submitted to the Court for approval:

```
INDICTMENT TERM AND NO.   :
CHARGE                    :
MAXIMUM SENTENCE          :
OTHER AGREED DISPOSITION  :

        SENTENCE
FINE AND COSTS            :
PROBATION OR IMPRISONMENT :
```
_____

```
INDICTMENT TERM AND NO.   :
CHARGE                    :
MAXIMUM SENTENCE          :
OTHER AGREED DISPOSITION  :

        SENTENCE
FINE AND COSTS            :
PROBATION OR IMPRISONMENT :
```
_____

```
INDICTMENT TERM AND NO.   :
CHARGE                    :
MAXIMUM SENTENCE          :
OTHER AGREED DISPOSITION  :

        SENTENCE
FINE AND COSTS            :
PROBATION OR IMPRISONMENT :
```
_____

```
INDICTMENT TERM AND NO.   :
CHARGE                    :
MAXIMUM SENTENCE          :
OTHER AGREED DISPOSITION  :

        SENTENCE
FINE AND COSTS            :
PROBATION OR IMPRISONMENT :
```

TERMS OR CONDITIONS:

    1.   To meet your family responsibilities.

    2.   To refrain from frequenting unlawful or disreputable places or consorting with disreputable persons.

    3.   To refrain from having in your posession a firearm or other dangerous weapon unless granted written permission by the court or parole officer.

    4.   To remain within the jurisdiction of the court and to notify the court or probation officer of any change in your address or your employment.

    5.   To report as directed to the court or the probation officer and to permit the probation officer to visit your home and place of employment at any time.

    6.   To refrain from using alcoholic beverages and/or drugs.

    7.   To refrain from violating any Municipal, County, District, State or Federal Laws, Ordinances and Orders and otherwise conduct yourself as a good citizen.

    8.   To notify the probation office within 72 hours if you are arrested or involved in any other trouble.

    9.   To pay above fine(s)/sums to the use of the County and costs within_____months from date of approval of this Plea Bargain by the Court.

    10.   Additional conditions and terms:

_____   _____
Defendant   District Attorney

_____   _____
Attorney for Defendant   Assistant District Attorney

COURT ACTION: _____

DATE:_____

ADDITIONAL TERMS OR CONDITIONS:

DATE: _____

Defendant
_____

Attorney for Defendant
_____

District Attorney
_____

BY: _____
Assistant District Attorney

COURT ACTION: _____

DATE: _____

STATE OF NEW MEXICO   COUNTY OF..

                    IN THE .... COURT

STATE OF NEW MEXICO   NO...
        -vs-

                        Defendant

PLEA AND DISPOSITION AGREEMENT

         The State of New Mexico and the defendant hereby agree to the following disposition of this case:

Plea: The defendant agrees to plead (*guilty*) (*no contest*) to the following offenses:

Terms: On the following understandings, terms and conditions:

         1. That no more severe than the following disposition will be made of the charges:.................. ....

         ----

         2. That the following charges will be dismissed, or if not yet filed, shall not be brought against the defen-

            dant: ....

         ----

         3. That this agreement, unless rejected or withdrawn, serves to amend the complaint, indictment, or informa-
            tion to charge the offense to which the defendant pleads, without the filing of any additional pleading. If
            the plea is rejected or withdrawn, the original charges are automatically reinstated.

         4. Unless this plea is rejected or withdrawn, that the defendant hereby gives up any and all motions, de-
            fenses, objections or requests which he has made or raised, or could assert hereafter, to be the court's entry
            of judgment against him and imposition of a sentence upon him consistent with this agreement.

         5. That, if after reviewing this agreement and any pre-sentence report the court concludes that any of its
            provisions are unacceptable, the court will allow the withdrawal of the plea, and this agreement shall be
            null and void. If the plea is withdrawn, neither the plea nor any statements arising out of the plea pro-
            ceedings shall be admissible as evidence against the defendant in any criminal proceedings.

         I have read and understand the above. I have discussed the case and my constitutional rights with my lawyer.
I understand that by pleading (guilty) (no contest) I will be giving up my right to a trial by jury, to confront, cross-
examine, and compel the attendance of witnesses, and my privilege against self-incrimination. I agree to enter my plea
as indicated above on the terms and conditions set forth herein. I fully understand that if, as part of this agreement, I
am granted probation, a suspended sentence or a deferred sentence by the court, the terms and conditions thereof are
subject to modification in the event that I violate any of the terms or conditions imposed.

---   ---
                 DATE   DEFENDANT

         I have discussed this case with my client in detail and advised him of his constitutional rights and all pos-
sible defenses. I believe that the plea and disposition set forth herein are appropriate under the facts of this case.
I concur in the entry of the plea as indicated above and on the terms and conditions set forth herein.

---   ---
                 DATE   DEFENSE COUNSEL

         I have reviewed this matter and concur that the plea and disposition set forth herein are appropriate and are
in the interests of justice.

---   ---
                 DATE   PROSECUTOR

                                        Approved:

APPROVED: COURT ADMINISTRATOR. OCTOBER 1. 1974   MAGISTRATE OR DISTRICT JUDGE

Bibliography

Abrams, N. Internal Policy: Guiding the Exercise of Prosecutorial Discretion. 19 UCLA L. Rev. 1 (1971).

Acceptance of Guilty Pleas. 14 Ariz. L. Rev. 543 (1972).

Accepting the Indigent Defendant's Waiver of Counsel and Plea of Guilty, 22 U. Fla. L. Rev. 453 (1970).

Adelstein, R.P. The Negotiated Guilty Plea: An Economic and Empirical Analysis. Unpublished Ph.D. dissertation. University of Pennsylvania, 1975.

Alschuler, A. The Defense Attorney's Role in Plea Bargaining. 84 Yale L.J. 1179 (1975).

Alschuler, A. The Supreme Court, The Defense Attorney, and the Guilty Plea. 47 U. Col. L. Rev. 1 (1975).

Alschuler, A.W. The Prosecutor's Role in Plea Bargaining. 36 U. Chi. L. Rev. 50 (1968).

A.B.A. Project on Minimum Standards for Criminal Justice, Standards Relating to Pleas of Guilty, February, 1967 (Tentative Draft).

A.B.A. Special Committee on Standards for the Administration of Criminal Justice Standards Relating to the Prosecution Function and the Defense Function, 1971.

American Friends Service Committee, Struggle for Justice, 1971.

Anderson R., and Associates, Guidelines for Determining the Impact of Legislation on the Courts, June 30, 1975 (report prepared for the Judicial Council, State of California, second year findings and recommendations by the Judicial Impact Analysis Project).

Anderson R., and Associates, Guidelines for Determining the Impact of Legislation on the Courts, June 30, 1974 (report prepared for the Judicial Council, State of California).

Andrews, B.G. The Role of the Prosecutor in Utah, 5 Utah L. Rev. 70 (1956).

Appellate Review of Constitutional Infirmities Notwithstanding a Plea of Guilty, 9 Hous. L. Rev. 305 (1971).

Arcuri, A. Police Perceptions of Plea Bargaining: A Preliminary Inquiry, 1 J. Police Sci. & Ad. 93 (1973).

Ariano F. and Countryman, J.W. The Role of Plea Negotiation In Modern Criminal Law, Chi.-Kent L. Rev. 116 (0000).

Arizona Proposed Rules of Criminal Procedure, 1972 (issued by the Arizona State Bar Committee on Criminal Law).

Bailey F.L. and Rothblatt, H.B. Successful Techniques for Criminal Trials (1971).

Baker, N. and DeLong, E., The Prosecuting Attorney, 24 J. Crim. L.C. & P.S. 1025 (1934).

Balch, R. Deferred Prosecution: The Juvenilization of the Criminal Justice System, 38 Fed. Prob. 46 (1974).

Barbara, J., Morrison, J., Cunningham, H. Plea Bargaining: Bargain Justice?, 14 Criminol. 55 (1976).

Barton, B.A. Plea Negotiations: The A.B.A. and National Advisory Commission Standards, May 10, 1974 (unpublished paper prepared for the Role Conflict Seminar sponsored by the Center for the Administration of Justice, Wayne State University, Michigan).

Battle, In Search of the Adversary System—The Cooperative Practices of Private Criminal Defense Attorneys, 50 Tex. L. Rev. 60 (1971).

Bazelon, D. New Gods and Old: Efficient Courts in a Democratic Society, 46 N.Y.U. L. Rev. 653, at 663 (1971).

Behavior Research Center of Pheonix, Survey of Arizona Superior Court Criminal Cases, 1971.

Benjamin, R.W. and Pedeliski, T.B. The Minnesota Public Defender System and the Criminal Law Process, L. Socy. Rev. 279 (0000).

Bequai, A. Prosecutorial Decision Making—A Comparative Study of the Prosecutor in Two Counties in Maryland, 4 Police L.Q. 34 (1974).

Berger, M. The Case Against Plea Bargaining, 62 A.B.A. J. 621 (1976).

Bing, S.R. and Rosenfeld, S.S. The Quality of Justice In the Lower Criminal Courts of Metropolitan Boston, September, 1970 (A report by the Lawyers' Committee for Civil Rights Under Law to the Governor's Committee on Law Enforcement and the Administration of Justice).

Bishop, A. Broken Bargains, 50 J. Urb. L. 231 (1972).

Bishop, A. Guilty Pleas in Missouri, 306 U.M.K.C. L. Rev. 304 (1974).

Bishop, A. Guilty Pleas in the Pacific West, 51 J. Urb. L. 171 (1974).

Bishop, A. Guilty Pleas in Texas, 24 Baylor L. Rev. 301 (1972).

Bishop, A. Guilty Pleas in Wisconsin, 58 Marq. L. R. 631 (1975).

Bishop, A. Waiver in Pleas of Guilty, 60 F.R.D. 513 (1974).

Blumberg, A. Criminal Justice (1967).

Bond, J.E. Plea Bargaining and Guilty Pleas (1975).

Bongiovanni, Joseph. Guilty Plea Negotiation, V. 7 Duq. U. L. Rev. 542 (1968-69),

Bormon, D. The Chillded Right to Appeal from a Plea Bargain Conviction: A Due Process Cure, 69 N.W.U. L. Rev. 663 (1974).

Borrego, T. Criminal Law: Plea Negotiations—Legitimizing the Agreement Process, 27 Okla. L. Rev. 487 (1974).

Breitel, C.D. Controls in Criminal Law Enforcement, 27 Chi. L. Rev. 427 (1960).

Bugliosi, V. and Gentry, C. Helter Skelter: The True Story of the Manson Murders (1974).

Bureau of Social Science Research, Summary of Pre-Trial Screening Evaluation Phase I, October, 1975 (manuscript prepared for the National Institute of Law Enforcement and Criminal Justice, Law Enforcement Assistance Administration, Grant No. 75NI-99-0079).

Burger, W. The State of the Judiciary—1970, 56 A.B.A. J. 929 (1970).

Busch, T. Prosecution in Baltimore Compared to the Houston System, 5 The Prosecutor 253 (1969).

Caldwell, J. and Flynn, L.J. Institutional and Policy Discretion, February 9, 1973 (report prepared for the Venture County Model Criminal Justice System Development Project by Public Safety Systems).

Carney and Fuller, A Study of Plea Bargaining in Murder Cases in Massachusetts, 3 Suf. L. Rev. 292 (1969).

Carpenter and Russel, An Act to Add and to Repeal Section 1192.5 of the Penal Code, Relating to Plea Bargaining, 5B No. 1449 (January 21, 1976).

Carr, W.S. and Connelly, V.J. Sentencing Patterns and Problems—An Annotated Bibliography, (1973).

Carstarphea, L.A. Sentence Bargaining at the Local Level: Perceptions and Attitudes of Judges, Prosecutors and Defense Attorneys, May 23, 1970 (unpublished thesis in the University of Georgia libraries).

Casper, J. American Criminal Justice—The Defendant's Perspective, 1972.

Casper, J. Criminal Justice—The Consumer's Perspective, NILE & CJ, February, 1972 (Superintendent of Documents, U.S. Govt. Printout).

Castberg, A.D. Prosecutorial Discretion: A Case Study, 1968 (unpublished Ph.D. dissertation at Northwestern University Library).

Ceriani, G.C. Prosecutorial Discretion In the Duplicative Statutes Setting, 42 U. Colo. L. Rev. 455 (1971).

Chalker, Judicial Myopia, Differential Sentencing and the Guilty Plea—A Constitutional Examination, 6 Am. Crim. L. Q. 187 (1968).

Chernoff, P.A. and Schaffer, W.G. Defending the Mentally Ill—Ethical Quicksand, 10 Am. Crim. L. Rev. 505 (1972).

The Chilling Effect in Constitutional Law, 69 Colum. L. Rev. 808 (1969).

Church, T. Eliminating Charge Reduction Bargaining: Criminal Justice Without Bargaining?, September 1975 (paper prepared for the 1975 Annual Meeting of the American Political Science Association).

Civil Consequences of Conviction for a Felony, 12 Drake L. Rev. 141 (1962).

Clark, C.E. and Shulman, H. A Study of Law Administration In Connecticut, 1973.

Cogan, N. Entry of the Plea of Guilty in Texas: Requirements and Post-Conviction Review, 29 S.W. L. J. 714 (1975).

Cogan, N. Guilty Pleas: Weak Links in the "Broken Chain," 10 Crim. L. Bull. 149 (1974).

Cohen, R.M. and Witcover, J. A Heartbeat Away: The Investigation and Resignation of Vice President Spiro T. Agnew (1974).

Comment: Constitutional Law—Plea Bargaining—New Jersey Statute Allowing A Defendant to Avoid the Death Penalty by Pleading Non Vult or Nolo Contendere Held Valid, 44 N.Y.U. L. Rev. 612 (1969).

Comment: Determining Voluntariness of Guilty Pleas in Alabama—The Boykin Standard, 5 Cumber.—Sam. L. Rev. 61 (1974).

Comment: Guilty Plea Is Not Invalid Because It Is The Product of a Plea Bargain, 2 Loy. U. L. J. 346 (1971).

Comment: Guilty Pleas in Illinois, The Enigma of Substantial Compliance, 24 DePaul L. Rev. 42 (1974).

Comment: In Search of the Adversary System—The Cooperative Practices of Private Defense Attorneys, 50 Tex. L. Rev. 60 (1971).

Comment: Plea Bargaining in Washington, 6 Gonz. L. Rev. 269 (1971).

Comment: Plea Bargaining Mishaps—The Possibility of Collaterally Attacking the Resultant Plea of Guilty, 65 J. Crim. Law 170 (1974).

Commonwealth of Virginia Division of Justice and Crime Prevention, Judicial Administration of Criminal Justice, October 31, 1974 (unpublished report submitted in Charlottesville, Virginia).

Competence to Plead Guilty—A New Standard, 1 Duke L. J. 149 (1974).

Constant, A. Determination of Sentence in Criminal Cases: The Guilty Plea and Related Factors, April 21, 1971 (unpublished paper in the University of Texas Law School Library).

Constitutional Law—Guilty Pleas—A New "Voluntariness" Standard?, 45 Tul. L. Rev. 1049 (1971).

Constitutionality of an Equivocal Guilty Plea—*North Carolina v. Alford*, 400 U.S. 25 (1970) Gonz. L. Rev. 8 (1972-3).

Convictions of Unincluded Lesser Offenses: Informal Amendments and Plea Bargains, 25 Hast. L.J. 1075 (1974).

Cook, J. Constitutional Rights of the Accused—Pre-Trial Rights, 1972.

Coon, The Indictment Process and Reduced Charges, 40 N.Y.S. B. J. 434 (1968).

Cooper, H.H.A. Plea Bargaining: A Comparative Analysis, 5 Intl. L. & Pol. 427 (1972).

Court's Duty to Advise or Admonish Accused as to Consequences of a Guilty Plea, 97 A.L.R.2d 549.

Criminal Defendant Entitled to Reasonably Competent Assistance of Counsel, 12 Am. Crim. L. Rev. 193 (1974).

Criminal Justice In Dade County—A Preliminary Survey (unpublished report by the American Judicature Society).

Criminal Law—Enforcement of Plea Bargaining Agreements, 51 N.C.L.R. 602 (1971).

Criminal Law—Federal Rules of Criminal Procedure—Discretion of Court to Refuse a Guilty Plea Under Rule 11, 20 Wayne L. Rev. 1359 (1974).

Criminal Law—Fifth Amendment—Guilty Plea Not Compelled Though Entered With Claim of Innocence to Avoid Possible Death Penalty—*North Carolina v. Alford*, 400 U.S. 25 (1970).

Criminal Law—Habeas Corpus Guilty Pleas—A Constitutional Objection to the Composition of a Grand Jury May be Waived by Counsel Without Consultation with Defendant when Counsel Conscientiously Considers that Course of Action to be in the Best Interest of Defendants—*Winters v. Cook,* 489 F.2d 174 (5th Cir. 1973) V. 8 Ga. L. Rev. 984 (Summer 1974).

Criminal Law—Plea Bargaining—Direct Participation By Trial Judge in Plea Bargaining Does Not Vitiate Voluntariness of Subsequent Guilty Plea, Ga. L. Rev. 5 809 (1970-71).

Criminal Law—Plea Bargaining—Withdrawal of Guilty Pleas, 74 W. Va. L. Rev. 196 (1971).

Criminal Law—Plea Negotiations Legitimizing the Agreement Process, 27 Okla. L. Rev. 487 (1974).

Criminal Law—Pleas of Guilty—Plea Bargaining—The American Bar Association's Standards on Criminal Justice and Wisc. Stat. Section 971.08, 1971 Wis. L. Rev. 583 (0000).

Criminal Law—Right to Appeal—Failure of Counsel to Advise Defendant of His Right to Appeal After a Plea of Guilty Held Insufficient Grounds to Require a Mongomery Hearing, 40 Ford. L. Rev. 949 (1972).

Criminal Procedure—Duty of the Trial Judge to Advise a Defendant of the Consequences of a Guilty Plea, 19 S.C. L. Rev. (1967).

Criminal Procedure—Guilty Pleas—Voluntariness Where Motivated by Desire to Escape Death Penalty Under Unconstitutional Statutory Scheme—*Brady v. United States,* 397 U.S. 742 (1970); *Parker v. North Carolina,* 397 U.S. 790 (1970), 47 Denver L.J. 540 (1970).

Criminal Procedure—Plea Bargaining—Implicit Restrictions on Defendant's Right to Appeal, 21 Wayne L. Rev. 1161 (1975).

Criminal Procedure—Plea Bargaining—Trial Judge's Participation in Plea Negotiations Does Not Render Plea Involuntary, 24 Vand. L. Rev. 836 (1971).

Criminal Procedure—Requirements for Acceptance of Guilty Pleas, 48 N.C. L. Rev. 352 (1970).

Criminal Procedure—Voluntariness of Guilty Pleas in Plea Bargaining Context, 49 N.C.L. Rev. 795 (1971).

Dahlin, D.C. The Public Defender's Office In San Bernadino County, California: A Role Analysis, 1969 (unpublished thesis in Claremont Graduate School Library).

Daray, J. Plea Bargaining In A California Legal System: A Case Study 1971 (unpublished Ph.D. thesis in Claremont Graduate School and University Library).

Dash, S. Cracks in the Foundation of Criminal Justice, 46 Ill. L. Rev., Northwestern U. 385 (1951).

Davis, A. Sentences for Sale: A New Look at Plea Bargaining In England and America, Crim. L. Rev. 150 (1971).

Davis, S. The Guilty Plea Process: Exploring the Issues of Voluntariness and Accuracy, 6 Val. U. L. Rev. 111 (1972).

Davis, S.M. The Guilty Plea Process: Exploring the Issue of Voluntariness and Accuracy, 6 Val. U. L. Rev. 111 (1972).

Davis, W.J. No Place for the Judge, 9 Trial 22 (1973).

Dean, J. The Illegitimacy of Plea Bargaining, 38 F. Prob. 23 (Sept. 1974).

The Defective Assistance of Counsel, 42 U. Cin. L. Rev. 1 (1973).

The Defense Lawyer's Role at the Sentencing Stage of a Criminal Case, 54 F.R.D. 315 (1968).

Discretion of Court to Refuse a Guilty Plea Under Rule 11, 20 Wayne L. Rev. 1359 (1974).

Don Vito, P. An Experiment in the Use of Court Statistics, 56 Judicature 56 (1972).

Dorsen, N. and Friedman, L. Disorder in the Court (1973).

Downie, Jr. L. Justice Denied—The Case for Reform of the Courts, (1971).

Eckhart, D.R. and Stover, R.V. Public Defenders and Routinized Criminal Defense Processes, 51 J. Urb. L. 665 (1974).

Effective Assistance of Counsel in Plea Bargaining: What is the Standard?, 12 Duq. L. Rev. 321 (1973).

Eiseland, G. The Guilty Plea In South Dakota, 15 S.D. L. Rev. 66 (1970).

Eisenstein, J. and Jacob, H. Felonious Justice, 1975 (unpublished manuscript).

Elderkin, E.J. Criminal Procedure: Meaning of Voluntariness As Pertaining to Withdrawal of Guilty Plea, 46 Calif. L. Rev. 471 (1958).

Ellenbogen, J. and Ellenbogen, E. Perspectives On Plea Bargaining, 1 Crime & Corrections 5 (1973).

Emory, H.M. The Guilty Plea As A Waiver of Rights and as an Admission of Guilt, 44 Temp. L. Q. 540 (1971).

Enker, A. Perspectives on Plea Bargaining, app. A, 108 in The President's Commission on Law Enforcement and the Administration of Justice, The Task Force on the Administration of Justice, Task Force Report: The Courts, 1967.

Enker, A.N. Address delivered in Charlottesville, Virginia, April 12, 1969, in Charles Whitehead (ed.), Mass Production Justice and the Constitutional Ideal (1970).

Equal Justice Task Force, Grosse Pointe Inter-Faith Center for Racial Justice, Study of 1970 Felony Defendants in Detroit Recorder's Court (1970).

Equivocal Guilty Pleas—Should They Be Accepted? 75 Dick. L. Rev. 366 (1970-71).

Erickson, W.H. Criminal Justice Standards—A Summary, 55 Judicature 369 (May, 1972).

Erickson, W.H. The Finality of a Plea of Guilty, 48 Notre Dame L. 835 (1973).

Fay, E.D. The "Bargained For" Guilty Plea, 4 Crim. L. Bul. 265 (1968).

Feeley, M. Coercion and Compliance: A New Look at the Old Problem, 4 L. & Socy. Rev. 505 (1970).

Feeley, M. The Effects of Heavy Caseloads, September 5, 1975 (unpublished paper prepared for delivery at the 1975 Annual Meeting of the American Political Science Association).

Feeley, M. Two Models of the Criminal Justice System: An Organizational Perspective, 7 L. & Socy. Rev. 407 (1973).

Feit, M. Before Sentence is Pronounced . . . A Guide to Defense Counsel in the Exercise of His Post-Conviction Responsibilities, 9 Crim. L. Bull. 140 (1973).

Ferguson, G. and Roberts, D. Plea Bargaining: Directions for Canadian Reform, 4 Can. B. Rev. 496-576 (1974).

Ferguson, G. The Role of the Judge in Plea Bargaining, 15 Crim. L.Q. 26 (1972).

Fertitta, R.S. Comparative Study of Prosecutor's Offices: Baltimore and Houston, 5 The Prosecutor 248 (1969).

Finkelstein, M. A Statistical Analysis of Guilty Plea Practices in Federal Courts, 89 Harv. L. Rev. 293 (1975).

Fischer, D.A. Beyond *Santabello*—Remedies for Reneged Plea, 2 U.S.F.V. L. Rev. 121 (1973).

Fisher, E. "Plea Bargaining" in Traffic Cases, The Prosecutor, No. 5, 1969, at 92-99.

Fletcher, Pretrial Discovery in State Criminal Cases, 12 Stan. L. Rev. 293 (1960).

Folberg, J. The "Bargained For" Guilty Plea—An Evaluation, 4 Crim. L. Bul. 201 (1968).

Frankel, Lawlessness in Sentencing, 41 U. Cin. L. Rev. 1 (1972).

Friendly, J. Is Innocence Irrelevant? Collateral Attack on Criminal Judgments, 38 U. Chi. L. Rev. 142 (1970).

Gallagher, K. Judicial Participation in Plea Bargaining: A Search for New Standards, 9 Harv. C. L. C.R. L. Rev. 29 (1974).

Gallagher, K. Voluntary Trap, 9 Trial 23 (May/June 1973).

Gaylin, W. Partial Justice, 1974.

Gentile, C.L. Fair Bargains and Accurate Pleas, 14 B. U. L. Rev. 514 (1969).

George, B.J. and Cohen, I.A. Prosecutor's Source Book, 1969 (Criminal Law and Practice—Sourcebook Series No. 1).

Gibbs, J.P. Needed: Analytical Typologies in Criminology, 4 Southwestern Social Science Q. 321 (March, 1960).

Goldstein, J. For Harold Lasswell: Some Reflections on Human Dignity, Entrapment, Informed Consent, and the Plea Bargain, 84 Yale L.J. 683 (1975).

Goodard, W.H. Criminal Procedure—Plea Bargaining, 60 Calif. L. Rev. 894 (1972).

Greene, H. Address delivered at a Courts Workshop in Charlottesville, Virginia, April 11, 1969, in Charles Whitehead (ed.) Mass Production Justice and the Constitutional Ideal (1970).

Greenwood, P., Wildhorn, S., Poggio, E., Strumwasser, M., DeLeon, P. Prosecution of Adult Felony Defendants in Los Angeles: A Policy Perspective, March, 1973 (prepared by Rand, Inc. R-1127-DOJ).

Grosman, B.A. The Role of the Prosecutor, Can. B.J. 580, (1968).

The Guilty Plea and Bargaining, 17 Loyola L. Rev. 703 (1971).

The Guilty Plea as a Waiver of Rights and as an Admission of Guilt, 44 Temp. L. Q. 540 (1971).

The Guilty Plea and Sentencing: Proposed Improvements, 115 Sol. J. 120 (1971).

Guilty Plea Bargaining: Compromises by Prosecutors to Secure Guilty Pleas, 112 U. Pa. L. Rev. 865 (1964).

The Guilty Plea in South Dakota, 15 S.D. L. Rev. 66 (1970).

Guilty Pleas—*McMann v. Richardson,* 397 U.S. 759 (1970); *Brady v. United States,* 397 U.S. 742 (1970); *Parker v. North Carolina,* 397 U.S. 790 (1970), 61 J. Crim. L.C. & P.S. 521 (1970).

Guilty Pleas—Voluntariness Where Motivated by Desire to Escape Death Penalty Under Unconstitutional Statutory Scheme, 47 Den. L. J. 540 (1970).

Haas, H. High Impact Project Underway in Oregon—"No Plea Bargaining Robbery and Burglary," 10 The Prosecutor 127 (1974).

Hall, D. The Role of the Victim in the Prosecution and Disposition of a Criminal Case, 28 Vand. L. Rev. 931, 953 (1975).

Halperin, D.J. Proposals For Improving Efficiency of the Superior Court, (a report to the Judicial Council of Maine), 1975.

Hartman, M. Query: Can Plea Bargaining Be Eliminated?, 59 Judicature 8 (June-July), 1975.

Heath, R.L. Plea Bargaining—Justice Off the cord, 9 Wash. L. J. 430 (1970).

Heberling, J. Judicial Review of the Guilty Plea, 7 Lincoln L. Rev. 137 (1972).

Hedblom, P.B. Criminal Law—Guilty Pleas—Where Strong Evidence of Actual Guilt Substantially Negated Defendants' Claim of Innocence and Provided Strong Factual Basis for the Guilty Plea, Defendant Being Represented by Competent Counsel, Court Committed No Constitutional Error in Accepting Guilty Plea Despite Defendant's Claim of Innocence and Fear of Death Penalty, and such was Voluntarily and Intelligently Pleaded. *North Carolina v. Alford,* 400 U.S. 25, 915 (Ct. 160, 27 L. Ed. 2d 162 (1970), 3 St. Mary's L.J. 127 (1971).

Henley, K. Plea Bargaining and the Courts of the District of Columbia, January 23, 1974 (unpublished paper in the Institute of Criminal Law and Procedure Library, Georgetown University Law Center).

Herrmann, J. The Role of Compulsory Prosecution and the Scope of Prosecutorial Discretion in Germany, 41 U. Chi. L. Rev. 468 (1973-74).

Hersey, J. Court-Oriented vs. Client-Oriented Justice, 31 Briefcase 271 (1972).

Heumann, M. A Note of Plea Bargaining and Case Pressure, 9 L. & Socy. Rev. 515 (1975).

Heymann, M. Plea Bargaining Systems and Plea Bargaining Styles: Alternate Patterns of Case Resolution in Criminal Courts, September, 1974 (unpublished paper prepared for delivery at the 1974 Annual Meeting of the American Political Science Association).

Hobbs, G. Judicial Supervision Over California Plea Bargaining: Regulating the Trade, 59 Calif. L. Rev. 962 (1971).

Hobbs, S. Prosecutor's Bias, An Occupational Disease, 2 Ala. L. R. 41 (1949).

Hoffman, (J.) Plea Bargaining and the Role of the Judge, 53 F.R.D. 500 (1972).

Improvident Guilty Pleas and Related Statements: Inadmissible Evidence at a Later Trial, 53 Minn. L. Rev. 559 (1969).

The Influence of the Defendant's Plea on Judicial Determination of Sentence, 66 Yale L.J. 205 (1956).

Jacob, H. and Eisenstein, J. Sentences and Other Sanctions Imposed on Felony Defendants in Baltimore, Chicago, and Detroit, 1974 (paper prepared for delivery at the 1974 Annual Meeting of the American Political Science Association).

Japha, A.F. Preliminary Report of the Drug Law Evaluation Project in New York, February 11, 1976 (unpublished report submitted by A.F. Japha, project director, to Gerald M. Caplan, Director, National Institute of Law Enforcement and Criminal Justice, LEAA).

Jenkins, S. Plea Bargaining and Its Consequences: A Study In the Criminalization Process, 1974 (unpublished Ph.D. dissertation available from Xerox University Microfilms).

Jooshin, H. "Do Lesser Pleas Pay?: Accommodations in the Sentencing and Parole Processes," Journal of Criminal Justice, Vol. 1 (1973), 27-42.

Judicial Participation in Guilty Pleas—A Search for Standards 33 U. Pitt. L. Rev. 151 (1971).

Judicial Plea Bargaining, 19 Stan. L. Rev. 1082 (1967).

The Judicial Research Foundation, Inc., Struggle for Equal Justice: A Report On Neglect and Crisis in the Lower Courts, March, 1969.

Judicial Supervision Over California Plea Bargaining: Regulating the Trade, 59 Calif. L. Rev. 962 (1971).

Kalmanoff, A. Criminal Justice, 1976.

Kalven, H. and Zeisel, H. The American Jury (1966).

Kaplan, K.J. Latitutde and Severity of Sentencing Options, Race of the Victim and Decision of Simulated Jurors: Some Issues Arising From the 'Algier's Motel' Trial, 7 L. & Socy. Rev. 87 (1972).

Kaplan, K.J. The Prosecutorial Discretion—A Comment, 60 N.W.U. L. Rev. 174 (1965).

Katsh, E., Pipkin, R.M., and Katsh, B.S. Classroom Strategies—Guilt By Negotiation—A Simulation of Justice, 3 L. in Am. Socy., 23 (1974).

Katz, L.R. Justice is the Crime, 1972.

Klein, A. Plea Bargaining, 14 Crim. L. Q. 289 (1972) [a Canadian Journal].

Klein, J.F. Habitual Offender Legislation and the Bargaining Process, 15 Crim. L. Quar. 417 (1972).

Klonoski, J., Mitchell, C., and Gallagher, E. Plea Bargaining in Oregon—An Exploratory Study, 50 Or. L. Rev. 114 (1971).

Knudson, S. Plea Negotiations in Denver, June, 1972 (paper prepared for the Institute for Court Management, University of Denver Law Center).

Koblenz, M.R. and Strong, Jr., C.P. Justice: A Word to Bargain—A Study of Plea Bargaining in the Prosecutor's Office, 8 The Prosecutor 388 (1972).

Koffer, Role Of the Trial Judge, 19 N.Y. Jud. Conf. Rep. 205 (1974).

Krantz, S. An Evaluation of the Kings County Plea Negotiation Conference Program, 1971 (unpublished manuscript prepared for CJCC, Boston University Law School).

Kress, J.M. The Agnew Case: Policy, Prosecution and Plea Bargaining, 10 Crim. L. Bull. 80 (1974).

Kress, J.M. and Newman, D.J. Two Perspectives on the Agnew Plea Bargain, 10 Crim. L. Bull. 80 (1974).

Kuh, R.H. Plea Bargaining—Guidelines for the Manhattan District Attorney's Office, 11 Crim. L. Bull. 48 (1975).

Kulig, F. Plea Bargaining, Probation, and Other Aspects of Conviction and Sentencing, 8 Creighton L. Rev. 923 (1975).

LaBelle, J.D. Negotiated Pleas.

Lachman, J. An Economic Model of Plea Bargaining In the Criminal Court System, 1975 (unpublished Ph.D. dissertation at the Michigan State University library).

Lachman, J. The Defendant's Decision to Plea Bargain: An Economic Analysis, June, 1975 (paper prepared for presentation at the annual meetings of the Western Economics Association).

Lachman, J. The Prosecutor's Decision to Plea Bargain: An Economic Perspective, in Conference on Modeling and Simulation: Proceedings. IEEE and University of Pittsburgh, 1975.

LaFave, W.R. The Prosecutor's Discretion in the United States, 18 Am. J. Comp. L. 532 (1970).

Lagoy, S., Senna, J. and Siegal, L.J. An Empirical Study On Information Usage For Prosecutorial Decision Making In Plea Negotiations, 13 Am. Crim. L. Rev., 435 (1976).

Lambros, Plea Bargaining and the Sentencing Process, 53 Fed. R. Decs. 509 (1971).

Landes, W.M. An Economic Analysis of the Courts, 14 J.L. & Econ. 61 (1971).

Law Enforcement and Planning Office, Honolulu, Hawaii, Deferred Prosecution and Deferred Acceptance of a Guilty Plea, 1971.

"The Legitimation of Plea Bargaining: Remedies for Broken Promises" 11 Am. Crim. L. Rev. 771 (1973).

Legrande, J.L. Basic Processes of Criminal Justice (1973).

Leonard, R.F. and Barber, J. Screening of Criminal Cases, (1972).

Leonard, R. "Deferred Prosecution Program," The Prosecutor No. 8, 1972 at 315.

Leonard, S.M. Judicial Enforcement of Nonstatutory "Immunity Grants": Abrogation By Analogy, 25 Hast. L. J. 435 (1974).

Levin, M. Delay and Related Policy Topics In Five Criminal Courts, Sept. 1973 (unpublished paper prepared for delivery at the 1973 Annual Meeting of the American Political Science Association in New Orleans).

Littrell, W. Constructing Crime: Police and Prosecutor's Management of the Charging Process, June, 1974 (unpublished Ph.D. thesis at the New York University Library).

McIntyre, D.M. A Study of Judicial Dominance of the Charging Process, 59 J. Crim. L.C. & P.S. 463 (1968).

McIntyre, D.M. and Lippmann, D. Prosecutors and Early Disposition of Felony Cases, 56 ABA J. 1154 (1970).

McMenamin, B. Plea Bargaining in the Military, 10 Am. Crim. L. Rev. 93 (1971).

Madigan, M.J. Honest Way, 9 Trial 18 (May/June, 1973).

Martin, W.L. Collective Sentencing Decision In Judicial and Administrative Contexts—A Comparative Analysis of Two Approaches to Correctional Disparity, 11 Am. Crim. L. Rev. 695 (1973).

Marcus, Constitutional Law—*North Carolina v. Alford*: The Protection of Constitutional Rights in Plea Bargaining, 7 N. Eng. L. Rev. 139 (1971).

Mather, L. Some Determinants of the Method of Case Disposition: Decision Making by Public Defenders in Los Angeles, 8 L. & Socy. Rev. 187 (1974).

Meglio, J.J. Comparative Study of the District Attorneys Offices in Los Angeles and Brooklyn, 5 The Prosecutor 237 (1969).

Mendes, R. and Wold, J. Plea Bargaining Revisited: New Uses For An Old Practice, April, 1974 (paper prepared for delivery at the annual meeting of the Western Political Science Association, April 4-6, 1974).

Mileski, M. Courtroom Encounters: An Observation Study of A Lower Criminal Court, 5 L. & Socy. Rev. 473 (1971).

Miller, J. The Compromise of Criminal Cases, 1 S. Calif. L. Rev. 1 (1927).

Mills, J. I Have Nothing to do With Justice, 70 Life 56 (March 12, 1971).

Mills, J. The Prosecutor: Charging and "Bargaining," 1966 U. Ill. L. F. 511 (1966).

The Mitre Corporation, National Impact Program Evaluation, A Primary Source Description of Impact City Felony Courts Prior to Program Initiation, June, 1975 (document prepared for the Law Enforcement Assistance Administration).

Morris, N. Are Courts Too Soft on Criminals? Probation and Plea Bargaining in Metropolitan Jurisdictions, 53 Judic. 231 (1970).

Morris, N. The Future of Imprisonment (1974).

Moskowitz, D.H. Lack of Counsel on Guilty Pleas in Pennsylvania, 36 Pa. Bar Assoc. Q. 309 (1965).

Moss, F.E. The Professional Prosecutor, 51 J. Crim. L. C. & P. S. (1960-61).

Mullady, Appellate Review of Constitutional Affirmities Notwithstanding A Plea of Guilty, 9 Hous. L. Rev. 305 (1971).

Myhre, Conviction Without Trial in the United States and Norway: A Comparison, 5 Hous. L. Rev. 647 (1968).

Nagel, S. and Neef, M. Plea Bargaining, Decision Theory, and Equilibrium Models, July, 1975 (unpublished draft for presentation at the Law and Society Association Conference on "Models of the Legal Process" at the University of Buffalo).

National Advisory Commission on Criminal Justice Standards and Goals, Report On the Courts (ch.3), 1973.

National Association of Attorneys General Committee on the Office of Attorney General, Report On the Office of Attorney General, February, 1971.

National Center for State Courts of New Jersey, A Study of Plea Bargaining In Municipal Courts for the State of New Jersey, August 31, 1974 (unpublished project manuscript).

National District Attorneys Association, Plea Bargaining: The Prosecutor's Perspective, 1973 (NDAA Manual).

Neubauer, D.W. Confessions In Prairie City—Some Causes and Effects, 65 J. Crim. L.C. & P.S. 103 (March, 1974).

Neubauer, D.W. Criminal Justice in Middle America (1974).

Neubauer, D.W. The Administration of Justice and the Role of the Prosecutor: Prairie City, 1972 (unpublished Ph.D. dissertation).

A New Ground for Withdrawal of Pleas of Guilty: Plea Involuntarity Induced by Defendant's Attorney, 36 Mo. L. Rev. 139 (1971).

Newman, D.J. Conviction: The Determination of Guilt or Innocence Without Trial, 1966.

Newman, D.J. Informal Bargaining, in Radzinowicz, L. and Wolfgang, M. (eds.) The Criminal in the Arms of the Law (1971).

Newman, D.J. Pleading Guilty For Considerations: A Study of Bargain Justice, 46 J. Crim. L.C. & P.S. 780 (1955-56).

Newman, D.J. Reshape The Deal, 9 Trial 11 (1973).

Newman, D. The Agnew Plea Bargain, 10 Crim. L. Bul. 85.

Newman, D.J. and NeMoyer, E., Issues of Propriety in Negotiated Justice, 47 Den. L. J. 367 (1970).

Note: Constitutional Law—Guilty Pleas Coupled With Claim of Innocence—Should They Be Accepted?, 22 Mercer L. Rev. 785 (1971).

Note: The Elimination of Plea Bargaining In Black Hawk County: A Case Study, 60 Iowa L. Rev. 1053 (1975).

Note: Plea Bargaining: The Case for Reform, 6 U. Rich. L. Rev. 325 (1972).

Note: Plea Bargaining—Proposed Amendments to Federal Criminal Rule 11, 56 Minn. L. Rev. 718 (1972).

Note: Prosecutor's Discretion, 103 U. Pa. L. Rev. 1057 (1955).

O'Brien, III, W.J. Constitutionality of An Equivocal Guilty Plea, 8 Gonz. L. Rev. 332 (1973).

O'Rourke, J. and Dell'Apa, F. Issues—Report of A Conference For Supervisory Board Members In Region 8 Law Enforcement Assistance Administration, 1973 (report of the 4th Annual Supervisory Board Conference).

Official Inducements to Plead Guilty: Suggested Morals For A Marketplace, 32 Chi. L. Rev. 167 (1964).

Ohlin, L.E. and Remington, F.J. Sentencing Structure: Its Effect Upon Systems For the Administration of Criminal Justice, 23 L. & Cont. Prob. 495 (1958).

Oliver, Constitutional Law–Criminal Law–Guilty Plea is Not invalid Because It is the Product of a Plea Bargain, 2 Loy. U.L.J. 346 (1971).

Owen, I. Defending Criminal Cases Before Juries–A Commonsense Approach, (1973).

Panel and Discussion: Minimum Standards on Pleas of Guilty, 51 F.R.D. 87 (1971).

Pareti, H. Constitutional Law–*North Carolina v. Alford:* The Protection of Constitutional Rights In Plea Bargaining, 7 N. Eng. L. Rev. 139 (1971).

Parker, J. Plea Bargaining, 1 Am. J. Crim. L. 187 (1972).

People v. Selikoff: The Route to Rational Plea Bargaining, 21 Cath. L. Rev. 144 (1975).

Persons Who Enter Guilty Pleas Are Not Foreclosed From Having a Federal Evidentiary Hearing on the Voluntariness of Their Plea, 15 Vill. L. Rev. 253 (1969).

Peterson, R.W. Bad Bargain, 9 Trial 16 (1973).

Pieczenik, R. Urban Justice: Understanding the Adjudication of Felony Cases In An Urban Criminal Court, 1974 (unpublished Ph.D. dissertation available from Xerox University Microfilms).

Pickett, M. Guilty Pleas and the Concept of Waiver, v. 5, Willamette L. J. 575 (1969).

Plea Agreements in Oklahoma, 22 Okla. L. Rev. 81 (1969).

The Plea Bargain in Historical Perspective, 23 Buf. L. Rev. 499 (1974).

Plea Bargaining, 8 Duq. L. Rev. 461 (1970).

Plea Bargaining: A Model Court Rule, 4 U. Mich. L. Rev. 487 (1971).

Plea Bargaining in Washington, 6 Gonz. L. Rev. 269 (1971).

Plea Bargaining: Justice Off the Record, 9 Wash. L.J. 430 (1970).

Plea Bargaining: Proposed Amendments to Federal Criminal Rule 11, 56 Minn. L. Rev. 718 (1972).

Plea Bargaining: The Case for Reform, 6 U. Rich. L. Rev. 325 (1972).

Plea Bargaining: The Judicial Merry-Go-Round, 10 Duq. L. Rev. 253 (1971).

Plea Bargains: Is Court Enforcement Appropriate? 17 Stan. L. Rev. 316 (1965).

Pleading Guilty: Illinois Supreme Court Rule 402 and the New Federal Rule of Criminal Procedure 11, U. Ill. L. F. 116 (1975).

Plea of Guilty is Invulnerable to Impeachment Where No Adequate Procedure Exists to Challenge the Voluntariness of a Confession Motivating the Plea, 46 Notre Dame L. 604 (1971).

Plea Withdrawal in Oklahoma, 23 Okla. L. Rev. 472 (1970).

Polstein, R. How to "Settle" A Criminal Case, Prac. Law. 35 (1962).

Post-Conviction Relief from Pleas to Guilty: A diminishing Right, 38 Brook. L. Rev. 182 (1971).

Pound, R. and Frankfurter, F. (eds). Criminal Justice in Cleveland (1922).

Pre-Plea Discovery: Guilty Pleas and the Likelihood of Conviction at Trial, 119 U. Pa. L. Rev. 527 (1971).

Pre-sentence Withdrawal of Guilty Pleas in Federal Courts, 40 N.Y.U. L. Rev. 759 (1965).

The President's Commission on Law Enforcement and the Administration of Justice, The Challenge of Crime In A Free Society (1967).

Profile of A Guilty Plea; A Proposed Trial Court Procedure for Accepting Guilty Pleas, 17 Wayne L. Rev. 1194 (1971).

Propriety and Prejudicial Effect of Showing, in Criminal Cases, Withdrawn Guilty Plea, 86 A.L.R.2d 326 (1962).

Prosecutorial Discretion—A Re-evaluation of the Prosecutor's Unbridled Discretion and its Potential for Abuse, 21 DePaul L. Rev. 485 (1971).

Prosecutor's Discretion, 103 U. Pa. L. Rev. 1057 (1955).

The Prosecutor's Duty to Disclose Exculpatory Evidence, 19 Okla. L. Rev. 425 (1966).

The Prosecutor's Role in California Sentencing: Advocate or Informant?, 20 U.C.L.A. L. Rev. 1379, 1396 (1973).

Pugh, Standards Relating to Pleas of Guilty, 57 F.R.D. 357 (1972).

Purves, R.F. That Plea Bargaining Business: Some Conclusions From Research, Crim. L. Rev. 470 (1971).

Pye, A.K. Address delivered in Charlottesville, Virginia, April 10, 1969, in Charles Whitebread (ed.), Mass Production Justice and the Constitutional Ideal (1970).

Recent Decisions, Criminal Law—Habeas Corpus—Guilty Pleas—A Constitutional Objection to the Composition of a Grand Jury May Be Waived by Counsel Without Consultation With Defendant When Counsel Consciously Considers That Course of Action to Be in the Best Interests of Defendant—Winters v. Cook, 489 F.2d. 174 (5th Cir. 1973), 8 Georgia L. Rev. 984 (1974).

Recent Decisions, Criminal Law—Plea Bargaining—Direct Participation By Trial Judge In Plea Bargaining Does Not Vitiate Voluntariness of Subsequent Guilty Plea, 5 Geor. L. Rev. 809 (1970).

Recent Developments, Criminal Procedure—Double Jeopardy—Retrial on greater charge after guilty plea to lesser included offense vacated held violative of fifth amendment double jeopardy clause, 7 Ind. L. Rev. 761 (1974).

Recent Developments, Judicial Plea Bargaining, 19 Stan. L. Rev. 1082 (1966-67).

Renfro, J.M. Judge Maneuvering In An Urban Court: The Philadelphia System, February 26, 1971 (unpublished paper in the University of Texas Law School Library).

Requirements for Acceptance of Guilty Pleas, 48 N.C. L. Rev. 352 (1970).

Restructuring the Plea Bargain, 82 Yale L.J. 286 (1972).

Retrial on Greater Charge After Guilty Plea to Lesser Included Offense Held Violative of Fifth Amendment Double Jeopardy Clause, 7 Ind. L. Rev. 761 (1974).

Ridley, H. Plea Bargaining: An Analysis of the Procedure From The Perspective of the Participants, 1975 (unpublished Ph.D. dissertation at the Emory University Library).

The Right to "No Trial" and the Right to "No Counsel," 4 Val. L. Rev. 163 (1969).

Rogers, The Rational Basis for Guilty Pleas and the Restrictive Scope of Direct Consequences, 31 Wash. & Lee L. Rev. 236 (1974).

The Role of Plea Negotiation in Modern Criminal Law, 46 Chi.–Kent L. Rev. 116 (1969).

Rosett, A. and Cressey, D.R. Justice By Consent: Plea Bargains In the American Courthouse (1976).

Rosett, A. The Negotiated Guilty Plea, 374 The Annals of the Am. Academy of Political and Social Science 70 (1967).

Rotenberg, D.L. The Progress of Plea Bargaining: The ABA Standards and Beyond, Institute of Judicial Administration (1972).

Rothblatt, H.B. Bargaining Strategy, 9 Trial 20 (May/June, 1973).

Scheff, T.J. The Societal Reaction to Deviance, 11 J. Soc. Prob. 401 (Spring, 1964).

Seventeenth Annual Report of the Temporary Commission of Investigation of the State of New York to the Governor and the Legislature of the State of New York, No. 92 at 196, April 1975 (legislative document).

Signorelli, E.L. Judicial Analysis and Critique of the New Drug and Sentencing Laws, 46 N.Y. St. B. J. 9 (1974).

Silverstein, L. Defense of the Poor in Criminal Cases in American State Courts, 1965 (in three volumes).

Skolnick, J. Justice Without Trial (2d ed. 1975).

Skolnick, J.H. Social Control of the Adversary System, 11 J. Conflict Resolution 52 (1967).

Smith, J.M. and Dale, W.P. The Legitimation of Plea Bargaining: Remedies for Broken Promises, 11 Am. Crim. L. Rev. 771 (1972).

Steinberg, H.B. The Responsibility of the Defense Lawyer in Criminal Cases, 12 Syrac. L. Rev. 442 (1961).

Steinberg, H.B. and Paulsen, M.G. A Conversation With Defense Counsel on Problems of A Criminal Defense, 7 Prac. Law 25 (1961).

Stone, W.R. Plea Negotiations Inventory, September 4, 1975 (unpublished paper presented to the Department of the Attorney General of Rhode Island).

Subin, I.H. Criminal Justice In A Metropolitan Court, NTIS, October, 1966.

Sudnow, Normal Crimes: Sociological Features of the Penal Code in A Public Defender Office, in Crime and Justice In Society (R. Quinney ed. 1969).

Supreme Court's Changed View of the Guilty Plea, 41 Mem. St. U.L. Rev. 79-90 (1973).

Thomas, An Exploration of Plea Bargaining, 1969 Crim. L. Rev. 69 (1969).

Thomas, E. Plea Bargaining: The Clash Between Theory and Practice, 20 Loy. L. Rev. 303 (1974).

Thomas, P. Plea Bargaining and the *Turner* case, 1970 Crim. L. Rev., 559 (1970).

Thomas, P. Judicial Approach to Plea Bargaining, January 10-13, 1972 (paper presented at the First South Pacific Conference, located at the University of Manitoba library, Canada).

Thompson, W.J. The Judge's Responsibility on a Plea of Guilty, 2 N. Virg. L. Rev. 62 (1959-60).

Trammell, G.W. Control of System Policy and Practice by the Office of the District Attorney In Brooklyn and Los Angeles, 5 The Prosecutor 242 (1969).

Treback, A. The Rationing of Justice, 1964.

The Trial Judge's Satisfaction as to the Factual Basis of Guilty Pleas, 306 Wash. L. Q. 66, (1966).

The Trial Judge's Satisfaction as to the Voluntariness and Understanding of Guilty Pleas, 1970 Wash. U. L. Q. 289 (1970).

The Unconstitutionality of Plea Bargaining, 83 Harv. L. Rev. 1387 (1970).

Underwood, R. Let's Put Plea Discussions and Agreements—On Record, 1 Loy. U. L.J. 1 (1970).

University of California, Berkeley, College of Engineering, Plea Bargaining: Structure and Process, August 15, 1975 (unpublished report to the District Attorney of Alameda County).

Vetri, D.R. Guilty Plea Bargaining: Compromise By Prosecutors to Secure Guilty Pleas, 112 U. Pa. L. Rev. 865 (1963-64).

Virginia Commonwealth's Attorney's Handbook, 1972 (sponsored by Virginia Council on Criminal Justice).

Voluntariness of Plea of Guilty Made in Response to Promise of Leniency, 35 N.Y.U. L. Rev. 284 (1960).

Weintraub, R.G. and Tough, R. Lesser Pleas Considered, 32 J. Crim. L.C. & P.S., 506 (1941).

Wexler, D.B. Cases and Materials On Prison Inmate Legal Assistance—Preliminary Report, 1971 (report sponsored by NILECJ).

Wheatley, J. Plea Bargaining—A Case for It's Continuance, 59 Mass. L. Q. 31 (1974).

White, W. A Proposal for Reform of the Plea Bargaining Process, 119 U. Pa. L. Rev. 439 (1971).

Williams, G. Discretion in Prosecuting, Crim. L. Rev. 222 (1956).

Williamson, Jr., T.S. The Constitutionality of Reindicting Successful Plea-Bargain Appellants On the Original Higher Charges, 62 Cal. L. Rev. 258 (1974).

Wishingrad, J. The Plea Bargain In Historical Perspective, 23 Buffalo L. R. 499 (1974).

Withdrawal of Guilty Plea to Defective Indictments, 21 Ohio St. L. J. (1960).

Withdrawal of Guilty Pleas in the Federal Courts, 55 Colum. L. Rev. 366 (1955).

Withdrawal of Guilty Pleas Under Rule 32(d), 64 Yale L.J. 590 (1955).

Wold, J. and Mendes, R. Perceptions of Bureaucratic Needs In A Criminal Justice System, September, 1975 (paper prepared for delivery at the 1975 Annual Meeting of the American Political Science Association).

Woodward, B. and Bernstein, C. The Final Days (1976).

Worgan, D.S. and Paulsen, M.G. The Position of A Prosecutor In A Criminal Case—A Conversation With A Prosecuting Attorney, 7 Prac. Law 44 (1961).

Arthur Young & Company, Judicial Weighted Caseload Project, May, 1974 (Final Report prepared for the Judicial Council of California).

Arthur Young & Company, Non-judicial Staffing Study, May, 1974 (final report prepared for the Judicial Council of California).

Younger, E.J. Position Paper On Plea Bargaining, December 5, 1975 (unpublished paper).

Zander, M. Acquittal Rates and Not Guilty Pleas: What Do the Statistics Mean?, Crim. L. Rev. 401 (1974).

Zander, M. Unrepresented Defendants In the Criminal Courts, Crim. L. Rev. 632 (1969).

Ziesel, H. deGrazia, J. and Friedman, L. Criminal Justice System Under Stress: A Study of the Disposition of Felony Arrests In New York City, Vera Institute of Justice, August 15, 1975 (unpublished manuscript).

Index

About the Author

David Arthur Jones is a professor who holds a joint appointment in the Graduate Program in Administration of Justice and in the Department of Sociology at the University of Pittsburgh. He is a practicing attorney who is a member of the Bars of Massachusetts, New York, the District of Columbia and the Supreme Court of the United States. Dr. Jones holds a Ph.D. in criminal justice from the School of Criminal Justice, State University of New York at Albany; a J.D. from Union University; and an A.B. from Clark University. He has been a faculty member at the University of Tennessee, State University of New York, Buffalo, Georgetown University Law Center, and The School of Justice at The American University. Professor Jones served as deputy director of the National Study of Plea Bargaining, and he has been a consultant to many federal, state, local and private criminal justice agencies. Dr. Jones is the author of *The Health Risks of Imprisonment* (Lexington Books, 1976) and of *Crime and Criminal Responsibility* (Nelson-Hall, 1978). He is or has been a member of numerous bar associations, the American Judicature Society, the Association of Trial Lawyers of America, the Academy of Criminal Justice Sciences, the American Academy for Professional Law Enforcement, and the National District Attorneys Association.